WOUNDED BY LOVE

Wounded by Love

The Life and the Wisdom *of* Saint Porphyrios

edited from an archive of notes and recordings by the Sisters of the Holy Convent of Chrysopigi

DENISE HARVEY (PUBLISHER) • LIMNI, EVIA, GREECE

Published by Denise Harvey (Publisher), 340 05 Limni, Evia, Greece
www.deniseharveypublisher.gr

First printed in March 2005
Reprinted in 2005, 2006, 2008, 2009, 2011, 2013, 2014, 2015, 2017 and 2018

This book was originally published in Greek
by the Holy Convent of the Life-giving Spring – Chrysopigi
under the title *Γέροντος Πορφυρίου Καυσοκαλυβίτου, Βίος καὶ Λόγοι* (2003).

The English translation is by Father John Raffan

Printed in Greece

ISBN: 978-960-7120-19-9

I have run to the fragrance of your myrrh, O Christ God,
For I have been wounded by your love;
do not part from me, O heavenly Bridegroom.

CONTENTS

NOTE ON THE ENGLISH TRANSLATION

The contents of this book come from an archive of notes and recordings compiled by two women who knew Saint Porphyrios for a period of more than three decades. Throughout this time they kept a record of his conversations, his reminiscences and his words of spiritual guidance. When, some ten years after the elder's death, these two women became nuns at the convent of Chrysopigi in Chania in western Crete, the archive was placed at the disposal of the convent.

Under the guidance of the abbess of the community, Mother Theoxeni, the material that had been collected was carefully transcribed and edited in such a way as to allow Saint Porphyrios to speak for himself. The prime concern was to present the words exactly as spoken, preserving their immediacy and authenticity. At the same time, however, the material, often collected at very diverse times and in different contexts, was arranged into chapters according to subject matter in order to make it more accessible.

The English translation similarly allows Saint Porphyrios to present himself and his teachings with a minimum of introduction. The figure of the 'elder' or *staretz* in the Orthodox Church has always been seen as a source of wisdom and guidance and as possessing a gift of speaking directly to the heart. The differences which distinguish the culture of Eastern Orthodoxy from that of Western Christianity will not prevent the western reader from responding to Saint Porphyrios's simple, lucid and vivid narrative.

Scriptural and other quotations have been identified and a number of short explanatory footnotes have been added where this seemed necessary. Biblical references are given to the Septuagint version of the Old Testament as used in the Orthodox Church, followed in brackets by a reference to the numbering in the Revised Standard Version where this differs from the Septuagint numbering. Books such as the Wisdom of Solomon which are not included in the western canon of Scripture are marked as [DC] = Deuterocanonical. The English translation of Scriptural passages is indebted to the Revised Standard Version, but very frequently deviates from this where a rendering of the Greek text of the Septuagint is required.

BIOGRAPHICAL NOTE

Saint Porphyrios was born in the village of Aghios Ioannis in the province of Karystia on the Greek island of Evia (Euboea) on the 7th February 1906. The name he received at birth was Evangelos. His parents, Leonidas and Eleni Bairaktaris, were poor farmers and had difficulty in supporting their large family. For this reason his father left for America where he worked on the construction of the Panama Canal.

Young Evangelos was the fourth child of the family. As a boy he looked after sheep on the hills and had completed only the first class of primary school when, at the age of seven, he was obliged on account of his family's extreme poverty to go to the nearby town of Chalkida to work. He worked there in a shop for two or three years. Thereafter he went to Piraeus to work in a general store owned by a relative.

At the age of twelve he left secretly to go to the Holy Mountain. His longing was to imitate Saint John the Hut-dweller* whose life he had read and for whom he felt a special affinity. The grace of God led him to the hermitage of Saint George in Kavsokalyvia† where he lived in obedience to two elders, natural brothers, Panteleimon, who was a father confessor, and Ioannikios, who was a priest. He devoted himself with great love and in a spirit of utter obedience to the two elders who had a reputation for being exceptionally austere.

He became a monk at the age of fourteen and took the name of Niketas. Two years later he took his final monastic vows of the Great Schema. Shortly thereafter God granted him the gift of clear sight.

At the age of nineteen he became very seriously ill and was obliged to leave the Holy Mountain. He returned to Evia where he went to live in the Monastery of Saint Charalambos at Levka. A year later, in 1926, and at the age of twenty, he was ordained priest at the Church of Saint Charalambos in Kymi by the Archbishop of Sinai, Porphyrios III, who gave him the name Porphyrios. At the age of twenty-two he became a confessor and spiritual father. For a time he was parish priest in the village of Tsakei in Evia.

He lived for twelve years in the Monastery of Saint Charalambos in Evia serving as a spiritual guide and confessor and then for three years

* See Appendix, p. 249.
† See Appendix, p. 250.

in the deserted Monastery of Saint Nicholas in Ano Vatheia.

In 1940, on the eve of Greece's entrance into the Second World War, Saint Porphyrios moved to Athens where he became chaplain and confessor in the Polyclinic Hospital. He himself said that he served there for thirty-three years as if it were a single day, devoting himself untiringly to his spiritual work and to easing pain and suffering.

As of 1955 he made his home in the tiny Monastery of Saint Nicholas in Kallisia on the foothills of Mount Pendeli. He rented this monastic dependency along with the surrounding area from the Pendeli Monastery and worked the land with great diligence. At the same time he carried out his copious work of spiritual guidance.

In the summer of 1979 he moved to Milesi, a village some thirty miles north of Athens and overlooking his native Evia, with the dream of founding a monastery there. To begin with he lived in a caravan under exceedingly adverse circumstances and later in a simple room constructed from breeze blocks where he endured without complaint his many health troubles. In 1984 he moved into a room in a wing of the monastery which was under construction. In spite of the fact that the elder was seriously ill and blind, he worked constantly and unstintingly for the completion of the monastery. On the 26th February 1990 he was able to see his dream becoming reality when the foundation stone of the church of the Transfiguration was laid.

During the final years of his earthly life he began to prepare himself for his death. His desire was to return to the Holy Mountain and to his beloved Kavsokalyvia where, secretly and silently, just as he had lived, he would tender up his soul to her Bridegroom. He was often heard to say, 'My desire now that I have grown old is to go and die up there.'

So it was that he came to his saintly end in his hermitage in Kavsokalyvia on the morning of 2nd December 1991.

The last words that were heard to pass from his lips were the words from our Lord's high-priestly prayer which he loved so much and repeated so often:

that they may be one. John 17:11, 22.

PART ONE

THE LIFE OF SAINT PORPHYRIOS
(1906–1991)

Saint Porphyrios
as a young monk

THE PATH TO THE HOLY MOUNTAIN

My dream was to imitate
Saint John the Hut-dweller

I'm from the village of Aghios Ioannis

There's a village in Evia called Aghios Ioannis; that's where I'm from. My parents were poor, and so my father left the village and went to America. He worked there as a labourer on the Panama Canal. In the village we children did chores from the earliest age. We would water the garden and the trees; we would bring in the animals; we would do whatever jobs the grown-ups told us to do.

When I was little I used to mind the flocks up on the mountain. I was slow-witted and shy. I went to school for only one year, and we learnt virtually nothing because the teacher was ill. While I was looking after the sheep, I read the life of Saint John the Hut-dweller, syllable by syllable. That's where my zeal to go and become a monk came from. Even though I knew nothing. I hadn't even seen a monk or a monastery. Nothing.

When I was seven my mother sent me to Chalkida to work in a shop. It sold everything. Shops at that time used to have ironmongery — keys, screws, locks and ropes and so on — but they'd also have sugar and rice and coffee and pepper and everything you'd find in a grocer's. It was a big shop. There were two other boys there. I went and joined them. I did whatever they told me to. Everyone bossed me about and I was never off my feet running to and fro. Before I arrived, the two other boys had worked out a system whereby they would go up to the balcony day and day about to water the basil plants belonging to the boss's wife. They had a rota. When I arrived they got me to do everything — to sweep the floor and water the flowers. It didn't cross my mind that it was unfair. I did everything. Wherever they told me to go, I went.

One day, just as I was finishing sweeping the shop, I noticed that some coffee beans had spilled on the floor next to where I had gathered my pile of rubbish. There would have been about fifteen beans in all. I bent down and picked them up and walked over to the sack with the coffee beans. My boss was in his office. It had windows all round and he saw me bending down and then walking over to the sack. He called out:

'Angelos!' — meaning me, that's what they used to call me when I was young — 'come over here!'

I went over.

'What have you got in your hand? What's that?'

'They're coffee beans. I found them over there and I picked them up,' I said.

He started to shout:

'Tasos! Aristos! Yiannis! Yiorgos!'

One was in the storeroom and the others in various parts of the shop. The boss kept shouting. They all gathered in the office. The boss opened my hand.

'Do you see that? What's that?' he asked.

'Coffee beans,' they answered.

'Where did you find them, Angelos?'

'They were littered on the floor and I picked them up and was about to throw them into the coffee sack,' I replied.

Well, my boss started to give us a lecture. What went on in that shop was nobody's business! Such wastage! Scoops would be tossed right, left and centre…

'Listen now,' he said, 'as from today you're going to organize a rota for the jobs in here. One week it will be Aristos, one week Tasos, one week Angelos — for the flowers and for everything.'

My boss's family was very fond of me. They would invite me up to their house and would get me to sing to them whatever hymns I knew. They looked on me with real affection. My action in picking up the beans had made an impression on them — because they didn't know me.

After two years I went to Piraeus to work in a grocer's shop owned by a relative. The grocer's shop was also a taverna. There was a little attic there where I slept at night. The shop was on a hill, in Tsamados Street. People would come by every day to do their shopping and many of the customers would sit down to have a drink or a snack since it doubled as a taverna.

I developed a deep desire to become a hermit

One day two elderly men came into the shop. They sat down and asked for two sardines and half an oka* of wine. I fetched their order at once. Then I heard one of them say to the other:

* A Turkish measure of weight and capacity; one oka equals about two thirds of a quart.

'You should see the wine I drank on the Holy Mountain! I haven't found wine like that anywhere.'

'So you've been to the Holy Mountain, have you?' asked the other.

'Yes,' he replied, 'I left my home in Mytilene once — Kalloni was my village — and I went off to the Holy Mountain. We used to drink *monoxylitiko** wine there. What a wine that was!'

'Did you go to become a monk?' queried the other man.

'Yes, I wanted to be a monk, but I wasn't able to, I wasn't up to it. How I regret now that I didn't stay there!'

I listened to all this with great attention because some time earlier a group of monks had passed by handing out booklets. One was about the life of Saint John the Hut-dweller, which, as I told you, I had stammered through syllable by syllable while I was looking after the sheep in the village. I had reread it up in the attic by the light of a little lantern — with considerable difficulty, because I hadn't learned to read properly. The life of the saint filled me with such enthusiasm that I wanted to imitate him. But about the Holy Mountain I knew not a thing.

'I went to become a monk, but I left,' continued the old man. 'How marvellous it was there! I saw monks, hermits, holy men, striving to love God and battling away in the wilderness with fasts, deprivations and prayers. But I left it all behind and returned to the world and snarled myself in a thousand cares and troubles. I remember it all constantly and I regret I didn't stay there, instead of landing myself back here in the world with all the troubles and trials of family and children. All these cares of life have brought me to my knees. Yes, I remember it all...'

Soon the two men got up and left, but my mind remained captivated by what I had heard. From that moment I was filled with zeal to go to the place he'd been speaking about. My mind became fixated on the idea that I could realize my dream of imitating Saint John the Hut-dweller. It became my all-consuming desire.

Two days later the elderly man came in again; he lived close by. I went up to him and, out of earshot of the others, I asked him:

'Tell me, *Kyr* Adonis, what are things like up there on the Holy Mountain. Is it a good place?'

'You heard about it the last time; I can't tell you anything at the moment.'

And he didn't tell me anything. He left. But I in the meantime could

* Wine produced in the Monoxylitis Monastery, a dependency of the Monastery Dionysiou on Mount Athos.

think of nothing else. I developed a deep desire to become a hermit. But how? I didn't know how to get to the Holy Mountain. I had no money. Nor did I know what to say to my boss.

Kyr Adonis came back once more to the shop. Once again I secretly queried him about the Holy Mountain and this time he told me everything. But how was I going to leave? And what was I going to say?

A little urchin for the love of Christ

For days on end I was downcast and lost in thought. My boss noticed it. He came up to me and said to me:

'Why are you looking unhappy? What's the matter?'

I'm afraid I couldn't help telling a lie. I said that when I had left the shop to go and fetch some food-supplies, I had heard from someone from my village that my mother was ill and I wanted to go and see her. He believed my story and gave me money for my ticket to go to my mother. He also gave me food to take to her and, showing his sympathy, he accompanied me out onto the road and wished me a safe journey.

I ran down to the boat. I had set off for the Holy Mountain! I had begun to realize my dream. The boat was to sail via Chalkida, Volos and then Thessalonica. But after the boat had put to sea I began to feel miserable. I wanted to reach my destination, but I was afraid and I felt sorry for my parents who, not knowing where I was, would be sick with worry. I couldn't do it. When the boat put in at Limni in Evia, I got off and took the next boat back to Piraeus.

I returned to the shop and announced that my mother had recovered. And so I carried on my work as before. But not exactly as before. I was pensive, I prayed continually, I ate little, I made prostrations, and as a result of all this I lost weight; I changed.

'What's the matter, Angelos?' people would ask me. 'What's wrong? We can see that there's something on your mind, my boy, and you've lost a lot of weight. You know we're fond of you and we want you here, but do you perhaps want to go back to your parents?'

'Yes,' I answered, 'I want to go home.'

'Go and see them then, if you like, and when you come back bring with you another good lad like yourself for the shop.'

And so once again they gave me money, food and sweets, some bottles of peppermint liqueur and various other items and my boss took me down to the boat and bought me a ticket for Chalkida.

It was a boat bound for Chalkida, Edipsos, Volos, Thessalonica, the

Holy Mountain and Dafni. The boat was called *Athenai.* I got on board and the boat set off. It was after dark when we left. We sailed all night. Eventually we arrived at Chalkida. When the boat had tied up the sailor shouted, 'Anyone for Chalkida, anyone for Chalkida?'

I kept my mouth shut and didn't say a word. I had snuggled up in a corner and kept quiet. The boat set sail from Chalkida. But when we arrived at Edipsos the sailors discovered me because they were checking the tickets there.

'Why didn't you get off at Chalkida?' they asked me.

'I was sleeping,' I replied.

'What are we going to do now?' they asked. 'You're going to have to pay.'

'I don't have enough money,' I told them.

'Never mind then,' they replied.

And so they took me along without paying. Money at that time was counted in five or ten cent pieces. One drachma at the most would have been all I had with me.

When we disembarked at Volos I was suddenly overwhelmed with melancholy. I started to cry and cry. I thought about how I was going to leave the world forever and about how my parents were going to lose me, and how they would be distressed and worried. I thought about my brothers and sister. Something seemed to be choking me and I wanted to go back. The boat berthed for several hours at Volos and everyone got off. Then the whistle blew and it pulled away for Thessalonica. I stayed on shore, intending to go back. I spent the night up on a hill, crying and praying.

The next day I found the boat that sailed the same passage to Thessalonica. I got on board. My money had finished and so, not having a ticket, I hid myself in the stern so that they wouldn't put me off the boat. At one point the sailors asked to see my ticket. Of course, I didn't have one and they berated me loudly. I sat on a bench on the port side of the ship weeping. As I wept I looked out at the sea and sang to myself a verse from a hymn I'd been taught by my father. He was a singer in the church and he used to sing this hymn whenever All-souls Saturday came round. The words ran:

> *Beholding the sea of life, swollen high and raging wild,*
> *And through temptations' lashing storm, racing on to the calm*
> *of Your haven fair,*
> *I cry, Lord, raise up my life from destruction and save me,*
> *O All-merciful.**

* Hymn from the Book of the Eight Tones (Resurrection Canon, Tone 6, *irmos* of the 6th Ode).

'My life, O Christ, is a tempestuous sea,' I said to myself, 'and, just as I am sailing on this rough sea, I ask You for Your divine providence to lead me to a harbour so that my soul can find stillness there — in the harbour that You are, You who are Peace.' I said all this, or rather sang it softly and wept because I was deeply affected by the fact that I was leaving the world, that is, I was leaving my parents. The world didn't matter to me. I wasn't concerned about the world, only about my parents. I was little and I remembered only my parents and I was pained that I was leaving them.

Midday came and people started eating on the deck; they sat together in their family groups as people used to do then. Opposite me was a woman with her husband and their three children. I was sitting looking out at the sea. At one point a lady came up — because the sailors had asked for my ticket and I didn't have one, people had seen that I was a poor boy — and she tapped me on the shoulder and gave me a piece of bread with three little bunches of white bait. In those days people used to fry white bait in little bunches of three tied together with a piece of broom grass which they passed through the fishes' eyes — they would then dust them with flour and fry them.

I said to her:

'Thank you. Thank you very much!'

Some of the other women who were nearby said to her:

'Well done! That was a kind thing to do. How come you thought of that? It didn't occur to us.'

The woman, however, turned round and said to them:

'No one should bother about children like that, little urchins, nor give them anything. But what are we to do? We're human too.'

When I heard the words 'little urchin', I, poor little wretch, suddenly felt a surge of happiness inside because I thought that I really am a little urchin. I had become a little urchin for the love of Christ. And I said to myself, 'O Christ, save me and guide me!'

Eventually we arrived in Thessalonica. We got off the boat. I didn't know where to go. I went to the church of Saint Demetrios and kissed the icons. I knelt down weeping and implored the saint to help me to become a hermit; that was my dream. Then I climbed up a hill and came to a little church, a country chapel. It was locked. But outside there was a wooden bench. I stayed there all night. I cried a lot. I wanted to go back, to go home to my parents. This was a sore temptation for me. Three times I went back. While I was weeping I kept repeating the words of the hymns of supplication to our Lady that my father had taught me: 'Do not despise my supplication, do what's profitable to my soul...'.* I said this again and again through my tears. And so I fell asleep.

I forgot to tell you what I did with the presents that my boss had given me supposedly to take to my family. I gave them away to some young conscripts on the boat. I gave away the chocolates and the bottles of rose and peppermint liqueur, and so I got rid of them. The soldiers were at a loss to understand why I was giving the things away — I was a little boy. But they took them all the same.

So, as I was saying, I fell asleep outside the little chapel. I woke up in the morning, I went down to the sea, got onto the boat — the temptation was too much for me — and returned once again to Piraeus. What can I say? It's a long story!

I took a firm decision to leave and not come back

Following all these futile journeys and about-turns, after some time had passed, I took a firm decision to leave and not come back. I resolved not to get off the boat again. Once again I embarked from Piraeus, without return, for the Holy Mountain. It was the third time I was setting out — the last after all my misadventures.

When we arrived in Thessalonica it was Saturday. At that time Thessalonica was dominated by the Jewish community. People didn't work on Saturdays. It was a ghost town. Everything was closed: neither boats nor sailings. We had arrived late on the Friday evening. Everyone got off the boat to buy something to eat. I didn't get off because I was afraid of temptation. I was frightened that something might happen to me and I wouldn't arrive at my destination. I gave someone fifteen cents and he brought me bread and mackerel and I ate. For the whole day we all waited in the harbour because, as I said, nobody was working.

As evening approached, monks started to arrive and board the boat. I watched them in awe. For the first time I was seeing monks in their cassocks. I had positioned myself by the gangway and from where I stood I could see them all passing by. At one point a tall elderly and venerable-looking monk with a long beard and with a haversack on his back walked up. He came towards me. He took a seat on a bench and motioned me to sit down too.

'Where are you going, my boy?' he asked.

* The hymn (*troparion*) which follows the Gospel in the Canon of Supplication (*Paraklisis*) to the Theotokos.

'To the Holy Mountain,' I replied.

'And what are you going to do there?'

Concealing the truth, I answered, 'I'm going to work.'

'Come to Kavsokalyvia,' he said. 'That's where I live with my brother in a hermitage in the desert. Come along, my boy, and we'll all glorify Christ together.' Then he asked me:

'What books do you read, my boy?'

'The Letter of Christ, the Letter of our Lady, and the Life of Saint John the Hut-dweller,' I answered. 'I haven't been much to school.'

He made no comment about the books, about whether they were good or not.

'Come with me,' he said. 'We've got work there and we'll pay you. And...we might even make a monk of you!'

As soon as I heard that word, a smile crossed my face. Then he said to me, 'Listen, my boy, don't be upset at what I'm going to tell you. Young boys are not permitted on the Holy Mountain. You're very young and they're prohibited from allowing you to enter.'

My face fell.

'But don't worry,' he said, 'we'll tell a little lie and God will forgive us. In God's eyes it won't be a lie but a truth, because you love Christ and you want to go to the Holy Mountain to worship Christ. So whoever asks you, "What's your relationship to the elder?" you'll reply, "He's my uncle." And I'll say that you're my nephew, my sister's son.'

Lots of other monks crowded onto the boat. Night fell. The monks all huddled close together and each took out his food. We sat close to them too. The elder gave me bread to eat.

'What's your relationship to the boy, holy confessor?' they all asked.

'He's my sister's son, my nephew. My sister has died and because he's an orphan I've taken him with me.'

A great miracle of God's providence

We sailed all through the night. In the morning at about ten o'clock we arrived at the port of Daphni. All the monks heaved up their haversacks filled with the items they had bought in Thessalonica for their various handicrafts. We walked down the ship's gangway. A rowing boat was waiting for us. My elder was given preference because he was a confessor and spiritual father. We clambered first into the little boat and arrived at the steps at Daphni. We got out. But then what happened? The elder distanced himself a little from me to find a spot to lay down his haversack and at that moment a tall guard, dressed in his white kilted skirt and crowned with his red fez and black tassel, grabbed hold of me and threw me back into the boat just as it was about to set out again to fetch more monks.

'What business do you have here?' he shouted. 'Children aren't allowed. Get back to the boat. Off you go!'

I started to cry; the boat began to pull out. At that moment, however, my elder noticed what was happening and ran shouting, 'Stop! Bring the boy back. He's mine.'

The boat rowed back and I was freed.

Then the Serdaris said to him — 'Serdaris' was what they called the guards on the Holy Mountain. At that time they wore white kilts and a red fez. Sterling fellows. They were present everywhere at all official ceremonies — so the Serdaris said to him, 'Father, you're not allowed to take the boy with you.'

'I've no choice but to take him. He's my nephew,' said the elder. 'He's my sister's boy and I can't leave him. He's an orphan. He's nowhere to go.'

'That's fine, but I'm the one who'll be in hot water if I let the boy in.'

'Don't worry. Whatever happens, refer the matter to me. I'll speak to the elders and you won't find yourself in any trouble.'

And so with the elder, 'my uncle', who indeed became my elder and spiritual father — Panteleimon was his name — we went up to the skete. By all this I want to show how God worked many miracles on me, unworthy as I am. His hand very manifestly protected me everywhere. And so in this case the hand of God led me into the hands of a holy elder and spiritual father who was to protect me. God had sent him and this elder saved me. It was a great miracle of God's providence. In many things God's providence has helped me but above all the great assistance I received was that I succeeded in going to the Holy Mountain at such an early age, in spite of the fact that it was forbidden. I knew nothing about monastic life. But God helped me.

As I told you, we arrived at the skete. From that time onwards it was a different life: a life in Christ, a life of worship, a life free of care, a life of resurrection!

THE HOLY MOUNTAIN – KAVSOKALYVIA (1918–1925)

My life on the Holy Mountain was prayer, joy and obedience to my elders

When I went to the Holy Mountain I was young and uneducated

If I were to tell you about my life on the Holy Mountain, my love and my
Heb. 11:32 devotion, *time would fail me to tell....* My love for you incites me to tell
you what I remember.

When I went to the Holy Mountain I was, as I told you, young and uneducated. I didn't know how to read; I read syllable by syllable. My elders — they were brothers, Elder Panteleimon the Confessor, and Father Ioannikios — asked me, 'Can you read?'

'A little,' I answered.

It was Saturday evening. They set me to read the Psalter. Shyly I started to stutter the words of the first psalm: *Ble...e...es...se...e...ed... i...is...th...e...ma...an...*

'That's fine, my boy, let me read now,' said Father Ioannikios, 'and
you can read another day.' He donned his glasses and started: *Blessed is*
Ps. 1:1 *the man who has not made his way...*

You can imagine my embarrassment. That was a lesson for me. 'I must learn to read,' I resolved.

And so I quickly set to work. Whenever I found a spare moment — and I had lots of free time — I would read the Psalter, the New Testament and the poetic canons from the daily offices to loosen up my tongue, and so from the countless times I read it, I learned the Psalter by heart. I read even during the night.

I felt that I was no longer on earth, but that I had been transported to heaven

One night there was a vigil service at the *Kyriakon*,* the church of the Holy Trinity. This was very shortly after I had arrived, during the first few

* The *Kyriakon* or *Katholikon* is the central church of the skete where the monks go on Sundays and major feast days.

days. Our skete was celebrating its feast day. My elders left in the early evening for the church and left me in the hermitage to sleep. I was young and they thought I might not be able to stay awake until the morning when the vigil would end.

After midnight Father Ioannikios came and woke me up. 'Wake up and get dressed,' he said, 'and we'll go to the church.'

I jumped up at once and in three minutes we had arrived at the Holy Trinity church. He ushered me into the church first. It was the first time I had been inside. I was overwhelmed! The church was filled with monks standing upright in an attitude of reverence and attentiveness. The chandeliers shed their light everywhere, lighting up the icons on the walls and on the icon stands. Everything was bright and shining. The little oil lamps were lit, the incense exuded fragrance and the singing resonated devoutly in the otherworldly beauty of the night. I was overcome with awe, but also with fear. I felt that I was no longer on earth, but that I had been transported to heaven. Father Ioannikios nodded to me to go forward and kiss the icons. I remained motionless. 'Take my hand, take my hand!' I gasped. 'I'm scared!' He took me by the hand and, gripping him tightly, I went up to venerate the icons. It was my first experience. It was engraved on my innermost soul. I will never forget it.

I went through a period of temptation

I was very happy and enthusiastic about my life there. In the beginning, however, I went through a period of temptation. I started to think about my parents. I felt sorely for them; I was pained that they didn't know where I was. I thought also about a cousin of my own age. I developed a desire to go to my village for a little and to bring my cousin to the Holy Mountain so that he too could experience this wonderful life. I felt that I had an obligation to bring him to Christ. I didn't say anything, however, to my elder. And so I started to lose my appetite for food, my face grew pale and I became melancholy.

My elder noticed all this. One day he called me over and said to me with concern, 'What's wrong, my boy? What's the matter with you?'

I told him everything. That was the end of it. I was freed. The temptation passed. My appetite returned and joy flooded my heart.

I continued in obedience to my elders. My face shone; I grew more handsome and good-looking. Although I had been thin and scrawny to begin with, I later became quite handsome. My face became angelic. How did I see it? I had gone to see my elder and as the sun struck his window it became a mirror for me. And when I saw my face I said to myself, 'Goodness! How the grace of God has changed me.' To begin with I thought about my parents and the thought of them tormented me. Later I didn't think about them. I remembered them only in my prayers, for the Lord to save them. At first I longed for them; later my longing was for my elders. I commemorated my parents in my prayer, but in a different way, only with the love of Christ. I started to fast more and to make greater ascetic effort, and I was filled with even greater mania and enthusiasm. I longed to be in the church continually and I wanted to do whatever the elders wanted, so that I could please them. There you see is the change, the transformation worked by the grace of God.

I loved my elders

As I have said before, my elders were Father Panteleimon and his brother Father Ioannikios. I loved them, though they were very strict. At the time I didn't realize this. Because I loved them I had the impression that they didn't treat me with austerity. I had great respect, devotion and love for them. My devotion was… was it that I saw the icon of Christ? such was my awe and such my devotion. After God came my elders. They were both priests. They came from the Karditsa area, from a village that is high up. What's the village called? It's worth recalling the name of the village… Yes, I remember! It's the village of Mesenikolas near Karditsa. That's where my woollen blanket is from, the one I slept in until recently. I was utterly obedient to them.

Obedience! What can I say? I truly knew the meaning of that word! I abandoned myself to obedience with joy and love. It was this absolute obedience that saved me and it was on account of this that God gave me His charismatic gift. Yes, I repeat, I was utterly obedient to my elders — not forced obedience, but with joy and love. I loved them truly. And because I loved them, this love made me sense and realize what they wanted. I knew what they wanted even before they asked, and not only what, but also how they wanted each thing. I went here and I went there. I was devoted to them. And so my soul was winged with joy when I was with them. I thought of no one else — not my parents, not acquaintances, not friends or the outside world. My life was prayer, joy and obedience to my elders.

If they said something to me once I would observe it always. For example, the elder once said to me, 'Wash your hands before you eat and every time we are about to go to the church, because we are entering a holy place and everything must be clean. Remember we are both priests and we celebrate the Liturgy; we need to have our hands clean and to have everything about us clean.'

And so every so often I would wash my hands with soap. There was no need for them to tell me a second time. Before I ate I would soap and wash my hands. If we needed something in the church, I would wash my hands. If I picked something up, then I would wash my hands. When delicate work was required in my handicraft, I would first wash my hands. I did the same with everything without the slightest thought of demurral. And remember that I had two elders and often they asked for conflicting things.

One day Father Ioannikios said to me, 'Take these stones from here and carry them over there.' I took them to the place he showed me. Then the father confessor came by. As soon as he saw them he scolded me angrily, saying, 'You crooked fellow! Why did you do that? Is that where we want these stones? Take them back to where you found them!'

Whenever he got angry he would use the phrase 'you crooked fellow' to scold me.

The next day Father Ioannikios passed by. He saw the stones in their original place and he fumed at me, saying, 'Didn't I tell you to take the stones over there?'

I hung my head and blushed; I made a penitent bow before him and said, 'Forgive me, Elder, I had carried almost all of them over, but the other elder saw me and said, "Take them back where you found them; that's where we need them." And so I took them back.'

Father Ioannikios said not a word.

They did things like this to me often. But I never suspected anything. I didn't think, 'Are you doing this to me to test me?' I never discerned, however, that they were testing me. But even if they were testing me, things occurred so naturally that I never realized it. That's important, because if someone knows he is being tested he can do even the hardest of tasks to show that he is being obedient. But if he is unaware that someone is testing him, and indeed sees that person agitated and angry, then he can't avoid reacting and thinking: 'Look at that now! Has this man been a monk here for all those years and yet he still cannot control his anger? Can this be possible? Can a monk be irascible and pray? How has he not managed to rid himself of anger? These men are very imperfect...'

At all events, I didn't think in this way, nor did I know whether they were testing me. On the contrary, I took great delight in these incidents, because I loved them. But they too had great love for me, even if they didn't openly display it. I loved both my elders, but I leaned particularly

for support on the one who was my spiritual father, Elder Panteleimon.
Ps. 62:9 Just as David says, *my soul has stuck fast behind You, Your right hand*
[63:8] *has supported me*, so my own soul stuck fast to my elder. This is quite
true! And my heart was with his heart. I watched him, I sensed him. He took me out and we went to the *Kyriakon* and from there we went to our various tasks together. It's incredible how much I sensed him. That sanctified me greatly. The fact that I stuck to him like a leech sanctified me. The fact that my heart was glued to his heart worked wonders for me. He was a very great saint!

And yet the elder said nothing to me. Not only did he not tell me where he came from, he didn't even tell me his surname. Nothing. He never said, 'in my village', or 'my parents',... 'my brothers'. He was always silent and always praying and always meek. If he got angry any time, his anger and everything he said was all feigned. I loved him and I believe that through my obedience to him and with my love for him the grace he possessed visited me and stayed with me.

I observed him in order to take something from him, to imitate him. I loved him; I revered him; I looked at him and received benefit. It was enough for me simply to look at him. We would go together on an entire expedition. We would walk from Kavsokalyvia up onto the mountain to cut holm oaks. All the way he would say nothing, not a word. I remember my elder showing me which oaks to cut. As soon as I cut one, I shouted with delight, 'Elder, I've cut it!' He said, 'Go there with your saw.' I cleared the brushwood round about so I could get in with my saw. He would then go to find me another. We would use the phrase 'with one puff', that is, at a single stroke. Again I would cry out, 'Elder, I've cut it!' With delight. These weren't natural things. It was my love; it was the grace of God that was transmitted from the elder to me, a humble boy.

Do you remember the story that's told about a group of monks who used to visit one of the Desert Fathers and inundate him with questions? One of the monks would sit saying nothing and simply looking into the elder's face. In the end the Abba turned to him and said, 'Why don't you ask anything? Have you no questions at all?' The monk replied, 'I wish for nothing more; it's enough for me simply to look at you, Elder.'* You see, he was gracefully enjoying him; he was 'inhaling' him, that is, he was breathing in the grace of God through him. Saint Symeon the New Theologian says the same thing. He confesses that he too received grace from his elder.

* A story told of Saint Anthony in the *Wisdom of the Desert Fathers*.

Whatever I did, I did with joy

My elders didn't give me heavy chores to do. I simply watered the garden and did my handicraft, that is, my woodcarving. Nor did they give me instruction. To begin with I went with them to the church services. Nothing more.

After some days the elder called me over and gave me a prayer rope and told me to repeat the prayer 'Lord, Jesus Christ, have mercy on me' every night. Nothing more. No instruction, no explanation. Before he gave me the prayer rope he said, 'Look! Make a bow, kiss my hand, and kiss the cross at the top of the prayer rope so that I may give you a blessing that God may help you.'

That was how I learned to pray with a prayer rope.

To begin with they didn't send me on errands outside the hermitage. Whatever jobs I did, I did in the house. Then I went out to the garden. I dug, watered, weeded and whatever else I could. Later I started to learn woodcarving. Once my chores were finished they got me to read the Psalter while they worked. I was conscientious in my work and I didn't want to disappoint them in any way. My only thought was how I could serve and please my elders in everything. Whatever they told me to do, I did, observing their instructions exactly. In order to be sure about what I was doing, I ran over in my mind again and again what they had said, learning it like a lesson. I worked over their words in my head. For example, my handicraft was woodcarving. I watched how the elders went about it and at night when I went to bed I went over the 'lesson' in my mind: we take the piece of wood, we cut it, we place it in water to soak, then we take it out and leave it to dry, then we cut it into shape, we plane it down, we smooth it with sand-paper, we take the rasp and we work it this way and that, then we take a crystallite sea stone that makes the wood shine (they called it adamantine), then we trace out the design, etc. I went over the whole process in my head so that I wouldn't forget the slightest detail and so that I would do the job exactly as they wanted. I was afraid I might make some mistake and upset them. And so whatever they told me, I learned by heart.

They explained to me why it was essential for me to learn a handicraft. They said:

'Be sure to learn your handicraft. Otherwise you can't survive here. This isn't a monastery, a coenobitic monastery that is, with lots of produce from fields, orchards and vineyards. Here you have to work to buy your biscuit.'

They explained this to me and taught me the art of woodcarving. And so as not to disappoint them, I mentally revised what I had learned at night when I went to bed, as I said. And so in the morning I was ready for work. Whatever I did, I did with joy. I said to myself, 'I'm going to become a monk, and I have to learn what that means.' I was inquisitive to learn everything in all its depth and breadth. I wanted to learn everything. I received my elder's blessing to read the Service of Monastic Tonsure and in two weeks I had learned it all by heart. It was not, of course, that I thought I would later become a preacher and that I would be able to make use of this knowledge, but simply out of love for Christ.

I accustomed myself not to leave my thoughts free
in order to acquire purity of mind

On the bench where I was working, where I was doing my woodcarving, I also had the Holy Scriptures. I opened them and read. I had the Gospels and I read them from the beginning of the Gospel according to Saint
Matt. 1:1 Matthew: *The book of the generation of Jesus Christ, Son of David, Son...* I
read, worked and repeated the words in my head. I repeated the words of the Gospels innumerable times and I remember them even now. What I wanted was to have holy words in my head. I never tired of repeating them again and again. I loved the divine words; I sensed them vibrantly and fathomed them ever more deeply. I would repeat them insatiably all day long. Even if I repeated them every day, I never tired of them.

I had great enthusiasm, and when my elders would leave in the morning and return at night, I would be free and would go to the little chapel, to Saint George's, and devote myself to prayer. I would go there. Yes...and what would happen! I would be so filled with exhilaration that I wouldn't eat. I didn't want to be distracted. You understand? I repeated the Jesus Prayer, I sang and I read. I went there on my own. I had a really good voice. It's true — I had a really excellent voice! I'm not telling you this now in order to compliment myself, but because that is how I felt. I had a very good voice, and as I sang the words sounded like laments. They were love songs...they were for Christ...they were whatever you like...you understand? My goodness! How many funeral services...how many...whatever you like. Suchlike things I sang. What can I do to make you...there! Suchlike things I say. Something I have experienced. You understand?

As time passed and I grew up a little and became stronger, the elders started to send me on errands outside the hermitage. In our hermitage, in Kavsokalyvia, we didn't have topsoil and we brought it in from a considerable distance lugging it on our shoulders. When I used to go in obedience to fetch earth and walked over towards Saint Niphon's cave, it was my habit not to leave my thoughts to roam freely, but to learn by heart passages of Holy Scripture, the psalms and the poetic canons. I did this in order to have purity of mind. I never imagined that I would ever use the things I learned by heart in the way preachers do to speak in public and give sermons. I never imagined that I would leave the desert. Such a thought never entered my head. I believed that there I would remain and there I would die. But without my realizing it and without my wishing it, I found myself outside the Holy Mountain.

I stretched forth my hand and preached a sermon

One day my elders sent me to bring earth over to the skete. Once I had walked some way along the path to Saint Niphon's chapel, I was, as usual, going over in my mind the words of Saint John's Gospel and gazing out at the Aegean Sea which stretched out in horizonless infinity. I stopped for a moment on a rock, breathed in the fragrance of the thyme, and, exhilarated by the exuberance of nature, I started to shout. I stretched forth my hand and preached a sermon. Yes, I assure you it's quite true! I laid down the sack I was taking to fill with earth and, standing on the rock, I stretched out my hand and, in a loud voice and speaking deliberately, I commenced:

And this is the judgment, that the light came into the world and men loved darkness rather than light for their works were evil; for everyone who does evil hates the light and does not come towards the light in case his works be reproved... John 3:19–20

I recited the passage to the end. And to whom did I address this sermon? To the empty air, to the sea, to the whole wide world. Without anyone to hear, I preached it in the midst of the wilderness.

Well, what sort of things should I tell you about? I tell you about the things that I loved. And I remember them so vividly!

I ran; I didn't walk

I didn't want at all to stay still. I wanted to be always on the move, watering plants and chopping wood. And everything was done with a bow and a blessing. I was filled with joy and exhilaration. I felt full and overflowing and I ran. I ran; I didn't walk. I was embarrassed, however, to let the elders see me running, and so I walked slowly to begin with and when I was out of sight I started to run. I took wings in order to go quickly and return quickly to my elders. A life free of care...what can I say! This life is truly angelic. And that blessed elder of mine was also full of eagerness for activity. He would say to me, 'Go here...go there...'. It's true, of course, that we had lots of jobs to do. They had given me responsibility for the hermitage. We kept a house well ordered and well looked after. We had olive trees, we had a few fruit trees and we had a vegetable garden.

The work naturally made me tired. I did lots of jobs. I went up to the mountain. My feet often got cut. How were my elders to know? They saw me as a child. When I came down from the mountain after walking for three hours, Father Ioannikios might say to me, 'Tomorrow we're going to make bread, so get ready now and go and fetch wood for the oven.'

So I would take a rope and go up the mountain for branches. I walked on paths, but also over rough ground. The elders would often send me to fetch logs or sticks and I would load them onto my back like a donkey. And fully loaded as I was and with my back aching, I would sit on the stone wall to rest. If the load were particularly heavy, I would say to myself, 'I'll show you, you old donkey!' I didn't know the meaning of laziness. Indeed, I didn't show any pity for my body. If my knees hurt, I wanted to take revenge on them. The more they protested and hurt, the greater the burden I loaded on my back. 'I'll show you, you old donkey!' I would repeat. I took revenge. I took revenge on my bad self. It's incredible that when I was a seventeen-year-old boy I loaded myself with a weight of almost two hundred pounds and carried it all the way for a distance, say, from Omonia Square up to the top of Lycavitos Hill.*

There was no question of laziness. I liked to pray even when I was tired. When I was exhausted I sought God even more. You must believe this and realize that it's truly possible. It's a matter of love. It's not simply that you work quickly. You do one job, then you begin another, you come back and do yet another, and you make sure that you finish them all: you water, you hoe, you bring earth and branches, you go up the mountain, you fetch wood for your woodcarving. With love you are in perpetual motion. You should see then where sins go. They all fall into a deep sleep. Do you hear? This is truly a life lost from the world, a blessed and holy life, a life in Paradise.

* Well-known landmarks in Athens, a steep climb of over one kilometer.

I can't give you an example of what real obedience is. It's not that we have a discussion about the virtue of obedience and then I say to you, 'go and do a somersault', and you obey. That's not obedience. You need to be entirely carefree and not thinking at all about the matter of obedience, and then suddenly you are asked to do something and you are ready to do it joyfully. If you are busy at work and not at all in a state of vigilance and readiness and someone humiliates you, then by your reaction you will show whether or not you have obedience.

I followed the instructions of my elders to the letter. They said to me, 'You won't speak and you won't say what we do or what order of prayer we keep in the hermitage. If you meet a monk on the road and he says, "your blessing", you will reply, "your blessing", with respect and Christ's love. And if he is an elder, you will kiss his hand. If he asks you, "How are your elders?" you will reply, "With your prayers they are well", and continue at once on your way — without any further conversation. And if he comes up behind you and approaches you and asks you something, don't stop and don't reply, because not all monks are good and you need to be careful. Whatever they ask you, you will reply, "I don't know, ask my elder, I don't know." Say, "your blessing", and leave. Don't let them tell you, "You know, woodcarving is not such a good handicraft, come and learn icon painting or music or suchlike." Don't listen to anything; continue your path.'

Once they sent me to Saint Niphon's, and on the way I met three men from the world — that's what people on the Holy Mountain call those who are not monks — and, as usual, when I approached them I said, 'Your blessing', and walked past. Since I had a really 'wild' appearance, one of the company commented, 'The poor boy, he doesn't seem to be quite right in the head.'

I had by this time walked on, but I had very sharp hearing. And when I heard this I was pleased by the humiliation. I smiled inwardly. 'He's right,' I thought. 'He's quite right. But what would he say if he knew my real madness!'

I didn't go out often, nor did my elders take me to the feast day celebrations. When a saint had his feast day the elders would go to the church dedicated to his memory and leave me at home.

The elders used to light a fire in the hermitage. I didn't want to be near it. I didn't approach the fire at all. The old men would sit close to the fire and I would sit further off. I was afraid. I was afraid the fire would spoil me and I said so to the elders and the dear men let me be. It's a matter of habit. If you once get accustomed to sitting by the fire, you cannot then inure yourself to hardship. If I ever caught a cold, I would drink a hot herbal infusion, make some five or six hundred prostrations, perspire profusely and then change my clothes; after that I would lie down on my mattress and I would get well again.

I was quite genuinely a 'wild' man. I was a wild goat of the forest. I ran around in the snow and across the rocks barefoot. You should have seen how red my heels and feet became! My elders didn't oblige me to be barefoot, and they themselves weren't barefoot. It was something I wanted myself. But on the other hand they didn't tell me not to take off my shoes. In the chapel and in the *Kyriakon*, however, I wore both socks and shoes — not my pig-skin moccasins. I remember something very lovely! It was springtime and the elders sent me to Kerasia. As I was running, I took off my moccasins because I wanted the soles of my feet to become as tough and resilient as moccasin soles in the snow and frost.

Because my elders saw me living like this, they took delight in me too. It may be that they humiliated me and scolded me; even when I did something good, they said that it was bad. Not always, of course, but they wanted to 'catch me out' when I wasn't expecting it.

My elders were exceedingly saintly. They instructed me in many ways, often with austerity. They never said, 'Well done!' They never praised me. Their counsels were always how to love God and how to humble myself, how I should invoke God to give strength to my soul and love Him greatly. That's what I learnt. 'Well done' were words I never heard, nor did I ever seek to hear them. Even at home I had never heard the words, 'Congratulations, that was well done.' My mother scolded me. My father was away; he was in America; he worked for years on the Panama Canal. That did me a lot of good. A person who is accustomed to humiliation attracts the grace of God. If my elders weren't scolding me I was disconsolate and thought to myself, 'Heavens above, couldn't I have found better elders than these?' I wanted them to castigate me, to scold me and to treat me harshly. Now I realize just how severe they were. At the time I didn't realize it because I loved them. Never would I have wanted to be parted from them.

Sometimes my excessive zeal would lead me astray

Sometimes my excessive zeal would lead me astray. I would do things without a blessing. That's egotism. I'll give you an example. Listen.

My elders would often be away working all day and would leave me alone in the hermitage. I would busy myself with my handicraft. My handicraft was woodcarving, as I have told you. They still hadn't shown me everything about the craft. They were afraid I might leave.

So one day I took a fine piece of white wood and traced out a design on it. I carved a very fine blackbird, full of movement, with its wings stretched back and pecking at a grape. The grape was hanging from the branch of a climbing vine that had two or three leaves and the blackbird was taking the grape in its open beak. It was very fine. I had finished it all off with sandpaper. When my elders returned I went to greet them with a bow. I took my carving with me and said to Father Ioannikios, 'Look what I've made!' As soon as he saw it his eyes glazed over and he started raging, 'Who told you to make that? Did you ask anyone?' He grabbed it and threw it on the floor, smashing it to smithereens. 'Go at once and tell the elder,' he said. I was mortified and I asked his forgiveness. Without realizing it, I had upset them. 'Why do you do things without asking? Go at once to the elder and show him the pieces and make confession.'

I went straight away to the elder and showed him the pieces and he said to me, 'You shouldn't have done that, my boy. Nothing gets done without a blessing. That way you can easily be led astray and lose the grace of God.' I made a bow of penitence and asked his forgiveness with simplicity and without passion. The reproach didn't vex me, on the contrary, I thought, 'My elders should have been harsher to me, they should have punished me.'

On another occasion, however, I was deliberately disobedient. One day, before the elders left for work, my spiritual father said, 'Do you see that book up on the shelf there? Don't touch it. It's not for you; you're too young. Later when you've shown improvement, when you're more humble, then you'll read it.'

That for me was law. I didn't so much as glance at it. But one day when the elders had left for Kerasia I was overtaken by curiosity. I went over and looked up at it. It was high up. I was small and couldn't reach it. I turned the matter over and over in my mind... Then I said to myself, 'At least let me see what it's about.' So I pulled across a stool, climbed up, reached for it and brought it down. What a pity! The letters were all jumbled up like a foreign language. It was written by hand. By hand — a large book, a very large, thick book. I couldn't understand all the strange abbreviations — later I learned to read them. But you should have seen the letters and the calligraphy! It was a manuscript. It was by Saint Symeon the New Theologian, a very big book with thick pages. It was also very heavy. So now I was going to read it, was I? I couldn't. I placed it back up on the shelf.

But after this I felt depressed, troubled and sad. I could neither work nor pray. Nothing. On other occasions when my elders were away I would go to the church and would be overcome by a sense of deep devotion and, since I had a good voice, I would sing. I sang hymns, keening away in a lament-like fashion. The hymns were deeply poignant and I enjoyed them and was moved by them. This time, however, after my disobedience, I did not go to the church. I went outside, sat on the wall and gazed glumly out at the Aegean Sea. I sat and looked at the sea. I didn't want even to repeat the 'Lord, Jesus Christ'. You see the state I was in? Great dejection. So that was that. I didn't go to the church and I didn't pray the Jesus Prayer. Melancholy took hold of me. Yes, of course, I had faith in God, but I didn't want to contravene the elders' instructions. I sensed the presence of God, but I didn't want to upset any person. I didn't want to cause anyone to be saddened. What was I to do...?

As evening fell the elders arrived back. What was I to do, poor wretch? I said to myself that I would tell them. But I couldn't bring myself to do it. I went to the church because I was obliged to go with the elders. We read Vespers and we read Compline. I said nothing. I went up to my cell, to my '*kavia*' — that's what we called the rooms. I didn't do my prostrations, or my rule of psalmody, or my prayer rope. I lay down and contemplated what I'd be like when I died, lying in my coffin. Needless to say, I was miserable. Next morning the bell rang. We went down to the church and I read. We finished Matins, said the dismissal and went out. We left the church to go to the refectory. I couldn't stand it any longer. I tugged a little at my elder's — that is my confessor's — sleeve, and I said to him:

'I want to see you for a minute, Elder.'

At once he turned back and we went into the church again and I told him:

'I'm very troubled,' I said. 'I've been disobedient. You told me not to touch that book and I had a look at it and since then I haven't been at peace: no 'Lord, Jesus Christ', no psalmody, no prayer, no prostrations.'

'Didn't I tell you so, my boy?' he said. 'Why did you do it?'

'Forgive me, Elder. Temptation got the better of me and I'm very sorry. Forgive me and with your prayers I'll be more careful in the future and I won't be disobedient.'

He read a prayer of forgiveness, and, do you know? All my tortured thoughts disappeared. That was one good thing. As soon as I confessed to the elder — glory to God — I got over everything immediately. Every time I confessed I was filled with a great sense of joy and I devoted myself passionately to prayer. I believed that I had told everything to God — that I was once again with God. You can't imagine how strongly I had that feeling! And nowadays I hear some monks saying, 'Make sure the elder doesn't hear about that!' Can you believe it? For us, on the contrary, the elder pervaded our whole being, into the inmost recess of our heart.

I loved the elders very much, though at that time all novices and those in obedience loved their elders. After God, what counted was the opinion of your elder. If you did anything contrary to that, any disobedience, you couldn't receive Communion or anything.

The secret of spiritual life is obedience

Many of those on the Holy Mountain lived secretly. They died without anyone knowing them. I too wanted to live secretly. I didn't want to be a preacher or anything. And it never crossed my mind to go out from the Holy Mountain. A young boy in a complete wilderness! To experience the sense of the desert and of helplessness I would climb up the mountain and stay there for hours. I wanted to live as a hermit. I found wild herbs and berries and ate them. I did this as a form of asceticism. I wanted to live on my own, just like the saint I had fallen in love with when I was little, Saint John the Hut-dweller. He was my favourite saint. He was the one I imitated. It made such an impression on me that he was able to endure staying close to his parents, setting up his little hut next to them, without revealing himself to them and giving them strength all the time: 'You pitched your tiny hovel by the gates of your parents.' That's what his *troparion* says:

With fervor from infancy
You longed and sighed for the Lord;
You left behind willingly
The world and all its delights
And struggled redoubtably.
You pitched your tiny hovel
By the gates of your parents;
Ambushes of the demons
You dispersed and defeated.
So rightly, John most blessed,
Christ's crown of glory was given you.

And another hymn* sung on his feast-day says the same:

Poor as another Lazarus,
You waited long and patiently
Before your parents' mansion gates
Within your tiny hut confined,
O Holy Father, saint most wise!
But now, O John, you've found a home,
A spacious, glorious dwelling-place,
Shared with the hosts of the angels
And all the saints in the heavens.

I told everything to my elder. Yes, whatever I was thinking. And he from time to time, when he saw me straying to extremes, would tell me:

'Delusion, my boy!'

My whole life was a paradise: prayer, worship, handicraft, and obedience to my elders. But my obedience was the outcome of love not coercion. This blessed obedience benefited me greatly. It changed me. I became sharp-witted, quick and stronger in body and soul. It made me know everything. I must glorify God day and night for granting me the possibility of living in this way in this life.

Obedience is something I have pored over and studied minutely. The other things that God has given me in my life came on their own. The gift of clear sight was also given to me by God on account of obedience. Obedience shows love for Christ. And Christ especially loves the obedient. That's why He says, *I love those who love me, and those who seek me*
Prov. 8:17 *will find grace.* Everything is written in Holy Scripture, but in a concealed manner.

I had great zeal for spiritual things

My elders never ordered me what to do. They gave me a prayer rope and told me, 'Say the prayer.' Nothing more. They saw that I was a fanatic and they didn't tell me much, not even what to read. They wouldn't let me read anything from the great Fathers which contain austerities, that is, Saint Ephrem, Saint Isaac the Syrian, Saint John of the Ladder, Saint Symeon the New Theologian and Evergetinos, etc. They had forbidden me. So, in obedience, I read only the lives of saints, the Psalter, the Book

* *Exapostilarion*, a hymn sung after the conclusion of the Canon during Matins. The Canon comprises a series of hymns based on the Biblical Canticles.

of the Eight Tones, and the *Menaia* containing the hymns for the days of each month, and that was where I learned to read from, because to begin with I wasn't able to. But I had great zeal for spiritual things. Every so often I would go to the chapel of Saint George, which I also helped to build, and I would sing lots of the sung parts of the services. Most of all I liked the Trinitarian canons. I liked also the hymns that are imbued with divine love, divine *eros*. It was a lament, a love song, call it what you like. I shed lots of tears, but they weren't tears of sadness, but tears of joy, divine joy. I was moved. I sang them beautifully! This was my life. I lived with the Lord's grace, not with my own strength. All these things were gifts of divine grace; they didn't come from my own ingenuity or from my learning — which I didn't have — nor, nor, nor... It was from the grace of God.

On some occasions, however, I strayed. I took some initiatives without asking my elders. Listen. In order to have purity of mind I started to learn Holy Scripture by heart. I started at the beginning, from the Gospel according to Saint Matthew. One day an opportunity arose and I recited to them the first chapter of Saint John's Gospel by heart. When they heard it, they scolded me because I had done it without a blessing.

I had waited for this moment with longing

Where should I start, my children, to tell you about how I became a monk? My life on the Holy Mountain is a long story.

When I had reached the age of fourteen, my elder called me and said to me:

'What are you going to do? What are your plans? Are you going to stay here?'

'I'm going to stay!' I exclaimed, beaming with pleasure and joy.

'Make a bow.'

I made a bow. Then he brought me a cassock of his own which was old and worn and which he kept for work. It was so patched and mended that the original cloth could barely be seen and the collar was greasy and stained by sweat. I had seen young monks in the *Kyriakon*; they had been handsomely dressed and I had dreamt of a cassock like theirs. What can I say? I had waited for this moment with longing. And young as I was, I had imagined the cassock I would be given to wear, and how fine and splendid it would be. But when the time came, what did I see? A patched old rag. I was disappointed a little — for five minutes. I was young at the time, you see, fourteen years old. I didn't say anything though; I didn't complain. When I saw the cassock, I felt suddenly crestfallen, as I said, but I quickly thought of the positive side.

'With your blessing,' I said and took it.

I didn't think about the matter again. I thought about the hermits who wore hair shirts and never took them off or washed them. God therefore gave me great consolation. I went to the reading desk. The Epistle of Saint John happened to open before me. And that same day, my God, You spoke to me! O my God, You spoke to me so much...

Two or three years later I was tonsured into the Great Schema

Two or three years later I was tonsured into the Great Schema.

The day before I received another special blessing. We had to go along with my elder to the Monastery of Megisti Lavra to obtain permission for the tonsure. The abbot who gave me the permission was very saintly. As we were walking from the place were Saint Neilos the Myrrh-streaming had lived towards the Lavra Monastery, I smelled for the first time the heavenly aroma. The fragrance flooded over me and I exclaimed about it to my elder. He smelled the fragrance in a simple, matter-of-fact sort of way, said nothing and walked on. That's how we must view these things, with simplicity. I smelled the fragrance for a second time at the relics of Saint Charalambos.

On the night of my tonsure all the fathers gathered in the church of the Holy Trinity, the *Kyriakon*. There they held a vigil service, chanting beautifully and devoutly while, filled with contrition, I stood unshod, in white socks. I made a prostration to all of the fathers and venerated the icons. Then the presiding elder addressed to me the special questions for the Great Schema. My eyes were filled with tears of emotion. Once the vigil was over we went to the hermitage. I was very happy, but silent. I wanted to be alone with God alone. When you are in that state, you don't want to sing or speak. You desire silence to hear in crystal purity the voice of Christ.

I loved the vigils on the Holy Mountain

The life of the Holy Mountain is a life of vigil and wakefulness. During the vigil service, when it is done properly, that is, when those participating are united in common worship, a spiritual atmosphere is created into which all enter easily and from which great spiritual benefit is derived. The soul is refined and the most suitable conditions for spiritual elevation and deep communication with the Lord are created. At two o'clock in the morning on the Holy Mountain a true earthquake takes place. I would always be filled with awe at that time. Prayer would cause the whole place to tremble, the entire spiritual world. Now that's what love for Christ is.

On the Holy Mountain I loved the vigil services very much. I became a different person. I was always very concentrated and focused. I had a great desire to hear the words. I didn't want sleep to snatch my mind away for even a moment. I didn't become heavy-eyed; I followed the services with irresistible devotion, with *eros*. When on occasion I would be sitting in the stalls at the side of the church, I didn't lean onto the back of the stall for fear of falling asleep. After the Divine Liturgy again I didn't want to sleep. The sense of love was what dominated, and that's why I kept awake.

The grace possessed by that saint radiated into my own soul too

In the *Kyriakon* where I went for vigils and other services I got to know holy men. Listen and I'll tell you about a hidden saint.

Up above our hermitage, very high up, there was a Russian, Old Dimas, who lived alone in a primitive hovel. He was exceedingly devout. Old Dimas remained virtually unknown throughout his life. No one mentions his name or speaks of his charismatic gift. Think of what it meant for him to leave Russia! Who knows how long his journey took. He left everything behind to come to the end of the earth, to Kavsokalyvia, and there he spent his whole life. And he died unknown. He was no egotist. On the very contrary, he was a fierce combatant. He had no one with whom to share his experiences and to whom he could say, 'I did five hundred prostrations today and this is what I felt...' He was a secret combatant.

Yes indeed, that is a perfect thing, perfect and selfless — selflessness, worship, holiness, face to face, without any obsequiousness towards men; the servant before the master. Nothing else at all: no abbot, no 'well done', no 'why is this thus?'. I saw a living saint. Yes, an unknown saint, poor and disdained. Who knows when he died? After how many days, or even months if it were wintertime, would we learn of it? Who would go all the way up there to his rude stone hovel? No one saw him. Often those hermits would be found two or three months after their repose.

The outpouring and superabundance of grace flowed over my pitiful self when I saw Old Dimas making prostrations and dissolving in tears in his prayer in the *Kyriakon*. With the prostrations of that man, grace overshadowed him so profusely that it radiated out even over me. It was then that the richness of grace was released over me also. Certainly, the grace existed before with the love I had for my elder. But it was then that I sensed the grace with exceptional intensity. Let me tell you how it happened.

One morning at about half past three I went to the *Katholikon*, to the Holy Trinity church, for the service. It was still early. The *simantron* had not yet been sounded. No one was in the church. I sat in the narthex beneath a stairway. I was hidden from sight and was praying. All of a sudden the church door opened and in walked a tall elderly monk. It was Old Dimas. As soon as he entered he looked around and saw no one. So then, holding a large prayer rope, he started to make rhythmic prostrations, rapid and numerous, and at the same time he repeated continually, 'Lord, Jesus Christ, have mercy on me… Most Holy Theotokos, save us.' After a short time he fell into ecstasy. I cannot, I simply cannot find words to describe to you his behaviour before God — motions of love and worship, motions of divine craving, of divine love and devotion. I saw him standing opening out his arms in the form of a cross, like Moses at the Red Sea, and he made a sound: 'Ouououououou!…' What was that? He was bathed in grace. He shone in the light. That was it! Immediately his prayer was communicated to me. Immediately I entered into the atmosphere surrounding him. He hadn't seen me. Listen. I was deeply moved and I started to shed tears. The grace of God came upon my pitiful and worthless self. How can I describe it for you? He transmitted the grace of God to me. The grace that that saint possessed radiated into my soul also. He transmitted to me his spiritual gifts of grace.

So Old Dimas had fallen into ecstasy. It happened without his willing it. He couldn't control his experience. That's not right either, what I'm saying. I can't express it. It is seizure by God, divine catalepsy. These things cannot be explained. They can't be explained at all, and if you explain them you fall very wide of the mark. No, they cannot be explained nor can they be rendered in books, nor can they be made comprehensible. You must be worthy to understand them.

Old Dimas transmitted to me the charisma of prayer and of clear sight

At four o'clock the bells rang. As soon as he heard the bells, Old Dimas made a few more prostrations and stopped praying. He sat on the low stone surround — I think there was a stone-built surround in the narthex — and in came Makaroudas — that was their affectionate name for

Makarios. He was nimble and soft-spoken. He was a little angel. How well he lit the oil-lamps! How well he lit the chandelier! And how well he snuffed out the lights again, one by one! How well he made his prostrations as he asked forgiveness right and left to take the service books in order to intone the words for the singers. How I loved him! He deserved to be loved, because he had the grace of God.

So Makarios, Makaroudas, entered into the main church. Old Dimas followed him, opened the door, and entered also. He stood and arranged himself in his stall, thinking that no one had seen him. I, too, concealed by the shadow of the stairway, stealthily and gingerly entered the main church. I went and venerated the icon of the Holy Trinity and returned and stood to one side. At the summons 'With the fear of God...' many of the fathers received Communion. I, too, made a prostration and received Communion. From the moment that I received Communion I was overcome by an intense joy, an enthusiasm.

After the service I went out into the forest alone, full of joy and exaltation. Madness! As I walked towards the hermitage I silently repeated the Prayers of Thanksgiving. I ran through the forest passionately, jumping for joy and stretching my arms out wide in enthusiasm and I shouted aloud, 'Glory to You, O Gooood! Glory to You, O Gooood!' Yes, my arms remained stretched out rigid, like a piece of wood and my body formed the shape of a cross. If you had seen me from behind, you would have seen a cross. My head was lifted up to the sky and my chest was expanded along with my outstretched arms ready to take off for the heavens. My heart wanted to fly. What I'm telling you is true, I experienced it. How long I remained in this state I don't know. When I came to, I lowered my arms and walked on silently with tears still in my eyes.

I arrived at the hermitage. I didn't eat anything as I usually did. I couldn't speak. I went to the chapel, but I didn't sing anything — none of the hymns of contrition that I usually sang. I sat in my stall and repeated the 'Lord, Jesus Christ, have mercy on me'. I continued in that state, but somewhat more calmly. Emotion was choking me. I dissolved in tears. They poured effortlessly from my eyes, on their own. I didn't want them, but it was emotion at the visitation of God. The tears did not stop until the evening. I couldn't sing or think or speak. And if anyone else had been there I wouldn't have spoken to him. I would have gone away to be on my own.

One thing is certain. Old Dimas transmitted to me the charisma of prayer and of clear sight at the time when he himself was praying in the narthex of the Holy Trinity church, the *Katholikon* of Kavsokalyvia.

What happened to me was something I had never thought of, neither had I ever desired it, nor expected it. My elders had never spoken to me of these gifts of grace. That was their way. They didn't teach me with words, only with their way of life. When I read the lives of the saints and ascetics I saw the gifts that God gave them. Believe me, I never thought that I would receive some charisma from God. It never crossed my mind. And that which I had never thought of appeared suddenly and I never gave any importance to it.

In the evening of the same day I went out of the church and sat on the low wall looking out to sea. It was approaching the time when my elders usually returned. While I was looking to see if they were coming, I saw them suddenly appear. I saw them descending some marble steps. But that place was far away, and I shouldn't normally have been able to see it. I saw them by the grace of God. I was filled with enthusiasm. It was the first time this had happened to me. I jumped up and ran to meet them. I took their haversacks.

'How did you know we were coming?' asked the elder.

I didn't reply. But when we arrived at the hermitage I approached the father confessor, Father Panteleimon, and secretly and out of the hearing of Father Ioannikios I said to him:

'I don't know how to explain this to you, but when you were on the other side of the hill I saw you loaded with your haversacks and I ran to meet you. The hill was like a pane of glass and I saw you on the other side.'

'All right, all right,' said the elder, 'don't give any importance to these things, and don't tell anyone, because the evil one is watching.'

I lived among the stars, in infinity, in heaven

The gift of clear sight, as I have told you, was something I had never desired. Nor, when I received it, did I attempt to increase it or cultivate it. I gave no importance to it. Neither have I ever asked, nor do I ask God to reveal something to me, because I believe that is counter to His will. But after the experience with Old Dimas I changed completely. My life became all joy and exaltation. I lived among the stars, in infinity, in heaven. I wasn't like that previously.

From the moment I experienced the grace of God all the gifts were multiplied. I became sharp-witted. I learned the Trinitarian canons, the Canon of Jesus and other canons. Simply on their being read and sung in the church I learned them by heart. I recited the Psalter by heart. I took care with some psalms that have similar words so that I didn't mix them up. I genuinely changed. I 'saw' lots of things, but I didn't speak, that is, I wasn't given the right to say anything, I wasn't 'informed' to speak. I saw everything, I registered everything, I knew everything. From my joy I no longer walked on the earth. My sense of smell was opened and I smelled everything, my eyes were opened and my ears were opened. I recognized things from far away. I distinguished the animals and the birds. From the sound of the call I knew if it was a blackbird or a sparrow, a finch or a nightingale, a robin or a thrush. I recognized all the birds by their song. At night and at dawn I delighted in the chorus of nightingales and blackbirds, all of them…

I became another, a new, a different person. I turned everything I saw into prayer. I referred it to myself. Why does the bird sing and glorify its Maker? I wanted to do the same. The same with the flowers: I recognized the flowers by their fragrances and I smelled them when I was half an hour away. I observed the grasses, the trees, the water, the rocks. I spoke with the rocks. The rocks had seen so much! I asked them and they told me all the secrets of Kavsokalyvia. And I was filled with emotion and contrition. I saw everything with the grace of God. I saw, but I didn't speak. I often went to the forest. I was greatly enthused by walking amidst the stones and the rushes, the thickets and the tall trees.

I fell in love with the nightingale and it inspired me

One morning I was walking alone in the virgin forest. Everything, freshened by the morning dew, was shining in the sunlight. I found myself in a gorge. I walked through it and sat on a rock. Cold water was running peacefully beside me and I was saying the prayer. Complete peace. Nothing could be heard. After a while the silence was broken by a sweet, intoxicating voice singing and praising the Creator. I looked. I couldn't discern anything. Eventually, on a branch opposite me I saw a tiny bird. It was a nightingale. I listened as the nightingale trilled unstintingly, its throat puffed out to bursting in sustained song. The microscopic little bird was stretching back its wings in order to find power to emit those sweetest of tones, and puffing out its throat to produce that exquisite voice. If only I had a cup of water to give it to drink and quench its thirst!

Tears came to my eyes — the same tears of grace that flowed so effortlessly and that I had acquired from Old Dimas. It was the second time I had experienced them.

I cannot convey to you the things I felt, the things I experienced. I have, however, revealed to you the mystery. And I thought, 'Why does this tiny nightingale produce these sounds? Why does it trill like that? Why is it singing that exquisite song? Why, why, why... why is it bursting its throat? Why, why, for what reason? Is it waiting for someone to praise it? Certainly not. No one there will do that.' So I philosophized to myself. This sensitivity I acquired after the experience with Old Dimas. Previously I didn't have it. What did that nightingale not tell me! And how much did I say to it in silence: 'Little nightingale, who told you that I would pass by here? No one comes here. It's such an out-of-the-way place. How marvelously you unceasingly carry on your duty, your prayer to God! How much you tell me, and how much you teach me, little nightingale! My God, how I am moved. With your warbling, dear nightingale, you show me how to hymn God, you teach me a thousand things, beyond number...'

My poor health does not allow me to narrate all this to you as I feel it. A whole book could be written about it. I loved that nightingale very much. I loved it and it inspired me. I thought, 'Why it and not me? Why does it hide from the world and not me?' And the thought entered into my mind that I must leave, I must lose myself, I must cease to exist. I said to myself, 'Why? Did it have an audience? Did it know I was there and could hear it? Who heard it as it was bursting its throat in song? Why did it go to such a hidden location? But what about of all these little nightingales in the middle of the thick forest, in the ravines, night and day, at sunset and sunrise? Who heard their throat-bursting song? Why did they go to such secret places? Why did they puff out their throats to bursting?' The purpose was worship, to sing to their Creator, to worship God. That's how I explained it.

I regarded all of them as angels of God, little birds that glorified God the Creator of all and no one heard them. Yes, believe me, they hid themselves so that no one would hear them. They weren't interested in being heard; but there in solitude, in peace, in the wilderness, in silence, they longed to be heard, but by whom? None other than by the Maker of everything, the Creator of all, by Him who gave them life and breath and voice. You will ask, 'Did they have consciousness?' What am I to say? I don't know if they did it consciously or not. I don't know. These, after all, are birds. It may be, as Holy Scripture says, that today they live and tomorrow exist no more. We mustn't think differently from what Holy Scripture says. God may present to us that all these were angels of God. We don't know about these things. At all events they hid themselves so that no one would hear their doxology.

So it is also for the monks there on the Holy Mountain; their life is

unknown. You live with your elder and you love him. Prostrations and ascetic struggles are all part of daily life, but you don't remember them, nor does anyone ask about you, 'Who is he?' You live Christ; you belong
to Christ. You live with everything and you live God, in whom all things Cf. Acts
live and move — in whom and through whom...you enter into the un- 17:28
created Church and live there unknown. And although you devote yourself in prayer to your fellow men, you remain unknown to all men, and perhaps they will never know you.

I got it into my head to leave for the desert, alone with God alone

I got it into my head to leave, to ask my elder for his blessing and a sack of dry biscuit and to disappear to praise and glorify God unceasingly. But I thought, 'Where will I go? I still haven't learned my handicraft properly.' They still hadn't taught me. Perhaps they were afraid I would leave. That was a widespread fear on the Holy Mountain. They wouldn't teach novices how to complete their handicraft so that they wouldn't leave. Because for a monk to know a craft means freedom, since he then has a way of buying his biscuit.

So this idea got into my head to leave for the desert, alone with God alone. Selflessly. Without pride, without egotism, without vanity, without, without, without... Do you believe it? That's where my ideal of selflessness came from. A number of ascetics who disappeared into the desert achieved this purity, this perfection. They sought neither the world nor anything at all... They dissolved in tears before God and prayed for the Church. They all were concerned first for the world and the Church and after that for themselves.

So, as I said, the aim of the nightingale became stuck in my head. What is his aim in bursting his throat in song in the wilderness? Worship, praise and doxology directed to God the Creator. So why should I not go into the wilderness to worship God in silence, lost to the world and the society of men? Is there anything more perfect? All these ideas I had derived from the nightingale. I dreamt up such plans! How I would go into the wilderness, how I would live joyfully, how I would die! I would eat wild herbs, I would do this and that! I would go as an unknown ragged beggar to some monastery to ask for a rusk of bread and I would eat it without saying who I am and where I stay. I made up a whole scenario. It was my secret.

I returned to my cell filled with all these emotions and dreams. I confessed them to the elder. The elder smiled. 'Deception!' he said. 'Get it out of your head. Don't ever think of these things again, because such thoughts will put an end to your prayer.'

And as I have told you many times, whatever I confessed to the elder finished there and then and I had a sudden feeling of joy. It was, it seems, the result of the elder's prayers.

So I lived in obedience in the earthly paradise of the Holy Mountain. I never wanted to leave from there. But God's plan was different.

God delivered me

It was a rainy day. When the rain stopped we saw from the workshop where we were working many of the fathers from the other hermitages walking towards Saint Niphon's to gather snails. Father Ioannikios saw the monks passing by and became agitated. He wanted me to go and look for snails too. I said to him, 'My elder told me not to go. I set out and he called me back. But if you want me to go, I'll be obedient and go.'

'Go,' he said. 'There are lots of snails out today.'

So I grabbed a shoulder bag and ran off. Or rather, to begin with I didn't run so that my elders wouldn't see me, but once I'd got out of sight, I started running. I climbed up high on some sheer rocks where not even the wild boars went, because when it rains the wild boars all get together and go off to eat the snails. I collected snails for three hours. I found a great many and filled the bag full. I was covered in sweat and as I was coming back down — by this time it was evening and the atmosphere had become chill and damp — I was caught in a freezing wind that was blowing off Mount Athos down to the sea. The bag on my shoulder was soaking wet and my whole back was frozen by the saliva from the snails.

As I was making my way down over difficult terrain I had to come down across a scree — a steep incline with small loose stones. When I was half-way down, the whole scree started to give way, rushing like a river from the top of the mountain and carrying with it stones and rocks and everything in its wake. This river of stones was about fifteen to twenty metres wide. My legs were buried up to my knees. I was stuck fast. With the sack still on my back and in danger of being killed, I shouted out: '*Panayitsa mou*! My Holy Lady!' All at once an invisible power threw me twenty metres across to the other side of the ravine onto some large rocks that, in turn, were on the point of rolling down the hillside. At the same moment down below the fathers who were returning from Saint Niphon's with their snails happened to be passing. They saw the treacherous landslide on the scree above and they shouted out, "Look out! Is there anyone up there?" I was now out of danger and hadn't suffered any ill. Only my moccasins had remained stuck in the landslide and my legs were cut and bruised. The fathers shouted up again, but I didn't shout back. I wanted to shout, but I couldn't. I was in a state of shock. I heard them, but I didn't reply. The bag, which remained unharmed on my back, would have weighed over a hundred kilos. When I recovered, I started to scramble from rock to rock until I reached the bottom. As soon as I had climbed down I encountered another danger: I saw a snake beneath a galingale plant. I was terrified…

God delivered me. I arrived back at the hermitage in a state of panic and collapsed. I told the elders all that had happened to me. I was in a state of shock. I told them about the landslide on the scree, about my shoes that had been lost, about the cuts on my legs, about the snake. My elder was very distressed and imposed a punishment on Father Ioannikios, forbidding him to celebrate the Liturgy for many months. Father Ioannikios was also deeply distraught at what had happened.

He kissed me on the forehead and we parted in tears

As a result of the cold I caught that day, I contracted pleurisy with a build-up of fluid and was in great pain. I had no strength and I didn't want to eat. The elders sent for Father Antonios, a tall and very saintly monk from the hermitage dedicated to the Holy Fathers of Athos. He was often called in to act as a doctor. He came and saw me and then returned to his hermitage to fetch a kind of hide they call an *ekdorion*. He put this on my back and all night it sucked the fluid from my back. The next day at about ten o'clock he took a pair of scissors, sterilized them with alcohol, and cut away the hide that had filled up with fluid and had become like a pillow along with my skin. The pain was excruciating. I was greatly debilitated and I fainted.

When I recovered a little I felt great joy because I was able to pray. I started to sing the words of the Little Canon of Supplication: 'From the countless multitude of my sins, both my soul and body are now weakened and both are sick…'* When Father Ioannikios heard me he came up to me and hugged me, and kissing me on the forehead and said, 'Forgive me, my boy!'

The elder came up and said to him fiercely, 'Bah! You crooked fellow!'

* The *Megalynarion* from the Little Canon of Supplication to the Theotokos.

I had no appetite, I didn't want to eat; I ate very little and every day my condition worsened. It seemed that I was going to waste away and die. The elders were afraid I might die and so was Father Antonios who was acting as doctor.

'The boy must leave,' said Father Antonios. 'He won't come through. He needs medicines that we don't have here. He's not eating, and it's certain that the longer he stays here the worse he'll get.'

Just think that I ate a mouthful of ground almonds and my stomach couldn't take them. Such was the extent to which I had weakened.

My elders wanted me very much, but they found themselves obliged to send me out into the world, because on the Mountain there was neither milk nor meat. And so they gave me permission to leave. They obtained the necessary papers for me to go back to my village for about two months until I would recover. And I left. Father Ioannikios took me to Daphni in a rowing boat. At that time we didn't have a motorboat at all. We didn't have either mules or motorboats then. Whatever the monks took up there, they carried on their shoulders, on their backs. So we arrived in Daphni. I was unable to stand upright; they laid me down in a room where the post-office was housed. After a short time I started to have excruciating pains in the kidneys. I cried from the pain. Father Ioannikios wept too. For all my pain, I found strength to comfort him:

'Don't cry, Elder, I'll get better; there's nothing the matter.'

And he comforted me through his tears saying:

'Don't cry, my boy. You'll get better.'

The boat arrived and they carried me on board. He kissed me on the forehead and we parted in tears.

EVIA (1925–1940)

Their hearts were softened
and without any external prompting
they desired to observe the fasts,
to enter the spiritual arena and to come to know Christ.

I had never imagined that I would return to the world

I had never imagined that I would return to the world. Kavsokalyvia was my home. It is true that I had asked God to send me an illness. And he gave me an illness. But I said, 'It's all very well, God, that you gave me the illness, but not that you take me away from the Holy Mountain.' But take me away He did. I left because of my illness; or rather they sent me away. God listened indeed, but not necessarily to my will. He gave me also something I didn't want, because, as I said, on account of my illness I left the Holy Mountain. And so after so many years I went back again to my home! I was in the boat for hours without end. Everything seemed strange to me. I hadn't seen little children and women for years.

I went to my village via the town of Chalkida. I passed through Aliveri and arrived at Aghios Ioannis, my village. First I went over to Perivolia. I found someone, my brother-in-law to be precise, Nikolas, Eleni's father, and I asked him which families were in the village. He replied that a little way off was Leonidas Bairaktaris, my father, and further down, other families, and he mentioned their names.

With my heart racing, I set out to meet my father. I hadn't seen him for many years. As I've told you, he'd been away in America for years. When I saw him I recognized him at once. But how could he possibly recognize me — a monk with long hair and a great long beard! I felt embarrassed, and so I had hidden my hair and beard inside the cassock I was wearing. Moreover, I was skin and bone as a result of my illness.

I greeted him and he said:

'Who are you? Where are you from?'

'I'm a monk,' I replied. Then I asked, 'Do you have any family? How many children do you have?'

'I had four, but one of my sons disappeared years ago. We lost him. He was working in Piraeus and he disappeared.'

‘In Piraeus? What was his name?’

‘Vangelis.’

‘Vangelis? He used to be a friend of mine.’

‘Tell me, do you know where he is?’

‘Alas, he died…’

‘He died?’

My father was heartbroken. He started to weep. I couldn’t bear it. If I had been made of steel I would have melted. I started to cry too. My heart was racing. I couldn’t bear to see his father’s heart so distressed and I revealed myself to him.

‘It’s me, father! Evangelos.’

Imagine what took place at that moment! Joy and tears mixed together. We embraced, and full of emotion we set out for the house to find my mother. My mother, however, was unforgiving. When she saw me she scolded me mercilessly. She regarded it as a great affront that one of her children had become a monk.

People came to see me

People learned about my homecoming. Various people would come to see me. I was a young man. Before I had become ill I had been very ruddy and handsome. But my face did not have a worldly beauty. It was a godly beauty. And now that I was back in the world everyone was commenting about me and about my hair. I hadn’t cut my hair from the day that I had left for the Holy Mountain. My hair had grown and now reached below my waist. There was a great fuss in the village. So, in order not to cut it, I boiled a pot of water, put my hair in and left it to boil for a long time. The hair was damaged and fell out. I was left almost bald.

So, as I said, people would come to see me in the village. It was put about there that Leonidas Bairaktaris’s son, who had disappeared and had been given up for dead, had returned from the Mountain where he had been a hermit. People came to see me out of curiosity. I said nothing; I felt acutely embarrassed. I went to the church in the village. Everyone poked fun at me. My mother was ashamed. She wept and bewailed her fate. The poor woman couldn’t bear to set eyes on me; she didn’t want me and forced me leave the house.

To begin with my aunt took me in. There I started to have good food — milk, cheese, eggs and meat — to recover from my illness. But I couldn’t stay there for long because I wanted, well…a different environment. What was I to do in the house? Moreover, I was embarrassed, because I had done nothing for my family... How could I now ask them to look after me?

When I felt better, I went straight back to the Holy Mountain

At a four or five hour walk from the village there was a monastery dedicated to Saint Charalambos.* One day I asked my father to take me there — not with a view to staying. I hadn't the slightest idea what I would find there or whether they would want me. In the meantime, we happened to meet Father Yiannis Papavasileiou in Aliveri. He telephoned the bishop — at that time there was a telephone line from Aliveri to Kymi — and told him that a monk from the Holy Mountain had arrived. The bishop said to him:

'Keep a hold on him, Papa Yiannis, don't let him leave us!'

The bishop of Kymi, Panteleimon Fostinis, had a great affection for monks.

My father took me and we set off. I went to kiss my mother's hand, but she pulled her hand away and wouldn't give it to me. My father, then, took me to the monastery of Saint Charalambos. The abbot gave me a warm welcome; he liked me and spoke to me. When I told him of my difficulties, he said:

'Stay here. We have eggs and milk, chickens and everything.'

And so I stayed there. The abbot was so fond of me that he cooked special food for me. To begin with, I didn't have any appetite for food, but gradually I recovered. My father also stayed with me initially to look after me. My father was a cantor and had had the good fortune to have been acquainted with Saint Nektarios.† He had a deep faith and was very devout.

When I felt better, I went straight back to the Holy Mountain. My elders were overjoyed. But after ten or thirteen days I suffered a relapse. I lost my appetite. I grew pale, lost weight and became exhausted with a diet of vermicelli soup and suchlike. I had, you see, become seriously ill. Once again I obtained permission to leave and set off for the Monastery of Saint Charalambos. There I had eggs, cheese, butter and so on, just as

* The Monastery of Saint Charalambos Lefkon, near the village of Avlonari, founded in 1040. Now a convent.

† Saint Nektarios (1846–1920), Bishop of Pentapolis in Egypt and founder of a well-known convent on the Greek island of Aegina, is one of the best loved modern saints of the Orthodox Church. He worked as an evangelist on the island of Evia from 1891–93 and it was doubtless at this time that he came into contact with Saint Porphyrios's father.

before. Once again I recovered and gained strength. After three months I returned once more to the Holy Mountain. Three times I went and returned, but each time after ten to thirteen days I suffered a relapse.

The third time my elders said to me:

'We have a responsibility for your health; we can't keep you. We love you and we want you, but God is showing that you must leave so that you don't die.'

Indeed, they added:

'We love you and if ever God grants you the possibility — and we believe that He will help you get well — and you wish to come here, then find another boy like yourself. We want you.'

And they sent me away. They said to me:

'We're afraid the other monks will blame us if you were to die here; you're such a young lad. We don't like at all having to send you away, but we have no other choice. You see that we have exhausted what our love can offer. You've gone away and returned three times and you haven't been able to make progress here.'

They gave me a blanket for the journey which I have kept and it is my best blanket. It's the one I had in my cell; I made my prostrations on it, I slept on it and I wrapped myself in it when I was standing to take a nap upright. That is, I slept awake! On that blanket I did all my spiritual exercises.

And so I left the Holy Mountain for good. I went to Saint Charalambos. All the people there wanted me; they were fond of me and were pleased that I had returned. Once again I started to eat milk, butter and eggs.

Let me tell you something important that I remember. There was a monk on the Holy Mountain who was called Father Joachim and he lived in the hermitage of Saint Neilos — the monks who were in obedience to him are still alive. Now, he wrote a letter to my mother and lambasted her severely, very severely. He wrote that even the wild beasts love their children. He wrote a lot, fine things certainly, but very pointed and harsh. And so my mother was really crushed.

Later, however, she changed. She devoted herself to the Church. When I was celebrating the Liturgy she would sit opposite me. She would cross her arms and pray. She was always looking at me. She didn't take her eyes off me at all. 'My priest', she would say proudly. In Tsakei, a village where I stayed for a short time after my ordination, they used to call her *papadia*, the 'priest's wife'. They would kiss her hand and she would glow with pride. I was with her when she died. 'I should have made all my children monks!' she used to say to me. 'I took it all very badly to begin with. I wish now all my children had become monks!'

Porphyrios III made me a priest

At the Monastery of Saint Charalambos I lived as a monk, with the same tactics as before. I loved reading the lives of saints, the poetic canons and so on. I learned passages of the New Testament and prayers by heart. I had known the Psalter by heart for years. I knew all the psalms. I was able to combine the different passages. The Psalter was the food of my thought. As I said, I lived in the monastery as a monk — a little monk with an old worn-out cassock — and I continued to go out at night and recite the Psalter because they didn't read it during the services in the monastery. I helped with the chores in the monastery. I was always on the move. They had given me the keys of the cheese-making workshop in the monastery because there were two or three elderly monks who needed help. All the dear monks there placed great trust in me... But while I was engaged in all the chores I didn't let my mind wander; I kept a strict control on it. Or rather, I didn't keep a strict control on it; it's just that my thoughts were on my love. It's like a girl who, let's say, falls ill with pleurisy, yet her mind remains fixed unswervingly on her lover. You understand? The loved one. Devotion to the lover, to Christ.

I became a priest in the monastery there. Listen and I'll tell you the story.

The bishop of Kymi, Fostinis, was always at pains to support and lavish care on students and teachers of theology. At the time there was a final-year theology student who had gone to stay in the bishop's accommodation while he was studying for his degree exams. Now it was the bishop's habit to get a discussion going with all the monks on some spiritual topic during or after their meal in the refectory. Let me give you an example: The bishop would ask, 'Tell me, which is the greatest virtue?' And then the monks would offer their opinions. There would be about fifteen around the table. The topics were various — about Scripture, religion or monasticism.

One evening when the discussion happened to centre around monasticism, the bishop sighed heavily and said:

'Ah, find me monks! There's nothing else I want. Good, faithful and patient monks. Nothing else. Just that. Then I can do wonders.'

At that point the theology student jumped up — he was from Kokla near Thebes — and said to him:

'Dearest Bishop, you're crying out for monks, and yet there's a monk up at Saint Charalambos who's pining away and you don't even know him.'

'Really!' exclaimed the bishop.

'Yes, there's a poor young lad who's come from the Holy Mountain. He's very good, but he's very weak — skin and bone — and the abbot has him doing chores.'

'Well then, you'll go down there at once and bring him here to me.'

So he came down with a letter addressed to the abbot asking for Niketas — that was what I was called then; it was my monastic name. I went at once to see the bishop and when I met him he put his hand on my head and said, 'How are you, my boy?' We went and sat together and he started asking me, 'Where are you from? How did you get to be here?'

And I told him in a few words how much I loved Christ and the ascetic life and how I had gone to the Holy Mountain as a boy. I explained to him how I had fallen sick and how my elders had sent me out into the world to recover. Well, well, well, what happened then! He summoned for me the best doctor in Kymi, who came and examined me and gave me a whole load of medicines. The bishop wanted me to stay there. But I was embarrassed to stay with the bishop. What I wanted was the forest, silence and simplicity. And I returned to Saint Charalambos.

The bishop visited the monastery regularly. The dear old man was very saintly. I recognized his saintliness with my charisma. One day he had come to Saint Charalambos and I heard him speaking and I liked very much what he said. I had never heard someone preaching a sermon in my life. The bishop had established a charitable foundation which he called the Holy Order of Saint Panteleimon and occasionally he would visit the monastery along with the children belonging to the Order.

On another occasion the bishop came to the monastery along with the Archbishop of Sinai, Porphyrios III. It was then they made up their minds to make me a priest. As you will understand, I didn't want to become a priest. I had learned that the right thing to do was to seek to remain as a monk and not to strive to become a priest or a bishop, and that when people start telling you to be ordained, you leave. That's what I knew. In the end, however, Porphyrios III made me a priest and gave me his name. I had fired him with enthusiasm. By the grace of God I revealed to him something personal about him as we were taking a walk on the hills together and he said to the bishop, 'Make sure you don't lose him.'

At the time I was twenty years old. I didn't want to become a priest, but I couldn't avoid it. The bishop insisted so much and the bishop is 'in the type of Christ'. You can't continuously repudiate your bishop; you can't damage your relationship with your bishop, otherwise your prayers don't rise to heaven, they remain fruitless. And so they made me a deacon on the Feast of Saint Paraskevi and a priest the day after on the Feast of Saint Panteleimon.

I heard confessions day and night non-stop

After two years they made me a confessor. On a great feast day when there were lots of people present they took me to the bishop's residence and they officially read the prayer for becoming a spiritual father. I was very young. What did I know about it! And, foolish wretch, I was thick-headed into the bargain. I was still uneducated; I didn't know the penitential canons. And, with incredible stupidity, what did I do? I bowed my head in obedience. Now I realize my folly. At the time I wasn't so aware of it.

How the monks and lay people that came for confession loved me! I heard confessions there day and night non-stop. I started early in the morning and I continued all through the day and throughout the night and the next day and the next night without interruption. I went forty-eight hours without eating. Fortunately, God took care of me and gave my sister the inspiration to bring me some milk to drink. There was a stairway with lots of steps leading up to the confessional and the people would come up to make confession. They waited all night long for their turn. When they left they would say to each other, 'Now there's a priest who's a knower of hearts!' I remember they used the Albanian word for priest, *priftis*. I stayed there for fifteen years.

When they would come I used to ask questions. I would ask: 'How old are you? Whom do you live with?' One would say, 'With my wife', another would say, 'With my parents', and another, 'I live on my own'. Then I would continue: 'What have you studied? What's your job? How long is it since you made confession? How long is it since you received Holy Communion?' and so on. And then depending on what he said to me I would speak to him a little and, because there was a queue waiting outside, I would say, 'What do you remember now, my child? What do you feel is weighing on your soul, on your conscience? What transgressions have you committed, what sins?' And he would gradually begin to confess his errors and I would help him along a little, having told him first that truly he must say everything just as he feels it.

To begin with, when I first started to hear confessions, I used to really 'scald' those who came to make confession. I used to have at my side Saint

Nikodemos's *Confessor's Guide** when someone would come for confession. If he confessed a serious sin then I would look up the book and would see that it wrote: 'Not to receive Holy Communion for eighteen years.' I didn't know; I was inexperienced. And so I imposed the corresponding penance. Whatever the book said was law. But then the people would come back the following year — they would come from various places, from various villages, from far and near — and when I asked them, 'How long is it since you made confession?' they would answer, 'I confessed to you this time last year.' Then I would ask, 'And what did I tell you?' They would reply, 'You told me to do a hundred prostrations every night.'

'And did you do them?'

'No.'

'Why not?'

'Well, you told me that I couldn't receive Communion for eighteen years so I thought to myself, "Since I'm damned anyway, I might as well forget about the whole thing."'

You understand? Then another person would come and say the same thing. So I thought, 'What do I do now?' It was then I began to become a little wiser. The confessor has the power to bind and to loose. I remembered one of Saint Basil's Rules, and I took that as my basic guideline and changed my tactics in confession. The Rule says: 'He who receives the power to bind and to loose, when he sees the great remorse of one of the sinners, let him reduce the time of the penance. Don't let him judge the penances in terms of time, but in terms of disposition.'

And so I started to encourage the people to read the poetic canons written in honour of the saints, to read short prayers, to make prostrations and to read Holy Scripture. And in that way they began to pay attention to the things of our religion. Their hearts were softened and without any external prompting they desired to observe the fasts, to enter the spiritual arena and to come to know Christ. And one thing I have understood is that when someone comes to know Christ and love Him and is loved by Christ, everything thereafter proceeds well in holiness and joy and everything is easy.

Before this magnificent vision I knelt down as unworthy

I remember many incidents from my life at the monastery of Saint Charalambos. Let me tell you about one. I've said before that I love the

* *Exomolgitarion.*

forest. I had become accustomed to solitude and I wanted to be on my own. I wanted to live out of doors, especially at night. So I climbed up into an evergreen oak, more than two and a half metres above the ground, and made myself a bed there out of the stems from a mastic shrub. I cut the stems and interwove them with the branches of the oak tree. I laid a blanket on top and wrapped myself in it. It was wonderful. I would climb a ladder that I had made myself, and once I was up I would pull up the ladder and no one would bother me. I had surrounded the bed with a wild clematis and its plentiful blossom produced a delightful fragrance. Beneath the evergreen oak there was a thick mastic shrub; it grew two or three metres from the roots of the oak. I would scramble up onto the bed. Once there, I was all prayer; I was a monk of the Holy Mountain. What I desired was solitude and the Psalter — and also the 'Lord, Jesus Christ…'. I would pray for hours up on the oak tree surrounded by the flowers of the clematis and lying on my mastic bed.

One evening when I had clambered up into this flowery bed I started to say my prayers. It was night-time and in the midst of the wilds. The moon washed creation in its light. The nightingales, which had just woken up and had started to sing, accompanied me. I recited numerous verses from the Psalter and most of all, 'Lord, Jesus Christ, have mercy on me'. At one point I stood upright and silently recited the office of Compline. When I began to say the Prayer to the Mother of God, I brought before my mind an image of our All-holy Lady: The most holy Theotokos on a glorious, divine and elevated throne and round about the orders of angels and archangels, the Cherubim and the Seraphim, the martyrs, the saints, the holy fathers and the prophets. Before this magnificent vision I knelt down as unworthy and began to say aloud: 'Spotless, undefiled, incorrupt, immaculate, pure Virgin, Bride of God and Lady…'. Awe and trembling had seized me when a ray of light emanating from our Holy Lady fell on my head which I had bowed low in humility because of my unworthiness.

As soon as I had finished the Prayer to the Mother of God and fell silent, I heard a sound beneath the tree and saw a man emerge. He said to me, 'Man of God, come down, I want to speak to you.'

I climbed down, and he greeted me and said, 'I'm very hungry.'

'I'll go and fetch you something,' I said.

'Listen and I'll tell you,' he said. 'I've come from America and I've killed my wife. They were hunting for me and I fled into the hills to avoid being arrested, but I'm dying of hunger.'

I went and brought him three *prosfora*.* He explained to me that his wife had had a lover, and that when he heard about it he came back and did what he had done. He had repented, but nevertheless he had done it.

'I beg you, man of God, don't tell anyone about me,' he implored and disappeared into the darkness.

When morning came the police arrived looking for him. They asked me if I had seen anyone and they described him to me.

'No,' I replied, 'I saw nothing.'

What that man confessed to me happened through the grace of our Lady.

What I tell you is true. The Most Holy Theotokos was there before me and sent her shining ray of light on me, a humble young monk — albeit a priest — about twenty-one years old.

'Come and let's do a blessing of water'

For a time I was appointed priest in a village in Evia. I'll tell you about one of the many incidents that took place there. One day a woman riding on the back of her donkey came towards the church where I was serving. As soon as she saw me, she dismounted and came up to me and said:

'*Pappouli*, my boy is sick.'

'What's the matter?'

'He's lost his voice.'

'Has he been like this for long?'

'Yes. He doesn't speak at all.'

The boy was about eighteen years old. I took my priest's stole and went down with her into the village. I arrived at her home. I saw the boy who quite genuinely wasn't speaking. I said to her, 'Come and let's do a blessing of water.'

She pulled across a chair and set a bowl of water and a towel on it. I started to read the service. The boy stood dumbly by. I finished the blessing and started to sprinkle the water around singing, 'Save, O Lord, Your people...'. When I then touched the boy on the forehead with the cross and the spray of basil, he said to me, 'Thank you very much!'

Thereafter that boy became very fond of me. Somewhat later he became godfather to a little boy and gave the child the name Porphyrios. Afterwards he came and said to me, 'I've given your name to a little boy.'

'Did you ask me?' I retorted.

* Round loaves stamped with a special seal for use at Holy Communion.

'I love you,' he said, 'and I wanted to give him your name.'

Listen to another similar story. This also happened in Evia.

Once a woman came to me with her daughter. The daughter was dumb. The mother said, '*Pappouli*, I'm very worried about my daughter. She hasn't spoken for a month.'

'What happened?' I asked her.

'We had tied a goat up down by the stream — there were lots of brambles there. And my daughter went down to fetch the goat. It was night-time. And when she came back she was dumb.'

I went and did a blessing of water for her. The mother, in fact, was the wife of a priest. I asked her:

'Which priest's your husband?'

'The priest from...'

'Oh, are you Father Christos's wife?'

'Yes, *Pappouli*.'

So I read the blessing and the priest's daughter recovered — through the grace of God, of course.

I went to Vatheia in Evia, to the Monastery of Saint Nicholas

After years had passed, and while I was still in Evia, I wanted to find a new place to collect my thoughts, like a hunted bird that wants to fly into God's embrace through prayer of the heart. I was alone and desolate.

I went to Vatheia in Evia, to the Monastery of Saint Nicholas, and I stayed there for ten days. It had some tumble-down cells full of large mice. But what happened? For two days there was a great storm and heavy seas. It rained unceasingly and the rain hammered on the walls and rattled against the windows as if it were hail. The wind howled furiously up in the huge plane tree. I heard its branches hitting against one another. The storm raged relentlessly there in the utter wilderness. All the elements of nature were roaring. And I was inside the poor, tiny, fresco-covered church of Saint Nicholas — a church sanctified many times over years before by the souls which I saw and sensed were bending down before the saints and unlocking their hearts.

There, in the wilderness, in the cold north wind, I was like a hunted little bird of the air. Imagine, what would a little bird caught in such a storm have done? Wouldn't it have sought to find a little nest, some cave to hide in? I did the same amidst the uproar and the storm, terrified by the elements of nature. I ran to find refuge; I ran to hide myself in the embrace of my heavenly Father. I sensed the pleasant warmth of Christ, my union with God. I felt great joy and exaltation and relief hiding myself away in God. I was unconcerned about the storm and the tempest, which are things of the world. My soul sought something higher, more perfect. I felt safe, comforted and at rest. I spent golden days there. I took advantage of a spell of dreadful weather.

That's how we should think always. And that's how we should live through difficulties and tragedies. We should see them all as opportunities for prayer, for approaching God. That's the secret: how the man of God will transform everything into prayer. That's what Saint Paul the
Col. 1:24 Apostle means when he says, *I rejoice in my sufferings*, in all the tribulations he encountered. This is how sanctification takes place. May God grant this to us. I ask for this fervently in my prayer.

I stayed for a considerable time — three whole years — in Vatheia in the Monastery of Saint Nicholas. I left just before the Italian invasion of Greece in 1940.

THE POLYCLINIC HOSPITAL IN ATHENS (1940–1973)

Blessed years, devoted to the sick and to suffering

I lived there for thirty-three years as if they were a single day

On the declaration of war I came to Athens. I was appointed chaplain to the chapel of Saint Gerasimos in the Polyclinic in Athens exactly at the time war was declared in 1940. I had a strong desire to work in a hospital. God fulfilled this desire and, to my great joy, I was appointed priest in the chapel in the Polyclinic in Athens. Since I have acquired the habit of always telling you about some event from my life, how I experienced it and felt about it, listen and I'll tell you the story from the beginning.

Once when I was in the skete of Kavsokalyvia I heard the interpretation of the Sunday Gospel by Nikiforos Theotokis* being read out in the *Kyriakon*. Theotokis emphasized how much good a person can do when he comforts souls that are in pain — people who are suffering from cancer, leprosy or tuberculosis. When I heard this I was deeply moved and was filled with enthusiasm — the reader was reading in a very animated way and, moreover, I always got inspired by everything. And I started to dream: If only I had been educated and knew how to preach then I could go to a hospital — a leper hospital or a sanatorium for consumptives... Such, approximately, were my thoughts. And when I desired something, I wanted to experience it. Whenever I had a strong desire to go to the desert, I would make myself experience the desert wherever I was. It was a vain fantasy, but nevertheless, I experienced it. I would have the sensation, for example, that I was up in Karmelion, up above Kerasia, where the church of Saint Basil is — the most peaceful place on the Holy Mountain. And I had the sensation that I was a hermit and I fantasized: 'That's how I'll read, that's how I'll light my lamp, that's how I'll say the prayer, "Lord, Jesus Christ", I'll do so many prostrations and I'll eat dry rusks and wild herbs.' And I made my dream reality. Vain fantasy! But nevertheless I satisfied myself briefly in that way and then the thought would go away. And at times of weakness — and it's at times of weakness that we give

* Nikiforos Theotokis (1731–1800), *Kyriakodromion*, 3 vols., Moscow 1796.

rein to thoughts that are not so good — I would think of such things that my soul desired and I would experience them.

That's how I lived at that time: I went to an island with lepers and I spoke to the lepers, I celebrated the Liturgy there and looked after them and helped those who were severely disabled. And I lived in my fantasy with the lepers. All this was then forgotten. It happened, however, that I myself became ill and three times my elders dispatched me back to the world to get well. But I failed to recover and in the end, as I have told you, they gave me their blessing to live outside the Holy Mountain in a place where there would be milk and eggs and meat and all the things that were required for my illness. For that reason I went to the Monastery of Saint Charalambos in Evia and stayed there for about fifteen years. Then I started to be deluged again by the ideas I had had on the Holy Mountain, namely, to go and work in a sanatorium. I thought of going to Pendeli. An acquaintance of mine had told me that they were in need of a priest. The sanatorium in Pendeli at the time was full of people suffering from consumption. I went to the director of the hospital and he told me, 'We've just appointed someone, Father, we've just got ourselves a priest.'

I told him about my yearning to work in a sanatorium and he said to me, 'Yes, I understand. I had the same aspiration and God brought me here.'

I then went down to Athens and there I met a priest from the Holy Mountain who was serving in the church of the Holy Cross at Stavros in the Spata area. I confided to him, 'Father Matthew, this is what I long to do. How should I go about it?'

'Listen, and I'll tell you,' he said. 'I was asked to go to a hospital, the Polyclinic in Athens, but I didn't accept. I preferred to come here to Stavros. Would you like me to speak to Professor Amilkas Alivizatos* and ask if they will take you there?'

'Let's go and see,' I said.

I went and saw. And, my goodness! What crowds of people and hustle and bustle…

'I wouldn't be suitable for this place, Father Matthew,' I exclaimed.

'Why wouldn't you be suitable?' he retorted.

And so we went to Professor Amilkas Alivizatos and spoke to him. Father Matthew left and the professor said to me, 'Come tomorrow.'

* Prof. Amilkas Alivizatos (d. 1969): Professor of Canon Law and Pastoral Theology at the Theological School of the University of Athens and President of the Polyclinic in Athens.

I went the next day and waited for the professor at his home. The maid showed me into the lounge and I waited for him to arrive because he had gone out. I took out my New Testament which I had in a pocket edition and started to read so as not to waste my time. When the professor appeared I closed the book. He came towards me, I greeted him and he said, 'What book was that, Father?'

'The New Testament, Professor,' I replied.

'Have you studied theology?'

'No,' I said.

'What education do you have?'

'The first class of Primary School and I didn't learn much there. What I have by way of education I learned in the desert in the Holy Mountain, in Kavsokalyvia. I had two elders I lived with.'

'Can you sing?'

'Yes, I can sing.'

'I've got a church, but I don't have a priest,' he said. 'I'm constantly finding priests and then they always leave.'

'I don't know, Professor, you must decide. I have a desire to serve in a hospital. It's a desire I've had from the time I was in the desert. When I had the desire then, I had no intention of leaving the Holy Mountain. Honestly! I never really thought of leaving the Holy Mountain to work in a leper hospital, but because I liked the idea when I heard it, I wanted to experience it and I experienced it in my fantasy. However, God has now granted me the possibility and I can now make the thing of fantasy a reality.

He asked me, 'What bishop have you been under?' I replied, 'The bishop of Kymi.' The professor then went through to another room and telephoned the Diocese of Kymi.

As I learned later from the bishop's chancellor Spyridon who happened to be present when the professor called, the bishop had responded saying, 'Excellent! The Polyclinic has found its priest at last!'

Amilkas returned and said to me, 'We must go and have you celebrate the Liturgy.'

I replied, 'I can't celebrate the Liturgy, Professor, because I'm afraid. I can't celebrate without the permission of the Archdiocese.'

'That's my business!' he responded. 'Your business is to celebrate the Liturgy.'

'But we must have permission from the Archdiocese,' I insisted.

'No,' he said. 'You will celebrate and we won't ask for permission.'

I wasn't happy, but in the end I gave in.

He got me to celebrate the Liturgy every day in the chapel of Saint Gerasimos in the Polyclinic.

'We'll appoint you as priest,' he said at last.

And so it was. But what happened then! There was an archimandrite, a graduate in divinity who had studied in London, who wanted to be priest at Saint Gerasimos's, but in the meantime Professor Amilkas had appointed me. The priest in question was most annoyed. He had spoken about it to Father Gervasios Paraskevopoulos, the Chancellor of the Archdiocese, and had been promised the post. But then they learned that I was serving there and so Father Gervasios summoned me to the Archdiocese. As soon as he saw me he started to vent his fury:

'I'll send you into exile,' he shouted. 'What on earth did you think you were doing? Are you really so ignorant? Don't you know that you have to have the permission of the local bishop?'

He really ranted and raved. I went to the professor and told him, 'The Chancellor really pulled me over the coals.'

'Come this way,' he said. And he took me up to the archbishop. At the time it was Chrysanthos of Trapezounta. It was 1940 — at the start of the Albanian War. His Beatitude asked me, 'What education do you have?'

'Your Beatitude,' I answered, 'I'm not educated. I learned to read in the desert.'

'How long did you attend school?'

'Only one year of primary school.'

He looked at the professor wryly.

'What can we do, Professor?' he said. 'It's the centre of Athens there in Omonia Square. People will think we're mad.'

'Not at all,' said Amilkas. 'He's the priest I want, he's the man for the job.'

'How's it to be done?' queried the archbishop.

His Beatitude then turned to me and asked:

'Do you know how to sing?'

'I've learned in a practical sort of way.'

'Listen, my child,' he said to me, 'this is a post that needs an educated person — a priest who's able to preach, because that area is a centre of vice and corruption and there must be someone who can speak and teach the people. Nevertheless, the professor wants you. So what I would say is this: you're not educated, but at least try to maintain a dignified bearing, and I would even go as far as to say that perhaps your manner is better than that of someone with a theological education who would preach to people with fine words.'

'With your blessing, Your Beatitude!' I replied.

And so it was. I bowed to take his blessing and left. The professor stayed behind with the archbishop.

The next day we had a Liturgy. I found myself once again in hot water because it happened that we had a memorial service. Father Gervasios learned about this too and was angered that I had done the memorial service because this was not allowed without a written letter of appointment. A long story... All these things, however, didn't unduly upset me; I got over them. The thing I couldn't get over was the thing I'll tell you about later.

I loved the church of Saint Gerasimos and the patients very much. I didn't forget anyone; I visited all the patients. After the Divine Liturgy I went round all the wards. And when I didn't have a Divine Liturgy in the morning, I would hear the confession of those who were waiting and then go to visit the sick. I lived there for thirty-three years as if it were a single day. I had a joyous, carefree life. I was so unknown and inconspicuous there in the Polyclinic that when I was very tired at mid-day and had lots of work in the evening, I wouldn't go home, but would stay there and no one would pay any attention to me. I hid myself away in a little anteroom, lined up chairs in a row and lay face down on them so that I wouldn't be cold and I slept a little and no one noticed me. I hadn't opened myself to any socializing, and so I was very much disregarded. I was uneducated, insignificant and poor. Other people were in charge of the administration of the chapel; I knew nothing. And yet I lived there for thirty-three years. Blessed years, devoted to the sick and to suffering. It was put about that I was a good confessor, and so many came for confession. Many broken and crushed souls came to pour out heartfelt tears before Saint Gerasimos. And with what faith they would make confession.

As I have told you, I have been hearing confession for more than fifty years. I would let the person making confession speak at length about whatever he wanted and at the end I would say something. While he was talking away — and not only about personal matters — I would observe what his soul was like. From his whole attitude I understood his state and at the end I would say something to be of benefit to him. And even the things that weren't of a personal nature nevertheless had some kind of relation to him, to the state of his soul. And all the people who came for confession were very happy with me because I didn't speak to them and they said freely whatever they wanted to. And if there was someone who had little connection with the Church or who mentioned to me some transgression of a somewhat more serious nature, I didn't draw attention to the matter particularly. If you make someone acutely aware of his fault, this provokes a reaction in him that makes him unable to give it up later. And at the end of the confession I would say something about the serious fault that he had made an effort to bring himself to confess. Thus I didn't show complete indifference, but nor did I emphasize it. It depended on the circumstances. I might even on occasion display indifference.

At the end I would say:

'My child, for everything you have said the Lord has forgiven you. Take care from now on, and be sure to pray so that the Lord will strengthen you, and then after so many days go and receive Communion.'

And so I wouldn't emphasize the specific fault. This is very important. Besides, the person is not exclusively responsible for his mistake.

Amid the hustle and bustle of Omonia Square I lived as if in the desert of the Holy Mountain

Amid the crowds, the people and the hubbub of Omonia Square I raised up my hands to God and I lived interiorly as if in the desert of the Holy Mountain. I would say to myself, 'I'm not cut out for being in the world; I'm made for the desert. In the desert, whatever you do, no one knows you.' And yet I lived in the world. I stayed there — there where God had brought me.

I loved everyone, I felt pained for everyone and everything moved me. This is something that divine grace had given me. I saw the nurses in their white uniforms, like alb-wearing angels, coming down to the church and tears came to my eyes when I saw them. I loved the nurses very much. And when I saw a nurse in uniform I thought of her as a sister of mercy, a sister of love on her way to celebrate a Liturgy in the temple of the love of God, in the hospital, serving the sick. An angel, an alben angel. How many things we pass over unnoticed! Again when I saw a mother breast-feeding her baby, I was moved. When I saw a pregnant woman, I wept. I saw the primary school teachers taking their pupils to the church and I shed tears at their work of love.

The greatest delight for me, of course, was the time of the Divine Liturgy. When I was reading, the congregation held its breath. I was carried away. I celebrated in a very devoted manner because I loved to celebrate the Liturgy. But the people were also inspired by the simple way I celebrated.

Because I was uneducated, I made great efforts. Highly educated people used to come and sing at the church of Saint Gerasimos. Many of them were university professors such as the Alivizatos brothers, Leonidas Philippidis, the professor of comparative religion, and others. Next to the Polyclinic was the Athens Odeon, the music school. The teachers from this school would also come to the church along with their families. The church choir was from the Royal Theatre. It was difficult for me, however, to keep in harmony with all the different Church Tones. So I decided to attend classes at the Odeon. I didn't waste any hours left at my disposal. I went and learned music with perseverance and zeal for hours on end. I did it to make things easier for the singers. I didn't want to upset the church choir. And it was, as I have said, a choir of professional standard. I wanted to be sure to intone confidently on the right note so that I wouldn't be tiresome and irritating to them. So I was obliged to go to the Odeon to learn music. But listen to my madness!

I wanted to learn to play the harmonium and I had an ulterior motive. When I would set up a monastery my intention was for us to have a harmonium in the *archontariki*, the official reception room, so that when we were there and would talk about various teachings or discuss some fine topic amongst ourselves, we would have the harmonium and we would use it to accompany our singing. The Odeon, however, did not have a harmonium and so they offered me the piano. I therefore learned the piano, but the instrument I liked was the harmonium. How God arranges everything! The staff in the Odeon were fond of me and they gave me a teacher who was truly saintly.

One day when I was celebrating I had been given a fine communion loaf — and what more precious gift was there at that time during the German Occupation when we were starving? I took it to my teacher and said to her with a smile:

'I've been given a fine communion loaf.'

'No, no,' she said, 'there's no way I can eat it.'

'Please take it,' I implored.

'No,' she said, 'it's not right.'

I felt embarrassed. I sat down at the keyboard and she gave me the lesson. At the end I said to her, 'I feel bad about this.' And the dear woman took the loaf.

But I didn't want to upset her at all about the lessons. So what did I do? When I had finished my modest prayer at night, until I fell asleep, I would arrange my hands as if on a piano and then I would go over the lesson in my head: C, B, A, G, G, G, E. And that's how I learned the lesson. Why did I do it? So as not to upset my teacher. That was something I had learned on the Holy Mountain. I am incapable of upsetting someone, because from my earliest age I learned to be obedient. This has caused me to make not a few mistakes in my life. When I see someone upset and pressurizing and imploring me to do or say something, I feel sorry for them and I do it, even if I don't want to.

To begin with when I was appointed there I experienced a great temptation

I haven't told you yet, however, that to begin with when I was appointed as priest in the Polyclinic I experienced a great temptation, but God helped me.

On the first Sunday I went to celebrate the Liturgy full of joy. My desire to work in a hospital was about to be fulfilled. God had given me this gift. But what happened to me! Just as I was about to begin, I heard the noise of a gramophone blaring out love songs from just outside the church: 'I love you, I love you...' etc. I started the service...the noise boomed on unabated. I read the prayers, the Divine Liturgy. Outside the crooning continued relentlessly. Inside the church was full of people. I came to the Holy Doors and said, 'Peace be to all', but the Liturgy was far from peaceful. When I finished in a state of despair, I consumed the Holy Gifts, took my vestments, folded them and went out at once. Opposite the church was a shop that advertised gramophones and gramophone records. I went politely to the shop-owner, Mr Kouretas (that was his name), and I asked him, if possible, to switch off the gramophone, at least during the Divine Liturgy.

'I've got my living to earn,' he replied. 'There's no way I can do what you want. I've children to look after and a rent to pay.'

'Please,' I insisted. 'It's distracting for me and it's not right.'

'Mind your own business!' was his response.

What was I to do now? I thought about leaving the church and looking for another one. But I felt under an obligation because I had been given the post even though I didn't have the formal qualifications — I didn't have a primary school leaving certificate or even a report card from one of the classes. What would I say to the archbishop who had done me the favour of giving his consent? What would I say to Professor Alivizatos who had done his utmost to have me appointed? I became deeply depressed. I sat in the sanctuary and thought. What would I do? I said to myself that I would have to leave; I couldn't stay any longer. How could I live in there? How could I celebrate the Liturgy? Especially as someone who had come from the desert, from complete and utter silence, how could I endure such a satanic noise? All the buses from Nikaia, from Peristeri and from Piraeus passed in front of the church door and you could hear the constant sound of their horns hooting as they went up and down. I resolved to leave. But how would I announce it? I returned home dejected. I didn't know what to do…

At the time I was living in the Lykavitos district, in Doxapatri Street. I went back there and wracked my brains… I didn't even want to eat. What was I to do? I had been so overjoyed that I had found a post in a hospital and that I would see sick people, that I would be able to look after them, to talk to them, to hear their confessions and give them Holy Communion. Now what? Only God could extricate me from this difficult situation. And so in answer to the dreadful problem I was facing, I said to myself: 'Whatever God says.'

'My God,' I said, 'I don't want You to speak to me; I don't want You to show me a sign. But with Your own love reveal to me something simple that will enable me to know whether I should leave or stay. Something very simple. I'm not asking for some miracle. I'm ashamed to.' And so I decided to fast for three days without even putting water in my mouth, praying in complete silence and waiting for an answer from God.

And the answer came. While I was in the chapel of Saint Gerasimos various people came in to light a candle. At one point a woman came in with her child. The boy would have been in the first year of secondary school. He was carrying his schoolbooks with him. One of them was his physics textbook. I asked him if I could have a look at it, because I was always curious to learn something new. As I was leafing through it I lighted on a page showing the following experiment: If you throw a small stone into a calm lake you see the water making ripples over a small area. If you then throw in a larger stone, the ripples become larger and extend over a larger area so that they outflank the first ripples. At that moment I received the answer to my dilemma. It was divine illumination. I reasoned as follows: the small ripples from the singing outside the church can be outflanked by the prayers of great spiritual intensity that are being said inside the church. And at the same time there came at once into my mind forcefully, very forcefully: 'And if you celebrate here and have your mind on God, who can cause you any harm?'

So I prepared myself to do just this — to abandon myself completely to Christ's love, to execute with great zeal and spiritual intensity the drama of the Divine Liturgy, the awesome drama of Golgotha. My joy was very great. I believed that God had found the solution for me. On the Sunday morning I arrived at the church full of hope. I gave the blessing to begin. My mind was focused solely on the divine worship. I felt that I was in heaven as well as on earth and with me was the congregation, God's flock, initiates in the mystery of His Word. I felt that we were all embraced by divine grace. Outside the gramophone was blaring furiously. I heard nothing. For the first time I experienced a Divine Liturgy like that. It was the most beautiful of my life. And from then onwards all the Divine Liturgies were the same.

I wanted to learn everything in all its depth and breadth

I experienced a great many things during the years I was at the Polyclinic. Greece, and especially Athens, was suffering from the hardships of the war and the occupation — the starvation and death that carried people away every day. I shared with them the communion loaves, the *prosphora*, and whatever else was brought to me. But even more the anguish in their souls made me suffer with them, as I saw into the depths of their souls with the gift of clear sight. Whenever someone came and told me about a bodily pain, I made it a matter for prayer. This fact also incited me to study. When I 'saw' a sick part of the body, I wanted to know its scientific name and the position of all the organs in the human body, the bile, the pancreas, etc. And so I bought medical textbooks on anatomy, physiology, etc., in order to study and understand. For a time, indeed, I attended classes at the Medical School to acquire a fuller knowledge. My thirst for learning extended to all fields. I wanted to learn everything in all its depth and breadth. If I visited a factory, I wanted to learn every detail about how it operated. If I visited a museum, I would spend hours examining the sculptures. I'll tell you about one incident I remember.

One Sunday afternoon I was passing the Archaeological Museum and since I had some free time I decided to go in. I walked through the rooms looking at the statues. In one of the rooms there was a group of people with a guide who was explaining things to them. There was complete silence. I went towards them. When the guide saw me, however, she whispered to them:

'A priest's just come in. I can't stand priests, but this one doesn't seem to be like the others.'

I came up closer and said:

'Good afternoon.'

'Good afternoon,' replied the guide.

'May I listen to what you are saying?' I asked.

'Of course,' she said.

We went from one statue to another. At one point we stood before a statue of Zeus. Zeus was on his throne and was in the act of hurling a thunderbolt at mankind. Once the guide had finished telling them what she knew, she turned to me and said:

'What do you have to say about this, *Pappouli*? How do you see the statue?'

'I don't know about these things,' I said. 'But as I see it, I marvel at the work of the artist and also at the human form, such a perfect divine creation. And I see that the artist who made it had a great sense of the divine. Look at Zeus. Although he is hurling his thunderbolt at mankind, yet his face is serene. He is not angry. He's impassionate.'

The guide, and indeed the whole group, was very pleased with my explanation. What does that tell us? It tells us that God is without passion, even when he punishes.

I had a great thirst for knowledge about everything, as I said. I once went to study poultry-farming. Truly! Another time I went to a teacher who taught bee-keeping. The teacher was from Corfu. There were various people in the class, boys and girls, young and old. When the lesson was over the teacher came up to me and said:

'Do you know what I've realized, Father? I can see that you'll be very successful as a bee-keeper.'

'How did you realize that?' I asked.

'From the way you look, from your attentiveness, I saw that you'll make a good bee-keeper. You'll do very well. You'll understand the bees, you'll talk to them and they'll talk to you.'

'That's quite right,' I said. 'I'll talk to the bees, I'll go up to the hive, I'll listen to them, I'll understand them, I'll be delighted with them — but I'll lose my cassock and my priest's hat!'

I wanted to be an ascetic, even if it was in the middle of Athens

My main work all those years since I became a spiritual father has been confession. Hours without end, days and nights without a break, I would hear confession, whether I was in Saint Charalambos in Evia, in Saint Gerasimos or in Saint Nicholas in Kallisia, or now, here in the monastery. Even when I had my illnesses — and they were very many and lasted for years — I received with Christ's love the souls that God sent me.

I wanted to be an ascetic, even if it was in the middle of Athens, and so I hid myself in the Tourkovounia hills. I lived there with my parents, my sister and my niece in a shack made of breeze blocks. At night we worked in silence and in prayer. We had knitting machines and we knitted vests and pullovers and we sold them. Our aim was to build a monastery with the money we set aside.

We also made incense. Precious incense. It was of my own invention, with my own recipes, my own concoctions, with fifty aromatic substances. I recognized the various incenses and their acidity by the fragrances. I had filled a jotter with my recipes — a jotter filled with recipes with which I made up fragrances for the incense. I put all the aromatic substances I had in a row — about fifty bottles in all: *routinol, rinanol, rinalil*, etc. And strangely, I knew all these bottles. I knew the fragrance of each one and its intensity and its acidity. I knew that if I needed ten parts of the one, from the other I needed two, or three or one and I made up some very fine, rare recipes. I had them all written down in a jotter, as I told you, but it was stolen. I know who stole it from me, but I don't want to say. That I can't say…

I was very simple

I was very simple and without worldly knowledge and without knowledge of social etiquette. I didn't know how to behave because I had grown up on a mountainside. I had spent a little time with my godfather in Piraeus, but I looked after myself there. The girls brought me food and I ate on my own and slept up in the attic. So I didn't know how to hold a fork or spoon at the table. Listen and I'll tell you something. I didn't generally go where I was invited. But once I was called to read a prayer for a sick woman who worked next to the Polyclinic near the Town Hall. A very fine, devout woman. But by the time we got to her house and read the prayer it was late and they insisted that I would stay and eat with them.

'No,' I said. 'I'm afraid I can't. I've got to leave.'

The woman's husband said:

'We'll be very offended if you don't stay, because we know you haven't eaten. We'll be very upset if you leave, Father. Do us the honour. We've got our little daughter too.'

They had a little girl. They hadn't been long married. A lovely little girl.

So I accepted. I said the grace, blessed the food and we began to eat. But their little daughter, seeing how I was eating, exclaimed:

'Mama, he's not holding his spoon properly!'

'Hush now, hush!' they said.

But hushed she wasn't.

'He's not holding his spoon properly.'

What an embarrassment! I looked at how they were holding their spoons and did likewise. Then they gave me something to eat with a fork.

At once the little one piped up:

'He's not holding his fork properly.'

Alas and alack! You see how simple I was...

Saint Gerasimos's walking stick

The place where we lived in the Tourkovounia was on a very steep incline. I would get up very early in the morning, set off for the church, for Saint Gerasimos's, and would return late in the evening. The road outside our house was very tricky and descended very abruptly. One morning I fell down and broke my leg. It was Sunday morning, the sun hadn't risen above the horizon and all was quiet. So some people heard my groans of pain and came out and called an ambulance. The ambulance came and took me to the hospital. I had broken my left leg at the shin. All the bones had been shattered. The pain was excruciating. When they got me to the Polyclinic they took me out of the ambulance and put me on a bed. The doctors decided to put my leg in plaster. The people in the church were waiting for me to go and celebrate the Liturgy. In the end they had to leave.

After two weeks, during which I had been lying in bed, while I was praying I happened to cast a glance at my leg. With the grace of God I saw that they had set my leg wrongly in the plaster. So I asked the doctors to remove the plaster. The consultant who heard about it said with a laugh:

'Instead of looking after the church for which he's responsible, that priest wants to criticize us, even though everything's been done properly and his leg's been x-rayed. What does he want now? Does he want to waste our time?'

Nobody showed any interest. I insisted on them looking at my leg. They paid no attention. When they brought me food at lunchtime, I didn't eat it and said that I demand that they take me for an x-ray. I insisted on this, because the leg would heal askew and would stay like that for good. The consultant sent a message, 'Tell him to occupy himself with his priestly duties! His leg's perfectly fine.'

Evening came and again they brought me food and again I didn't eat, insisting that they take a look at my leg. The next morning the consultant came by and said irately:

'What's all this nonsense, Papa? Are you trying to waste our time in here?'

In the end they took me down to the x-rays. They saw that they had indeed set my leg askew and, what's more, it had healed. The consultant started to laugh:

'Poor Papa,' he said. 'You must be a real sinner! Now I realize it too. Now you'll see what you have to go through! We'll have to break your leg again and reset it properly.

They started to hammer the plaster to break it. I said nothing, but only prayed silently.

'So you're not saying anything now,' he said to me. 'But now I'm going to forgive all your sins!'

With a sudden movement they pulled and removed the plaster. I was in great pain. Two doctors held my leg and the consultant started punching my shin with his fist to break it.

'Now you'll see, Papa!' he said. 'I'll forgive all your sins, and all my own will be forgiven as well!'

They set about breaking the bone; it had already healed a little and I was in unbearable pain. I bit my lip. In the end they broke it. They laid me down once again under the x-ray, pulled my leg and brought it back onto its axis. Then they carefully put on the plaster and sent me back to my bed.

For two or three months — I can't remember exactly — I remained stretched out in bed. After that they got me to sit up and gave me two crutches to walk with. I didn't want them. The consultant said to me:

'Take them to stand up, because you've been lying down so long.'

I didn't use the crutches for long because I was soon able to keep my balance on my own. I was wary of the crutches in case I would get used to them and wouldn't be able to do without them.

Then the consultant said to me:

'Be sure to buy a walking stick.'

'No,' I said, 'I don't need one.'

'You're a priest,' he said, 'and yet you're so disobedient! Listen to me, otherwise you'll fall and break all your bones.'

So I was obliged to ask my sister:

'Would you buy me a walking stick. We're poor, but you'll have to get me a walking stick so that I can get rid of those crutches.'

It was eleven o'clock in the morning and I went down on the crutches to the hospital chapel.

My sister got ready at once to set off to Aiolos Street to buy a walking stick. Just as she was about to leave, a woman holding a walking stick in her hand entered the church.

'Is this Saint Gerasimos's here?' she asked.

'Yes, dear, this is it,' answered the lady who acted as caretaker.

'Where's the icon of the saint?'

'Over there,' she said pointing to the icon.

The unknown visitor knelt down before the icon of the saint and with tears in her eyes started to address the saint out loud in such a way that we could all hear:

'Dear Saint, I didn't know you. I'd never heard of you. I hadn't even heard your name. And yet you did me the honour of visiting me and you asked me to bring the walking stick I had bought in Jerusalem to your house. And here I've brought it to you, my dear Saint. You said, "I want you to bring me the walking stick tomorrow morning!" I didn't know where you were, but I asked and now I've found you.'

I was sitting with my sister and the caretaker in the seats next to the candle bench. The woman approached us and said:

'What's all this about? Why did the saint ask for my walking stick? What does he want it for?'

The caretaker replied:

'Listen and you'll see why the saint wants your walking stick. He doesn't need it himself, but the saint has a servant and his servant is this priest here that you see. He's broken his leg and he's been suffering dreadfully for months. Today is the first day he's out of bed and the doctors have told him to get a walking stick. And look, his sister was just about to go to Aiolos Street to buy him a walking stick. Come, then, take the walking stick from the saint and give it here to his servant.'

The woman, overcome with emotion, brought me the walking stick and kissed my hand.

'Take it, Father,' she said, 'and forgive my sins. I bought it in Jerusalem. It's from the Holy Sepulchre. I come from the Probona district at the bottom of Patisia. That's where I live. I saw the saint there in my sleep.'

I thanked her. I took the walking stick and, setting aside my crutches, used it at once. I called it Saint Gerasimos's walking stick and was very fond of it. I take care of it so that I don't lose it. It's very miraculous. When someone has a pain somewhere, I tap the painful spot a little with the walking stick and they get better. It's truly miraculous. Can you believe it! The saint took care of someone as insignificant as myself! He appeared as large as life to the woman who had heard neither of Saint Gerasimos nor of me. The saints work the most incredible miracles. That's why we must honour them. And I venerate Saint Gerasimos who, with his saintliness and grace, is the staff of the sick.

'He rains on the righteous and unrighteous'

Many people would come to the church of Saint Gerasimos in the Polyclinic to light a candle. Some would stay for confession, others took a blessing, while others would light their candle, make the sign of the cross and leave. People of every kind would come: men and women, young and old, educated and uneducated. People of all walks of life lived in the Omonia area.

On the Feast of the Theophany, after the Great Blessing of the Water, it was the custom to go round and bless people's homes by sprinkling the Holy Water. One year I also went and did the blessing. I would knock on the doors of the flats, and when the door was opened I would enter singing: 'When in Jordan you were baptized, O Lord...'. As I was going down Maizon Street I saw an iron gate. I opened it and entered the courtyard, which was full of mandarin, orange and lemon trees, and walked towards the stairway. It was an outside stair that went up to a first floor and also down to a basement. I went up the stair, knocked at the door and a woman appeared. When she opened the door for me I started as usual to sing: 'When in Jordan you were baptized, O Lord...'. She stopped me abruptly. In the meantime, however, my voice had been heard and girls started coming out of the rooms from right and left in the corridor. 'I see what's happened,' I said to myself, 'I've stumbled on a house of ill fame.' The woman stood in my way barring my entrance.

'Go away,' she said to me. 'It's not right for these girls to kiss the cross. Let me kiss the cross and then, please, go away.'

I assumed a serious and reprimanding attitude and said to her:

'I'm afraid I cannot leave! I am a priest and I have come to bless the house.'

'That's all very well, but there's no way these girls can kiss the cross.'

'But how do we know who should kiss the cross, the girls or you? Because if God were to ask me who should be allowed to kiss the cross, I might reply that the girls should kiss it and not you. Their souls are in a better state than your own.'

She blushed for a moment. So I said, 'Let the girls come and venerate the cross.'

I signalled to the girls to come forward and started to sing 'When in Jordan you were baptized, O Lord...' with even greater gusto than before, because I felt a sense of joy that God had so arranged things for me to come to these souls.

They all kissed the cross. They were all immaculately turned out with their coloured skirts and so on. And I said to them, 'Blessings on you all, my children. God loves all of us. He is very good and *sends rain on the righteous and the unrighteous*. He is the Father of us all and is concerned Matt. 5:45
for each one of us. Only we too must try to come to know Him and to love Him and to become good. Love Him and you'll see how happy you'll be.'

They looked at me with puzzlement. But something remained in their troubled little souls.

'I'm delighted that God granted me the honour of coming here today to bless you,' I said to them as I turned to go. 'Blessings on you for many years!'

'For many years!' they replied, and I left.

The prayers were most magnificent

On various occasions, apart from Feast of the Theophany, I would be asked to go and do a service of blessing in homes. Once during the time of the German occupation a representative of the Red Cross came to the Polyclinic to take me to do a service of blessing.

'You'll have to go and get a priest from St Constantine's,' I said. 'The house belongs in that parish.'

'No,' he replied categorically, 'you're the priest who's to come. There's a reason for it, and willy-nilly you'll come along with me to Third September Street!'

And so submissively I went along with him, taking with me the cross, my monastic headgear and my good cassock. When we arrived, I was taken aback. I found myself face to face with a company of highly sophisticated ladies and gentlemen, including the Chancellor of the University who taught philosophy — Beis, I think, was his name. As soon as I entered the room I introduced myself confidently and shook hands with everyone. But I, an unlettered soul, had failed to bring a book with me. When I saw the people dressed in finery and the platters piled with choice sweets at the time of the Occupation I started to quiver with nervousness.

'Let's do the Service of Blessing,' I said to them.

I put on my outer cassock, donned my monastic veil and took the cross in my hand. I started the service without a book, and, summoning up courage, I began to say the prayers clearly and distinctly, word by word. As I progressed the words began to flow more confidently, but I kept my gaze fixed on the bowl of water in front of me.

'Peace be to all'…'Let us bow our heads to the Lord'…'Incline your ear and hear us, O Lord, you who deigned to be baptized in Jordan and sanctified the waters; bless all of us who signify our humility of mind through the bowing of our necks, and grant that we may be filled with your sanctification through our partaking of this water and our being sprinkled therewith; and may it be for us, O Lord, for health of soul and body. For you are the sanctification of our souls and bodies, and to you we give glory and thanksgiving and worship, together with your Father who is without beginning, and your all-holy and good and life-giving Spirit…'

I said it all like a bishop. When I finished the Blessing of the Water, I didn't go to sprinkle water on their heads and present the cross for veneration — many people don't like that — but I simply held the cross in my hand and looked to see who would come forward. The Cabinet Minister present came forward first and the others followed. I pronounced blessings on them: 'May God bless you, illuminate and strengthen you.' But I was constantly overwhelmed by the feeling that I was uneducated. Before leaving, I made the sign of the cross in the air, blessed them, and said, 'Good day to you, my children!' And there were university professors there!

'The prayers were most magnificent,' said the University Chancellor. 'I was most gratified. I enjoyed the Service of Blessing immensely, and you recited it all so well by heart. Are you a divinity graduate? I noticed, however, that you made a mistake in the Gospel reading. You said "became [*egeneto*] well", but the correct reading is "would become [*egineto*] well".'

'Thank you very much,' I replied. 'I'm an unlettered priest.'

This is the Gospel we read on the Sunday of the Paralytic. It goes as follows:

At that time Jesus went up to Jerusalem. Now there is in Jerusalem near the Sheep Gate a pool which is called in Hebrew 'Bethesda' and which is surrounded by five covered colonnades. Here a great number of disabled people used to lie ⊠ the blind, the lame, the paralyzed ⊠ waiting for the moving of the water. From time to time an angel would descend into the pool and stir up the water. The first person into the pool after the distur-
John 5:1–3 *bance of the water would become well, from whatever disease he had.*

Let me remind you of the *Kontakion* Hymn of the Sunday of the Paralytic:

> *By your divine authority, O Lord, raise up my soul,*
> *as once you raised up the paralytic,*
> *for my soul lies woefully paralyzed*
> *through all kinds of sins and wrongful actions,*
> *so that once healed I may cry out,*
> *Compassionate Lord, glory, Christ, to your Power.*

This is a good *Kontakion* to remember and recite as a prayer.

I saw Christ so vividly

In the church — the Church of Saint Gerasimos, I mean — I used to get very moved. As I heard the Gospel reading I was deeply affected. This happened because I saw the image before me, Christ himself.

One Good Friday we were doing the service. The church was packed with people. I was reading the Gospel, and when I came to the phrase, *Eli, Eli, lama sabachthani, that is, My God, My God, why have you forsaken me?* I was unable to finish it. I didn't read the words '*why have you forsaken me?*' I was overcome with emotion. My voice broke. In front of me I saw the whole tragic scene. I saw that face. I heard that voice. I saw Christ so vividly. The people in the church waited. I said nothing. I was unable to continue. I left the Gospel on the reading stand and turned back into the sanctuary. I made the sign of the cross and kissed the Holy Table. I brought to my mind another image, a better one. No, not a better one. There was no more beautiful image than that one, but the image of the Resurrection came to my mind. At once I calmed down. Then I returned to the Holy Doors and said:

Matt. 27:46

'Excuse me, my children, I got carried away.'

Then I picked up the Gospel Book and read the passage from the beginning. But at that moment the whole congregation was moved to tears.

That was bad. A person may think what he will. But it is not good to allow ourselves to be carried away. We need to be restrained.

What God's love and providence does

The years after the war were very difficult and people struggled hard to make a living. As I've told you, I was in the Polyclinic at that time. I remember many incidents from those years. Listen and I'll tell you about one.

Effi was seventeen years old and used to spend the summer with her parents and her brother at Boyati.* They had a vegetable garden and they used to sell the produce. One evening Effi's mother sent her down to a shop close by to buy some paraffin-oil for the lamp. At that time, remember, they didn't have electricity. On her way back to the house Effi met a boy who was in her class at school. They exchanged a few words about their lessons. The place where they had stopped to speak was behind a parked lorry. At that moment Effi's brother passed by and saw them speaking. He misconstrued the situation because he thought their conversation wasn't so innocent and he told their mother.

'Effi has shamed us,' he said, 'she was speaking to a boy on the street.'

When Effi arrived home her mother scolded her angrily and beat her. Moral principles were very strict at that time. Effi was deeply mortified. She was aggrieved and indignant at the injustice and her brother's suspicion.

The next day her father, who had been away from home, returned. He treated her differently, with understanding and kindness.

'I don't believe all that,' he told her. 'Come on. Let's go and water the vegetable garden. You watch and when you see that one section has been watered, tell me, and I'll turn the water into the furrow round the next section.'

So that's what they did. Effi, however, had not slept at all the previous night. Her distress and the injustice were choking her. She was in despair and decided to put an end to her life. And as she set out for the vegetable garden with her father she made up a plan. She would take some weed-killer and, in the evening when they were finished with the watering, she would drink it secretly and die. She thought to herself, 'Then I'll see, will they love me?' So she took the weed-killer and put it in her pocket and waited for night to fall to drink it. The difficult moment was not long in coming. Her father, suspecting nothing, said to her, 'Go down to the bottom of the garden and turn off the water.'

She went quickly. She was out of sight. There was no one near her. Her father was a good many yards away. Trembling, she put her hand into her pocket. At that precise moment she heard footsteps. Before she could move an unknown priest suddenly appeared before her. He greeted her and said:

'Dear Effi, you know how wonderful Paradise is — light, joy and delight. Christ is all light and he scatters joy and delight on everyone. He is waiting for us in the next life to give us the gift of Paradise. But there is

* A district north of Athens, now more commonly known as Aghios Stephanos.

also hell, which is all darkness, sadness, distress, anxiety and depression. If you swallow what you've got in your pocket you'll go to hell. So throw it away at once so that we don't lose the beauty of Paradise.

Effi was lost for words to begin with, but after a little while she said to the priest, after she had, unconsciously, thrown away the poison:

'Wait and I'll call my father to see you.'

She ran up the garden. She was lost from sight as she ran through the high maize stalks to find her father. She found him and said to him:

'Father, come quickly and see a priest who has come to the bottom of our garden.'

When they arrived at the place where they expected to find the priest waiting, there was no one there.

For a long time Effi was unable to explain all that had happened that evening. She couldn't explain the disappearance of the priest. She wanted to find him again because he had saved her life.

In the meantime, every winter the whole family went to stay in Athens. Effi frequently visited her godmother who was a very devout woman and she would stay with her for long periods. Her godmother often used to entertain priests, monks and theologians in her house. Once when Effi went to see her godmother she learned that there was a visitor in the lounge. Effi didn't know who it was. Her godmother came into the kitchen at one point and said to her:

'Effi, my dear, prepare a sweet-meat and a cup of coffee and bring it into the lounge for our visitor.'

Effi prepared everything. She took a little time, however, and just as she was carrying it through, her godmother appeared again and said to her:

'No, not on that tray. Use the silver tray, because it's an important visitor.'

Effi returned to the kitchen, changed the tray and carried it into the lounge. But what did she see! The tray nearly dropped from her hands. She saw before her the priest who had appeared to her on that difficult evening in their vegetable garden.

'I'm Father Porphyrios,' I said to her with a smile.

And so we got to know each other and ever since we have developed a great friendship. Effi got married and had lots of children. God gave her His blessing. You see the means the God can employ when He wants to save a person?

SAINT NICHOLAS KALLISIA (1955–1979)

Some great pain, some problem led them to set out on the rough track leading to Saint Nicholas.

We lived for more than twenty years in that deserted area

God fulfilled my desire to work in a hospital. I spent thirty-three years at the Polyclinic. But I cherished within me another deep desire — to find a site and build a monastery. After some searching I found Saint Nicholas at Kallisia. It was a dependency of the Holy Monastery of Pendeli.

One day I went there by the grace of God. The church appeared from far off. When I arrived, I went in. It was a place of prayer, old and with a few icons. Outside were a few small, smoke-blackened rooms. In the meantime, night had fallen. I was alone. There was no way I could go back to Athens. I lay down to sleep in the church. After a short time I heard a characteristic tapping. It came from the wall above my head. The icon of Saint Nicholas was hanging there. The tapping was coming from the icon. I felt that the saint wanted me to go and live there.

I went and I brought my parents, my sister and my niece. As a monk, I realized that monks who live on their own in the 'world' lose their way. We had great peace there. We lived very nicely, even though the conditions were primitive. We lived for more than twenty years in that deserted area. At that time it was a true wilderness. The whole area around Saint Nicholas was covered in vegetation. There were old and young pine trees, plane trees, bushes here and there, thyme plants disseminating their fragrance, cyclamens growing out of the cracks in the rocks, anemones and other wild flowers according to the season. It was a paradise; exceedingly beautiful. I wanted to create a monastery there. But God did not permit it.

Saint Nicholas is not very far from Pendeli, and in particular from the Social Services Centre known as 'PIKPA', but at that time there was no road. You had to walk on foot or go by donkey for an hour along a rough track and then follow a goat path for another twenty minutes in order to get to Saint Nicholas which was built on a rocky hillock. We gradually opened up a narrow pathway so that we could have easier access and bring in essential provisions — whatever we could not supply from our garden.

I enjoyed the garden. I bought a hand-held cultivator to prepare the ground as well as possible. The garden had everything: tomatoes, aubergines, pumpkins, onions, garlic and so on. My great love was for the trees. I was filled with joy to look at them. I planted four hundred trees: walnut trees, plum trees, pear trees, apple trees, peach trees, almond trees, hazelnut trees, medlar trees and pomegranate trees. I loved the work. I always said and still say: 'Work as if you were immortal, and live as if you were on the point of death.' That is, plant walnut trees, fig trees and olive trees, even if you're ninety years old. Is it possible for your heart not to leap as you plant them? Even if passers-by see you tiring yourself out and say, 'poor, wretched soul'.

To protect the trees from diseases, we would spray them with sulphur and copper sulphate. I used to come up from Pendeli with a sack on my back with the saplings. I lavished great care on them. I employed workers as well because I didn't have much time as I was still working at the Polyclinic. It was my duty to be in Saint Gerasimos's early in the morning and so I left for Athens the previous evening. When someone would come to talk to me and our conversation went on until late, I would leave Saint Nicholas at midnight.

We had water in abundance for our vegetables at Saint Nicholas. Down in a valley with lots of plane trees there was a spring. I installed a pump there to pump the water high up the hill to a cistern I made to collect the water there. And it was drinking water, of course. In order to have a little cool water in the summer, because we didn't have a refrigerator, I put water in a long-necked little earthen-ware pitcher which I had bought in Aegina and that kept the water cool.

I also sold chickens. I had rented a plot of land belonging to the Holy Monastery of Pendeli opposite the Observatory and I kept about a thousand chickens there. We couldn't have any more because the plot of land was small. As I have told you, I had in mind to build a monastery and so I found various ways of collecting money for that purpose.

We were quite isolated in Kallisia and so we wanted to hear a service or Divine Liturgy on one of the Athenian radio stations and also to hear the weather forecast and the news, to learn what was going on in the world and what to pray for. So I decided to make a radio of my own invention. I placed an aerial on a pine tree fifteen metres high and I fixed a cable to the wall of the church and tied it to a wild pear tree. This primitive radio had no on/off switch, so it played day and night without stop, but I had adjusted it to play quietly so that it wouldn't annoy us.

When I wasn't required at Saint Gerasimos's, I would celebrate at

Saint Nicholas. Gradually people started to come there to attend church or to make confession. We became one big family with all these people, the family of Kallisia.

They were glorifying God for the miracle

Other people, however, would also come from time to time. Some great pain, some problem led them to set out along the rough track leading to Saint Nicholas.

So one day a woman with her husband and four little children arrived. They were young and hadn't been many years married. To begin with they hadn't wanted children. Then they decided, 'Let's have a child.' And they had one set of twins and then another so that they ended up with four children. So they had all come there and the young woman — she was thirty years old — said to me:

'Elder, I'm in great pain. I'm not at all well.'

As she was speaking to me, I looked at her carefully and put my hand below her chin.

'Here,' I said to her, 'do you feel a constriction?'

'Yes,' she replied.

'And you are overtaken by a kind of sadness, which completes its cycle. That is to say, to begin with you feel a constriction and then a feeling of sorrow comes over you and you can't move. You move, you might even laugh, but inside you experience this state.'

'Yes,' she confirmed to me.

I painted her condition to her so very well. She felt pleased. Then I put my hand once more on her neck.

'Don't imagine there's anything the matter with you,' I said to her. 'You've no longer got any of these symptoms.'

I still had my hand on her neck and suddenly I said to her:

'There! It's all gone now.'

Because I saw it. As I saw, her neck had nothing the matter with it.

She also said to me: 'It's all gone now. I feel perfectly well in myself.'

Then I said to her: 'Kneel down.'

She knelt down and I placed one hand in front of her neck and the other on the back of her head and started to say, 'Lord, Jesus Christ, have mercy on me.' Then I remained in silence for a short time. Then, as she was kneeling there, she cried out, 'Ah!' as she felt relief.

'Off you go now then. Get up now,' I said to her. 'There are other people waiting now.'

She kissed my hand and left. She went a little way off and started something of a commotion among all the people there. Her husband, too, was overjoyed. They were glorifying God for the miracle.

You should see the pain which some people have to bear!

Another time Costas's parents came from Xylokastro. You should see the pain that some people have to bear! They are good people, but both their children, Costas and Maria, became fanatic followers of Sai Baba of India. Costas was a medical student. He left home along with his sister just before Easter. As they were leaving the house, the father said to his daughter:

'Joyous Resurrection, Maria!'

'The Resurrection has come, father, but people haven't recognized it,' she replied.

In the meantime their parents continually gave them money. Now they have stopped this because they were using it for their 'god'. Costas went to Thessalonica to spread his propaganda. Indeed, he was beaten up there. He tried to proselytize some young people there, and their parents got hold of him and beat him up.

These good people brought me a periodical. On the cover there is a photograph of Sai Baba. He has created a new religion in which they believe that he is the new Christ who came into the world to save it and to lead it to truth. They say he is the 'new God'. Sai Baba is alive now. He is married and has his wife and two children next to him. At the bottom of the photograph we see lots of young people who are his followers; many of them, indeed, are educated people. How did these educated young people end up there? On another page they are kissing his feet. 'The days of that Christ' — the true Christ, that is — 'are over now,' he tells them. 'This is another age,' he tells you. Everything now is changing. It's like a fairy tale. Perhaps Sai Baba is mad. They say he has collected a lot of money.

I'll tell you about another related incident.

One day an officer in the Greek Navy took me down to the waterfront at Oropos. We walked along the breakwater where a man was fishing. I said to the officer:

'Go and get me one of the fish that man is catching.'

The fisherman, however, replied:

'The basket is empty. I've been here since the morning and I've caught nothing. Go and leave me in peace…'

I said to him:

'Throw your hook into the sea.'

'Go away,' he said to us in an aggravated tone of voice.

We turned to go. But at that moment, just as the fisherman threw his line into the sea he felt a bite on it. He drew in the line and a large fish was struggling on the hook. He shouted out to us:

'Don't go! Come here. Don't go away. I've caught a fish.'

The officer said:

'I know why that happened, Father. It happened so that I would believe in you, that you are of God, and so that the fisherman would believe. Up till now I believed in the new Christ, the Sai Baba of India. Now I believe in the true Christ.'

We remained for hours in the divine light...

At Saint Nicholas in Kallisia I devoted most of my time to confession. There was, of course, also lots of time for prayer, especially at night. I'll tell you about an incident in relation to this.

Once — it was late evening — my sister and I decided we would go together to pray in the church of Saint Nicholas. We said we would eat first and wait for everyone to go to sleep and then we would get up and go into the church in secret. We closed the door and started to pray: 'Lord, Jesus Christ...' After a short time we were flooded by a light, a divine light. We continued the 'Lord, Jesus Christ...' and we experienced a joy, an ineffable joy. We remained there for hours in the divine light and then, as the light gradually left, we continued the 'Lord, Jesus Christ, have mercy on me.' Then we returned to the room. Our mother was awake and waiting for us and as soon as we opened the door, she said:

'Where did you go? Is that why you sent me off to bed? Did you think I didn't see you? I saw you through the window. I saw everything. I saw a light, a light that descended from heaven and entered the church. I watched it and I started weeping. Look! My eyes are filled with tears.'

The old lady was of a grouchy disposition but very pious. Even though the door was closed, she saw the light. The light had flooded the church.

Another time when we were living in Pendeli — it was a great feast, Christmas or Easter, I can't remember — the old lady got up and said:

'I'm going to go over to Saint Nicholas's. His oil-lamps have gone out, or so I feel.'

It was an hour and a half there and another hour and a half to come back on foot. She went and discovered the church bathed in light and the lamps lit.

THE HOLY MONASTERY OF THE TRANSFIGURATION – MILESI (1979–1991)

I would like the monastery to be a place to which people with sorrows and afflictions can come for refuge and find comfort, strength and healing

I harboured the desire to create a monastery

An old dream of mine, as I have told you, was to create a monastery, a place that would be a spiritual workshop where souls would be sanctified and cultivated and glorify the name of God unceasingly. I would like it to be a place to which people with sorrows and afflictions can come for refuge and find comfort, strength and healing.

For years while we were living with my sister and niece in the Tourkovounia area we had knitting machines and we worked. Yes, we knitted vests. We collected money for this purpose. We were very thrifty in relation to food, clothes and everything. So we purchased the first plots of land with this money. Thereafter money and labour were contributed and continue to be contributed by Christians who appreciate the value of the project.

For years I searched to find the right site. I never wanted to resort to real estate agents. I went to various places. I wanted the place to be sheltered from the wind but to have a view. I prayed as I was accustomed to do for God to guide me. I wanted the grace of God to assure me about this. I prayed 'Lord, Jesus Christ…' constantly. Finally God showed the present site on the hilltop at Milesi as the place to build the monastery. A shepherd told me the place was called 'Saint Sotira'. I liked the site and asked if it was for sale.

'Yes,' they told me. 'It belongs to Mr Baloka from Milesi, and he's promised it to his daughters, Eleni and Spyridoula. It's them you'll have to get in touch with.'

I then went close to the site and prayed. I wanted to know if it had water. I saw that it did have water, and indeed very good water. That pleased me very much. But I saw that the water was very deep underground and I thought: 'How can this water be brought to the surface?' I saw water in other places; it was the same water. Lower down, at a distance of about one and a half kilometers from the hilltop, the water was not so deep down. So I thought I would buy a plot of land there and drill a well and pump the water up to the site where I would build the monastery. So, with God's illumination, I secured the water.

Then I checked to see that a road could be opened up to bring in electricity and a telephone line. I looked to see if it was south-facing, if it was sheltered from the wind, and whether it was exposed to the north wind or was damp. I wanted to see the path of the sun so that in winter there would not be rooms that didn't see the sun. For months I went and observed how the sun was at sunrise, at mid-day and at sunset, so that we could build in such a way that the sun would fall on the building both at sunrise and at sunset — so that the last ray of light would fall on the monastery. All these things proved favourable. At once I set in motion the process of purchasing it. We bought it and started the work.

I bent down and drank the water mentally

We started digging the foundations and building without water. It wasn't easy to obtain a reliable supply of spring water at the outset. So we constructed a large cistern which held six hundred and forty cubic metres of rain water. In spite of this, the water from the cistern was not enough, and for five or six years we were obliged to buy water from Kifisia. We spent a lot of money each year on water. We had planted trees which we watered with purchased water. It was necessary, therefore, for us to exploit the water which I saw beneath the site. But for this a lot of money was going to be required because the water was very deep down and a suitable person would have to be found to do the work. The matter occupied my mind. A solution would have to be found. God found the solution. Listen to what happened.

One day a man came to ask my advice about a certain matter. For his benefit Christ revealed to me certain things about his family affairs. He was taken aback and said to me:

'No one apart from my wife knows about these things you are telling me. They are very secret.'

In his enthusiasm he said to me:

'What would you like me to bring you, Elder?'

'Nothing,' I replied.

'Have you water at the monastery?' he asked.

'No,' I said, 'we don't.'

'Then I'll bring up water for you. I have well-drilling equipment.'

'What will it cost?' I asked him.

'Nothing,' he replied. 'I'll meet all the costs of drilling, and I'll bring a pump.'

'Very well,' I said. 'You are saying this before Christ.'

And he left.

A few days later he appeared with a drilling machine. He drilled down to a depth of thirty-eight metres, but he came on a hard rock and didn't want to proceed any further. I implored him and he brought another, better, drill and went down to a depth of eighty metres, but without finding water. Again he came upon a hard rock and the drill wouldn't progress any further. In despair he said to me:

'I can't find any water, Elder. I going to leave.'

'You mustn't leave!' I told him.

'I'm going to have to leave,' he repeated.

Then, because I was blind, I asked one of the sisters and she took me down behind the point where they were drilling, about twenty-five metres from the drill-head, to a place hidden among the pine trees so that they wouldn't see me. There I prayed and went and found the stream of water mentally. I made the sign of the cross and prayed. From there I measured mentally how deep down the water was, just as I was accustomed to do. Because on other occasions, when I was younger, I had found water for people who asked me to. And not only did I find it, but I tasted it mentally to check the quality of the water, whether it was good, whether it was sea water, salty or fresh and so on. I took a measuring stick and measured downwards — mentally, that is. I measured, 'one, two, three…' The water was very deep down, and so I started to count with a ten metre measuring stick — mentally, of course. I said, 'Ten, twenty, thirty, forty, fifty, a hundred…' I felt great exultation. I had found the water, even though it was so deep down! I felt an inexpressible joy. Immediately I thought of tasting it to see whether it was good. I bent down and drank it mentally. It was exceedingly good! Pleased and excited, I returned to my cell. After a short time I called in Nicholas Mitas — that was the name of the man with the drilling equipment — and I said to him:

'You'll have to go very deep down.'

'It'll be solid rock, Elder,' he replied. 'There won't be any water. I don't have that many pipes. I'm going to leave.'

'You won't leave,' I told him. 'Go and bring pipes. I won't let you leave.'

The next day he brought pipes and went down to the depth I had told him. There he found a spring with an abundant flow of good and satisfying water. He was pleased himself. And we were all overjoyed. It was a blessing of the Lord. A spring of holy water. We sang a service of *Paraklisis* at the church of the Transfiguration of the Saviour in thanksgiving to the Lord for the great miracle. It was a miracle of the Transfiguration of the Lord.

In the 'University of the Church'

When I first thought of creating a women's monastery, many ideas came into my mind. A very great many. Most importantly I wanted to gather around me a number of nuns who would love me in Christ and whom I would love in Christ. I wanted them all to be true nuns imbued with the spirit of monastic life, without jealousies, and without such things that women usually have. I wanted them to have love and good order among themselves. Also I wanted us to have a handicraft which would occupy us for two or three hours a day in the morning.

But the centre of gravity I wanted to place on the 'University of the Church'. By that I mean the hymns, canons, midnight offices, mid-hour offices, the Psalter, Paraklitiki, Menaion, Theotokarion, Triodion, Pentecostarion — all the service books of the Church. I wanted us, if possible, to read everything that is prescribed in the Book of Liturgical Order, the so-called Typicon. I thought of reading the sections from the Psalter before mid-day so that we wouldn't read them during the night and make the sisters tired. Devotion to and occupation with the hymns and readings is a great thing in my view — a very great thing, because in that way a person is sanctified without realizing it. He acquires love and humility and everything as he hears the words of the saints in the various liturgical books. We need to dwell on this. This needs to be our daily occupation and delight in the Church. And then again every day, at some point before meal-time or in the afternoon, we would read for an hour or an hour and a half from the great Fathers of the Church. In the evening we would read again all together. And also privately in our cells, but again at a specified time. There needs to be a time-table.

Many convents have the habit of striking the bell three times at a certain hour, and wherever each sister happens to be, she kneels down, and for ten minutes repeats the prayer, 'Lord, Jesus Christ...'. In practice this is difficult. But do you know how wonderful it is to be watering the garden and, as soon as you hear the bell, to kneel down? Or else for all the nuns to come out and kneel down in silence? For ten minutes we say with intensity the 'Lord, Jesus Christ...' all together, wherever we happen to be, as one person, united with Christ in prayer of the heart, and then we continue our work. The monastery needs to become a school. Do you know what it means to be a school?

We need to have a lively interest in what we are doing. It's no use being half asleep. Even if you're uneducated, or whatever, you'll come to the reading desk. And after one, two, three, four, five or ten times you'll wake up. You'll learn the 'Our Father' and the Creed. You'll have another sister who'll show you. In one, two or three years you will have learnt to read. I would like, of course, all the sisters to read well, that is, clearly and distinctly and from the heart.

I believe that the Lord would work many miracles through this our love

My dream for the monastery was for it to exist in a state of paradise; for services and confession to take place twenty-four hours a day; for there to be lots of priests and confessors so that they could alternate, just like doctors on duty in a hospital, so that people wounded by various afflictions, of body and of soul, and by the injuries of sin could come there at any time of day or night; for there to be a telephone which would be answered day and night by the sisters, so that they could offer comfort to all those brought to despair by the various traumas of life and lead them by their words to Christ, the great Comforter, so that in this way their souls might be saved and filled with the heavenly light which divine grace would give them.

And I myself would like to hear the confessions of the people who would come. When someone who was sick would come — and above all those who were sick through the work of the tempter — I would hear their confession and then the sisters would come and sing with devotion a service of supplication on their behalf. That is to say, I would get the sick person to kneel down and I, wearing my priest's stole, would sit in a chair and read prayers while at the same time the sisters would with one voice sing the service of supplication. I believe that the Lord would work many miracles through this our love. Many of the sick would become well through the grace of God. For example, a father would come in distress and say, 'My child suffers from giddy spells and falls to the ground.' We would keep the child in the monastery for some time. All the sisters, who are one spirit, one soul and one heart with their elder, would kneel down and the prayer of all would influence the situation. A gathering of nuns in prayer has great power, it works wonders, and that is what I desire and long for. That is what I want to do in the monastery.

And there is something else I would like in the monastery. I would like to build a fine, large church. Some day many people may come here to make confession, to receive Holy Communion, to pray and to exercise themselves in the prayer of the heart. My dream is for spiritual fathers, who have immersed themselves deeply and vigorously in mystical theology in the desert of the Holy Mountain, to come and teach prayer of the heart in the rooms under the church; for them to come, albeit for one day. Of course, there are many who don't want either to open themselves or reveal themselves. Even those, however, we could bring one day and have them leave the next. What relief would be given in this way to all those souls that are tortured by the passions and the other trials of life!

The monastery must receive souls with the fear of God and inspire, not with teaching and sermons, but with prayer, fear of God and example. This is an exceedingly delicate matter. For example, when someone comes to the monastery we should offer him hospitality, but it is not necessary to say many words. The hospitality should be given through the church. That is to say, we should take our guest to prayer: to the services of Vespers and Compline. We should read the services very clearly and distinctly. We should sing reverently and a sense of order and silence should predominate. We may say a few edifying words. We will offer also material things, something to eat and drink, for example, but what will preponderate will be silence and what will speak will be example. Our disposition will teach the person more than anything else. It's not necessary to deviate from this tactic. This, rather than words, will be of benefit. If we maintain a good order and are devoted to Christ, the whole monastery will be sanctified. This, of course, needs to be done simply and naturally and without anxiety and effort on the part of the sisters. This, I believe, is the best form of missionary activity.

Very soon birds will start to come to the monastery. They will hear the bell and they will come to eat. They will sit outside and listen to the Vespers. They are our companions from the forest who will come to participate in our prayer.

Christ is Risen!

Today a number of my spiritual children visited me in my cell* and we sang together three times the hymn, 'Christ is Risen'. The Easter greeting I gave them was: 'I pray that the Resurrection of our Lord Jesus Christ may raise up in our souls every noble and beautiful sentiment. And may it lead us all to holiness and to triumph over our 'old self', *together with*

* This took place at Easter 1989.

the passions and the desires. This is what the Lord asks. This is why we Gal. 5:24
pray that His Resurrection may help us, that it may give us grace to put to flight and mortify our *old self*, and become worthy of His Church. So we Rom. 6:6
pray for the Lord to help us. The greatest miracle worked by Christ is His Resurrection. Don't let us ever forget this. Many happy returns!'

One of them said that today all things are praying — the earth, the sky, the stars, the fragrant flowers, the bubbling streams, the trilling nightingales, the fluttering butterflies — all are singing 'Christ is Risen'. And he got so excited that he started shouting out in joy, 'Christ is Risen!'

I got enthused in the same way on the Holy Mountain. It was Easter. I climbed up on my own towards Mount Athos to a height of about eight hundred metres. I had the Old Testament with me and I looked at the clear, blue sky, at the sea which stretched out endlessly, at the trees, the birds, the butterflies and all the beauties of nature, and I shouted full of enthusiasm: 'Christ is Risen!' As I shouted like this I stretched out my arms passionately and they remained stuck firm. I had gone mad! I opened the Old Testament a little and my eyes fell on the words from the Wisdom of Solomon:

O God of my fathers and Lord of mercy, who made all things by your word, and by your wisdom formed man to have dominion over the creatures you have made, and to rule the world in holiness and righteousness, and to pronounce judgment in uprightness of soul, give me the wisdom that sits by your thrones, and do not reject me from among your servants. For I am your slave and the son of your maidservant, a man who is weak Wisd. 9:1–5
and short-lived, with little understanding of judgment and laws. [DC]

I became completely absorbed in these divine words. I stayed for hours without being aware of the passing of time. My elders wondered where I was…

Listen to how the wise Solomon continues:

…and with you is Wisdom, who knows your works and was present when you made the world, and who understands what is pleasing in your sight and what is right according to your commandments. Send her forth from the holy heavens, and from the throne of your glory dispatch her, that she may be with me and toil, so that I may learn what is pleasing to you. For she knows and understands all things, and she will guide me Wisd. 9:9–11
chastely in my actions and guard me with her glory. [DC]

Do you realize how important these words were for me?

She '*understands what is pleasing in your sight*', and '*what is pleasing to you*'. Seek these things, devote yourselves to these things, and fill yourselves with fervent desire for these things. Without realizing, you will fall in love with Christ.

KAVSOKALYVIA – 1991

I ask all of you to forgive me
for whatever I have done to upset you

My dear spiritual children,

Now while I am still of sound mind I wish to give you some advice.

From the time that I was a little boy I was always given to sins. And when my mother sent me up to watch the flocks on the hillside — my father had gone to America to work, because we were poor — while I was looking after the animals, I read syllable by syllable the life of Saint John the Hut-dweller and I fell in love with Saint John and as a young boy that I was — twelve or fifteen years old, I can't recall exactly — I prayed very intensely; and wanting to imitate Saint John, with great effort I secretly left my parents and came to Kavsokalyvia on the Holy Mountain and placed myself in obedience to two elders — they were brothers — Panteleimon and Ioannikios. It happened that they were very devout and virtuous and I loved them very much, and so, with their prayers, I was utterly obedient to them. This helped me immensely. I also felt a great love for God. My time on the Holy Mountain passed very well for me. But, by God's disposition, for my sins, I became very ill and my elders told me to go to my parents in my village, Aghios Ioannis in Evia.

And while from the time I was a little boy I had committed many sins, when I returned to the world, I continued to commit sins, which up to the present time have become very many. People, however, looked on me favourably and all proclaim that I am a saint. But I feel that I am the most sinful person in the world. Of course, I have confessed as many sins as I could remember, and I know that for those that I have confessed, God has granted me forgiveness. But now I have a sense that my spiritual sins are also very many, and I ask for all of you who have known me, to pray for me, because — when I was alive — very humbly I prayed for you. But now that I am going to leave for heaven, I have the sense that God is going to say to me: 'What do you want here?' I have only one thing to say to Him: 'I am not worthy, Lord, to be here, but do for me whatever your love wishes.' What will happen thereafter, I do not know. I desire, however, for God's love to do its work.

And I always pray for my spiritual children to love God, who is everything, so that He may grant us to enter into His earthly uncreated Church. Because we need to start from here.

I always attempted to pray and to read the hymns of the Church, Holy Scripture and the lives of our saints. And I pray that you will do the same.

I ask all of you to forgive me for whatever I have done to upset you.

Priest-monk Porphyrios

*In Kavsokalyvia on the 4th/17th June 1991**

* Saint Porphyrios, sensing that his life was approaching its end, went to the Holy Mountain in 1991 where, on the 2nd December, he fell asleep in the Lord in his hermitage of Saint George, Kavsokalyvia. This letter, which he left as a spiritual testament, was dictated to one of the monks there.

The dual dating refers, first, to the Old (Julian) Calendar date, and, second, to the New (Gregorian) Calendar date.

PART TWO

THE WISDOM OF SAINT PORPHYRIOS

Saint Porphyrios
at Kallisia

ON THE CHURCH

On entering into the uncreated Church we come to Christ; we enter into the realm of the uncreated

...the mystery of faith is great

The Church is without beginning, without end and eternal, just as the Triune God, her founder, is without beginning, without end and eternal. She is uncreated just as God is uncreated. She existed before the ages, before the angels, before the creation of the world — *before the foundation of the world* as the Apostle Paul says. She is a divine institution and in her *dwells the whole fullness of divinity.* She is an expression of the richly varied wisdom of God. She is the mystery of mysteries. She was concealed and was revealed *in the last of times*. The Church remains unshaken because she is rooted in the love and wise providence of God. Eph. 1:4 Col. 2:9 1 Pet. 1:20

The three persons of the Holy Trinity constitute the eternal Church. The angels and human beings existed in the thought and love of the Triune God from the beginning. We human beings were not born now, we existed before the ages in God's omniscience.

The love of God created us in His image and likeness. He embraced us within the Church in spite of the fact that He knew of our apostasy. He gave us everything to make us gods too through the free gift of grace. For all that, we made poor use of our freedom and lost our original beauty, our original righteousness and cut ourselves off from the Church. Outside the Church, far from the Holy Trinity, we lost Paradise, everything. But outside the Church there is no salvation, there is no life. And so the compassionate heart of God the Father did not leave us exiled from His love. He opened again for us the gates of Paradise in the last of times and appeared in flesh.

With the divine incarnation of the only-begotten Son of God, God's pre-eternal plan for the salvation of mankind was revealed again to men. In his epistle to Timothy the Apostle Paul says: *Incontrovertably, the mystery of faith is great. God was revealed in flesh, justified in Spirit, seen by angels, preached among the gentiles, believed in throughout the world, taken up in glory.* The words of the Apostle Paul are dense in meaning: divine, heavenly words! 1 Tim. 3:16

God in His infinite love united us again with His Church in the

person of Christ. On entering into the uncreated Church, we come to
Christ, we enter into the realm of the uncreated. We the faithful are
Cf. Col. 3:9, called to become uncreated by grace, to become participants in the di-
Rom. 6:6, vine energies of God, to enter into the mystery of divinity, to surpass
Eph. 4:22 our worldly frame of mind, to die to the 'old man' and to become im-
mersed in God. When we live in the Church we live in Christ. This is a
very fine-drawn matter, we cannot understand it. Only the Holy Spirit
can teach us it.

In the Church we are all one and Christ is the head

The head of the Church is Christ and we humans, we Christians, are the
Col. 1:18 body. The Apostle Paul says: *He is the head of the body, of the Church.*
The Church and Christ are one. The body cannot exist without its head.
The body of the Church is nourished, sanctified and lives with Christ. He
is the Lord, omnipotent, omniscient, everywhere present and filling all
things, our staff, our friend, our brother: the pillar and sure foundation
of the Church. He is the Alpha and the Omega, the beginning and the
end, the basis — everything. Without Christ the Church does not exist.
Christ is the Bridegroom; each individual soul is the Bride.

Christ united the body of the Church with heaven and with earth:
with angels, men and all created things, with all of God's creation —
with the animals and birds, with each tiny wild flower and each micro-
Eph. 1:23 scopic insect. The Church thus became *the fullness of Him who fills all in
all*, that is, of Christ. Everything is in Christ and with Christ. This is the
mystery of the Church.

Christ is revealed in that unity between His love and ourselves: the
Church. On my own I am not the Church, but together with you. All together we are the Church. All are incorporated in the Church. We are all
one and Christ is the head. One body, one body of Christ: *You are the*
1 Cor. 12:27 *body of Christ and individually members of it.* We are all one because
God is our Father and is everywhere. When we experience this we are in
John the Church. This is our Lord's wish for all the members of the Church as
17:11, 22 expressed in His great high-priestly prayer: *that they may be one.* But
that's something you can only understand through grace. We experience the joy of unity, of love, and we become one with everyone. There
is nothing more magnificent!

The important thing is for us to enter into the Church — to unite ourselves with our fellow men, with the joys and sorrows of each and everyone, to feel that they are our own, to pray for everyone, to have care for their salvation, to forget about ourselves, to do everything for them just as Christ did for us. In the Church we become one with each unfortunate, suffering and sinful soul.

No one should wish to be saved alone without all others being saved. It is a mistake for someone to pray for himself, that he himself may be saved. We must love others and pray that no soul be lost, that all may enter into the Church. That is what counts. And it is with this desire one should leave the world to retire to a monastery or to the desert.

When we set ourselves apart from others, we are not Christians. We are true Christians when we have a profound sense that we are members of the mystical body of Christ, of the Church, in an unbroken relationship of love — when we live united in Christ, that is, when we experience unity in His Church with a sense of oneness. This is why Christ prays to His Father saying, *that they may be one*. He repeats the prayer again and again and the apostles emphasize it everywhere. This is the most profound aspect, the most exalted meaning, of the Church. This is where the secret is to be found: for all to be united as one person in God. There is no other religion like this; no other religion says anything of this sort. They have something to say, but not this mystery, this exquisite point of the mystery which Christ demands and tells us that this is how we must become, that he wants us to be His.

We are one even with those who are not close to the Church. They are distant on account of ignorance. We must pray that God will enlighten them and change them so that they too may come to Christ. We see things in a human light, we move on a different plane and imagine that we love Christ.
But Christ, who *sends rain on the righteous and on the unrighteous*, tells us: Matt. 5:45
Love your enemies. We need to pray that we may all be united, united in Matt. 5:44
God. Then, if we live out this prayer, we will achieve corresponding results; we will all be united in love.

For the people of God there is no such thing as distance, even if they be thousands of miles apart. However far away our fellow human beings may be, we must stand by them. Some people regularly telephone me from a town on the edge of the Indian Ocean — Durban is what it's called, if I am pronouncing it correctly. It's in South Africa, two hours drive from Johannesberg. Indeed, a few days ago they came here. They were taking a sick person to England and they came here first to ask me to read a prayer. I was very moved.

When Christ unites us, distances don't exist. When I leave this life it will be better. I'll be closer to you.

In the Church we progress towards immortality

The Church is the new life in Christ. In the Church there is no death and no hell. Saint John the Evangelist says: *Whoever keeps my word will*
John 8:52 *never taste death.* Christ does away with death. Whoever enters into the Church is saved; he becomes eternal. Life is one, an unbroken continuity: there is no end, no death. Whoever follows Christ's commandments never dies. He dies according to the flesh, according to the passions, and, starting from this present life, is accorded to live in Paradise, in our Church, and thereafter in eternity. With Christ, death becomes the bridge which we will cross in an instant in order to continue to live in the unsetting light.

From the moment I became a monk I believed that death does not exist. That's how I felt and how I always feel — that I am eternal and immortal. How magnificent!

In the Church which possesses the saving sacraments there is no despair. We may be deeply sinful. But we make confession, the priest reads the prayer, we are forgiven and we progress towards immortality, without any anxiety and without any fear.

When we love Christ, we live the life of Christ. If, by the grace of God, we succeed in doing this, we find ourselves in a different state, we live in another, enviable state. For us there is no fear: neither of death, nor of the devil nor of hell. All these things exist for people who are far from Christ, for non-Christians. For us Christians who do His will, as the Gospel says, these things do not exist. That is, they exist, but when one kills the old self
Gal. 5:24 *along with the passions and the desires*, one gives no importance to the devil or to evil. It doesn't concern us. What concerns us is love, service to Christ and to our fellow man. If we reach the point of feeling joy, love, worship of God without any fear, we reach the point of saying, *It is no*
Gal. 2:20 *longer I who live; Christ lives in me.* No one can prevent us from entering into this mystery.

The Church is Paradise on earth

With the worship of God you live in Paradise. If you know and love Christ, you live in Paradise. Christ is Paradise. Paradise begins here. The Church is Paradise on earth, exactly the same as Paradise in heaven. The same Paradise as is in heaven is here on earth. There all souls are one, just as the Holy Trinity is three persons, but they are united and constitute one.

Our chief concern is to devote ourselves to Christ, to unite ourselves to the Church. If we enter into the love of God, we enter into the Church. If we don't enter into the Church, if we do not become one with the earthly Church here and now, we are in danger of losing the heavenly Church too. And when we say 'heavenly' don't imagine that in the other life we will find gardens with flowers, mountains, streams and birds. The earthly beauties do not exist there; there is something else, something very exalted. But in order for us to go on to this something else we must pass through these earthly images and beauties.

Whoever experiences Christ becomes one with Him, with His Church. He experiences a mad delight. This life is different from the life of other people. It is joy, it is light, it is exultation, it is exaltation. This is the life of the Church, the life of the Gospel, the Kingdom of God. 'The Kingdom of God is within us.' Christ comes within us and we are within Him. This occurs just in the way a piece of iron placed in the fire becomes fire and light; once it is removed from the fire it becomes iron again, black and dark. Cf. Luke 17:21

In the Church a divine intercourse occurs, we become infused with God. When we are with Christ we are in the light; and when we live in the light there is no darkness. The light, however, is not constant; it depends on us. It is just like the iron which becomes dark when removed from the fire. Darkness and light are incompatible. We can never have darkness and light at the same time. Either light or darkness. When you switch on the light, darkness vanishes.

Let us love the Church fervently

In order for us to preserve our unity we must be obedient to the Church, to her bishops. When we are obedient to the Church we are obedient to Christ Himself. Christ wishes for us to become one flock with one shepherd. Cf. John 10:16

Let us feel for the Church. Let us love her fervently. We should not accept to hear her representatives being criticised and accused. On the Holy Mountain the spirit in which I was nurtured was orthodox, profound, holy and silent — without conflicts, without disputes and without censurings. We should not give credence to those who make accusations against the clergy. Even if with our own eyes we see a priest doing something we judge negatively, we should not believe it, nor think about it, nor talk about it to others. The same is true for the lay members of the Church and for every person. We are all the Church. Those who censure the Church for the errors of her representatives with the alleged aim of

helping to correct her make a great mistake. They do not love the Church. Neither, needless to say, do they love Christ. We love the Church when we embrace with our prayer each of her members and do what Christ did — when we sacrifice ourselves, remain ever vigilant, and do everything in the manner of Him who *when He was abused did not return*
1 Pet. 2:23 *abuse, and when He suffered did not threaten.*

We need to take care also to observe the formal aspects: to participate in the sacraments, especially the sacrament of Holy Communion. It is in these things that Orthodoxy is to be found. Christ offers Himself to the Church in the sacraments and above all in Holy Communion. Let me tell you in all humility about a divine visitation I experienced myself so that you see the grace of the sacraments.

Some time ago a tiny pimple appeared on my back which started to cause me a lot of pain. It was very small, the size of a pin head, yet the pain spread across a large area on the left hand side of my back. It was excruciating. Now we had done a service of Anointing for the Sick in my room in Milesi. And so as I was suffering greatly, they took the Holy Oil and made the sign of the cross with it over the spot and the pain vanished immediately. I was so grateful for this visitation of God that I would say to whoever came to see me:

'Take some of that Holy Oil there, and use it for whatever pain you have.'

Excuse me for telling you this, but it's to the glory of God.

'...all were filled with the Holy Spirit'

At Pentecost the grace of God was poured out not only on the apostles, but on all the people who were around them. It affected believers and unbelievers. Listen what the Acts of the Apostles says: *And when the day of Pentecost had come, they were all together in one place. And suddenly from heaven there came a sound like the rush of a violent wind...and all were filled with the Holy Spirit and began to speak in different tongues, according as the Spirit gave them utterance...the crowd gathered and were confused because each one heard them speaking in*
Acts 2:1–6 *the native language of each.*

Whereas Peter the apostle was speaking his own tongue, the language was instantaneously transformed in the mind of the hearers. In an ineffable way the Holy Spirit made them understand his words in their language, mystically, imperceptibly. These miraculous things happen through the action of the Holy Spirit. For example, the word ‘house’ would be heard by the person who spoke French as ‘*maison*’. It was a kind of gift of clear sight; they heard their own language. The sound struck their ears, but in their minds, through divine illumination, the words were heard in their own tongue. The Church Fathers don’t reveal this interpretation of Pentecost very clearly, they are afraid of distorting the mystery. The same is true of the Revelation of Saint John. The uninitiated are unable to comprehend the meaning of the mystery of God.

A little further on we read, *and fear came upon every soul.* This ‘fear’ Acts 2:43
was not exactly fear. It was something else, something alien, something incomprehensible, something...something we cannot say what. It was awe, it was a sense of being filled, it was grace. It was being filled with divine grace. At Pentecost the people suddenly found themselves in such a state of assimilation to God that they were overcome with confusion. So when the divine grace overshadowed them it made them all mad — in a good sense — it enthused them, filled them with God. This has made a great impression on me. It was what I sometimes call a ‘state’. It was enthusiasm. A state of spiritual madness.

And breaking bread in their various homes, they shared food in great joy and simplicity of heart, praising God and having goodwill towards all the people. And every day the Lord added to the Church those who were being saved. Acts 2:46–7

The ‘breaking of bread’ was Holy Communion. And the number of those who were being saved increased continually, since people saw all the Christians in a state of ‘*great joy and simplicity of heart*’ and ‘*praising God*’. The ‘*great joy and simplicity of heart*’ is like the ‘*fear came upon every soul*’. It is an enthusiasm and again a madness. When I experience this, I feel it and weep. I go to the event, I experience it, I feel it and am filled with enthusiasm and weep. This is divine grace. This is also love towards Christ.

What the apostles experienced amongst themselves when they felt this great joy happened then to all those who were beneath the upper room. That is, they loved each other, they took joy in one another: the one had become united with the other. This experience radiates outwards and others experience it.

And the heart and soul of the multitude of those who had believed were one; and not one of them said that any of his possessions were his own, but they had everything in common. The Acts of the Apostles speak of a Acts 4:32
coenobitic life. Here is the mystery of Christ. This is the Church. The best words about the first Church are here.

The Christian religion transforms people and heals them

Our religion is the religion of religions. It is from revelation, the authentic and true religion. The other religions are human, hollow. They do not know the greatness of the Triune God. They do not know that our aim, our destiny, is to become gods according to grace, to attain likeness with the Triune God, to become one with Him and among ourselves.
John These are things the other religions do not know. The ultimate aim of
17 : 11, 22 our religion is *that they may be one*. Here the work of Christ finds completion. Our religion is love, it is *eros*, it is enthusiasm, it is madness, it is longing for the divine. All these things are within us. Our soul demands that we attain them.

For many people, however, religion is a struggle, a source of agony and anxiety. That's why many of the 'religiously minded' are regarded as unfortunates, because others can see the desperate state they are in. And so it is. Because for the person who doesn't understand the deeper meaning of religion and doesn't experience it, religion ends up as an illness, and indeed a terrible illness. So terrible that the person loses control of his actions and becomes weak-willed and spineless, he is filled with agony and anxiety and is driven to and fro by the evil spirit. He makes prostrations, he weeps, he exclaims, he believes he is humbling himself, and all this humility is a work of Satan. Some such people experience religion as a kind of hell. They make prostrations and cross themselves in church and they say, 'we are unworthy sinners', then as soon as they come out they start to blaspheme everything holy whenever someone upsets them a little. It is very clear that there is something demonic in this.

In fact, the Christian religion transforms people and heals them. The most important precondition, however, for someone to recognize and discern the truth is humility. Egotism darkens a person's mind, it confuses him, it leads him astray, to heresy. It is important for a person to understand the truth.

Long ago when people were in a primitive state they didn't have houses or anything. They would go into caves without windows. They would block up the entrance with stones and branches so that the wind didn't blow in. They didn't realize that outside there is life, oxygen. When he is enclosed in a cave, a person is worn down, he becomes ill, he is destroyed, whereas when he is outside he is revitalized. Can you understand the truth? Then you are out in the sun, in the light; you see all the magnificence of creation; otherwise you are in a dark cave. Light and darkness.

Which is better? To be meek, humble, peaceful and to be filled with love, or to be irritable, depressed and to quarrel with everyone. Unquestionably the higher state is love. Our religion has all these good things and is the truth. But many people go off in another direction.

All those who deny this truth are psychologically ill. They are like those children who became delinquent or anti-social because they lost their parents, or because their parents divorced or quarrelled. And all those confused people find their way into various heresies. The confused children of confused parents. But all these confused and anti-social persons have a strength and perseverance and achieve a great many things. They succeed in bringing normal and peaceable people into subjection. They influence other like-minded people and they prevail in the world because they are in the majority and find themselves followers. Then there are others who, although they do not deny the truth, are nevertheless confused and psychologically ill.

Sin makes a person exceedingly psychologically confused. And nothing makes the confusion go away — nothing except the light of Christ. Christ makes the first move: *Come unto me all you who labour...* Then we Matt. 11:28
accept this light with our good will, which we express through our love towards Him, through prayer, through our participation in the life of the Church, and through the sacraments.

Often neither labour, nor prostrations, nor crossing ourselves attract God's grace. There are secrets. The most important thing is to go beyond the formal aspects and go to the heart of the matter. Whatever is done must be done with love.

Love always understands the need to make sacrifices. Whatever is done under coercion always causes the soul to react with rejection. Love attracts the grace of God. When grace comes, then the gifts of the Holy Spirit come. *The fruit of the Spirit is love, joy, peace, long-sufferance, gentleness, goodness, faith, meekness, self-control.* These are the things which Gal. 5:22–3
a healthy soul in Christ should have.

With Christ a person is filled with grace and so lives above evil. Evil does not exist for him. There is only good, which is God. Evil cannot exist. While there is light there cannot be darkness. Nor can darkness encompass him because he has the light.

ON DIVINE *EROS*

He who loves little, gives little. He who loves more, gives more.
And he who loves beyond measure, what has he to give?
He gives himself!

Christ is our love, our desire

Christ is joy, the true light, happiness. Christ is our hope. Our relation to Christ is love, *eros*, passion, enthusiasm, longing for the divine. Christ is everything. He is our love. He is the object of our desire. This passionate longing for Christ is a love that cannot be taken away. This is where joy flows from.

Christ himself is joy. He is a joy that transforms you into a different person. It is a spiritual madness, but in Christ. This spiritual wine ine-
Ps. 22:5 briates you like pure unadulterated wine. As David says, *You have*
[23:5] *anointed my head with oil and your cup intoxicates me most mightily.*
Spiritual wine is unmixed, unadulterated, exceedingly strong, and when
you drink it, it makes you drunk. This divine intoxication is a gift of God
Matt. 5:8 that is given to the *pure in heart.*

Fast as much as you can, make as many prostrations as you can, attend as many vigils as you like, but be joyful. Have Christ's joy. It is the joy that lasts forever, that brings eternal happiness. It is the joy of our Lord that gives assured serenity, serene delight and full happiness. All-
John 16:24 joyful joy that surpasses every joy. Christ desires and delights in scattering
& 1 John 1:4 joy, in enriching his faithful with joy. I pray that *your joy may be full.*

This is what our religion is. This is the direction we must take. Christ is Paradise, my children. What is Paradise? It is Christ. Paradise begins here and now. It is exactly the same: those who experience Christ here on earth, experience Paradise. That's the way it is, just as I tell you. This is right, it's true, believe me! Our task is to attempt to find a way to enter into the light of Christ. The point is not to observe all the outward forms. The essence of the matter is for us to be with Christ; for our soul to wake up and love Christ and become holy. To abandon herself to divine *eros.* Thus He too will love us. Then the joy will be inalienable. That is what Christ wants most of all, to fill us with joy, because He is the well-spring of joy. This joy is a gift of Christ. In this joy we will come to know Christ. We cannot come to know Him unless He first comes to know us. How does David put it? *Unless the Lord builds the house, they labour in vain that build it; unless the Lord guards the city, the watchman stays awake in vain.* Ps. 126:1 [127:1]

These are the things our soul desires to acquire. If we prepare ourselves appropriately, grace will bestow them on us. It's not difficult. If we acquire grace, everything is easy, joyful and a blessing from God. Divine grace is constantly knocking at the door of our soul and waiting for us to open so that it can enter our thirsty heart and fill it. The fullness is Christ, our Holy Lady, the Holy Trinity. What marvellous things!

If you are in love, you can live amid the hustle and bustle of the city centre and not be aware that you are in the city centre. You see neither cars nor people nor anything else. Within yourself you are with the person you love. You experience her, you take delight in her, she inspires you. Are these things not true? Imagine that the person you love is Christ. Christ is in your mind, Christ is in your heart, Christ is in your whole being, Christ is everywhere.

Christ is life, the source of life, the source of joy, the source of the true light, everything. Whoever loves Christ and other people truly lives life. Life without Christ is death; it is hell, not life. That is what hell is — the absence of love. Life is Christ. Love is the life of Christ. Either you will be in life or in death. It's up to you to decide.

One thing is our aim — love for Christ, for the Church, for our neighbour. Love, worship of, and craving for God, the union with Christ and with the Church is Paradise on earth. Love towards Christ and towards one's neighbour, towards everyone, including enemies. The Christian feels for everyone, he wants all to be saved, all to taste the Kingdom of God. That is Christianity: through love for our brother to arrive at love for God. To the extent that we desire it, to the extent that we wish it, to the extent that we are worthy, divine grace comes through our brother. When we love our brother we love the Church and therefore Christ. And we too are within the Church. Therefore when we love the Church we love ourselves.

There is one thing, O Christ, that I want, one thing I desire, one thing I ask for, and that is to be with You

Let us love Christ and let our only hope and care be for Him. Let us love Christ for His own sake only. Never for our sake. Let Him put us wherever He likes. Let Him give us whatever He wishes. Don't let's love Him for His gifts. It's egotistical for us to say: 'Christ will place me in a fine

mansion which He has prepared, just as the Gospel says: *In my Father's*
John 14:2–3 *house there are many mansions...so that where I am you may be also.* What we should say rather is: 'My Christ, whatever Your love dictates; it is sufficient for me to live within Your love.'

As for myself, poor soul...what can I say...I'm very weak. I haven't managed to love Christ so very fervently and for my soul to long for Him. I feel that I have a very long way to go. I haven't arrived at where I want to be; I don't experience this love. But I'm not discouraged. I trust in the love of God. I say to Christ: 'I know I'm not worthy. Send me wherever Your love wishes. That's what I desire, that's what I want. During my life I always worshipped You.'

When I was seriously ill and on the point of leaving this life, I didn't want to think about my sins. I wanted to think about the love of my Lord, my Christ, and about eternal life. I didn't want to feel fear. I wanted to go to the Lord and to think about His goodness, His love. And now that my life is nearing its end, I don't feel anxiety or apprehension, but I think that when I appear at the Second Coming and Christ says to me: *Friend,*
Matt. 22:12 *how did you get in here without a wedding garment?* I will bow my head and I will say to Him: 'Whatever you want, my Lord, whatever your love desires. I know I am not worthy. Send me wherever your love wishes. I am fit for hell. And place me in hell, as long as I am with You. There is one thing I want, one thing I desire, one thing I ask for, and that is to be with You, wherever and however You wish.'

I try to give myself over entirely to the love and worship of God. I have consciousness of my sinfulness, but I live with hope. It is bad to despair, because someone who despairs becomes embittered and loses his willingness and strength. Someone who has hope, on the contrary, advances forward. Because he feels that he is poor, he tries to enrich himself. What does a poor man do? If he is smart, he tries to find a way to become rich.

And so in spite of the fact that I feel weak and that I haven't achieved what I desire, I nevertheless do not fall into despair. It is a consolation to me, as I've told you, that I don't cease to try continually. Yet I don't do what I want to. Pray for me. The point is that I cannot love Christ absolutely without His grace. Christ does not allow His love to show itself if my soul does not have something which will attract Him.

And perhaps I lack that something. And so I entreat God and say, 'I'm very weak, O Christ. Only You with Your grace will be able to allow me to say along with Saint Paul the Apostle, *It is no longer I who live;*
Gal. 2:20 *Christ lives in me.*

That is what preoccupies me. I try to find ways to love Christ. This love is never sated. However much you love Christ, you always think that you don't love Him and you long all the more to love him. And without being aware of it, you go higher and higher!

When Christ enters your heart, your life changes

When you find Christ, you are satisfied, you desire nothing else, you find peace. You become a different person. You live everywhere, wherever Christ is. You live in the stars, in infinity, in heaven with the angels, with the saints, on earth with people, with plants, with animals, with everyone and everything. When there is love for Christ, loneliness disappears. You are peaceable, joyous, full. Neither melancholy, nor illness, nor pressure, nor anxiety, nor depression, nor hell.

Christ is in all your thoughts, in all your actions. You have grace and you can endure everything for Christ. You can even suffer unjustly. You can endure injustices for Christ, and indeed with joy. Just as He suffered, so you too can suffer unjustly. Did you choose Christ in order to avoid suffering? What does Saint Paul say? *I rejoice in my sufferings*. This is our Col. 1:24
religion: for our soul to awake and love Christ and become holy, to give herself over to divine *eros*. And so He, too, will love her.

When Christ enters your heart, your life changes. Christ is everything. Whoever experiences Christ within himself, experiences ineffable things — holy and sacred things. He lives in exultation. These things are true. People have experienced them — hermits on the Holy Mountain. Continually and with longing they whisper the prayer: 'Lord Jesus Christ...'.

When Christ enters your heart, your passions disappear. You are unable to swear, or hate, or seek revenge or anything. How could there be hatreds, dislikes, censures, egotisms, anxieties, depressions? What holds sway is Christ — and longing for the unsetting light. This longing makes you feel that death is a bridge that you will cross in an instant in order to continue the life of Christ. Here on earth you have an impediment and so you need faith. This impediment is the body. After death, however, faith is abolished and you see Christ as you see the sun. In eternity, of course, you will experience everything more intensely.

When you don't live with Christ, however, you live immersed in melancholy, affliction, anxiety and vexation. You don't live aright. Then many irregularities appear in your body, the endocrine glands, the liver, the bile, the pancreas, the stomach. They tell you: 'In order to be healthy, have a full breakfast of milk, egg, butter and toast.' But if you live properly, if you love Christ, you are fine with an orange and an apple. The great medicine is for you to devote yourself to the worship of Christ. Everything is healed. Everything functions normally. The love of God transforms everything; it sanctifies, amends and changes the nature of everything.

Our soul will be greatly comforted when we yearn for the Lord. We will not then concern ourselves with everyday and lowly things, but with spiritual and higher things. We will live in the spiritual world. When you live in the spiritual world, you live in the world in which your soul delights and for which it longs. This does not mean that you are indifferent towards others. You wish for everyone to find salvation, light and sanctification and for everyone to enter into the Church.

Love for Christ is insatiable

Christ is the summit of desire; there is nothing higher. All sensible things lead to satiety, but with God there is no satiation. He is everything. God is the summit of desire. No other joy, no other beauty, nothing else can rival Him. What is higher than the highest?

Love for Christ is something else. It is without end, without satiety. It gives life; it gives strength; it gives health; it gives, gives and gives. And the more it gives, the more the person wishes to fall in love. Human love and passion, by contrast, may be destructive and even drive a person mad. When we love Christ, all other loves abate. Other loves have a point of satiety. The love of Christ has no point of satiety. Fleshly love has a point of satiety. Thereafter jealousy and disgruntlement may set in, and may even lead to murder. Love in Christ knows no alteration. Worldly love remains for a time, and is gradually extinguished, whereas divine love continually grows and deepens. Every other kind of love can lead a person to despair. Divine *eros*, however, raises us up into the sphere of God; it bestows on us serenity, joy and fullness. Other pleasures enervate us, but of this pleasure we can never have enough. It is an insatiable pleasure, which you never tire of. It is the highest good.

At one point only does satiety cease: when a person is united with Christ. He loves, loves and loves, and the more he loves the more he sees that he wants to love even more intensely. He sees that he has not achieved union, that he hasn't abandoned himself to the love of God. Constantly he has the inclination and joyous longing to reach Christ, the summit of desire. He fasts, makes prostrations and prays ever more intensely, and yet he is never satisfied. He fails to realize that he is already in possession of this love. He does not feel that what he desires has filled him, that he has received it, that he experiences it, that he lives it. All ascetics yearn for this divine *eros*, this divine love. They are intoxicated with divine inebriation. With this divine intoxication the body may grow old and pass away, but the spirit becomes youthful and blossoms.

The hymns of our Church are filled with divine *eros*. Listen to the Canon of the Holy Apostle Timothy:

> *Burning for the highest of desires*
> *And therewith through love co-mingled,*
> *You led a life concordant with this craving,*
> *O man possessed by God,*
> *Your eyes transfixed forever on your love,*
> *And with His aspect sated.**

How marvellous are the words of this hymn! 'Co-mingled' (συγκραθείς) means at one, united with your lover, and 'sated' (πιμπλάμενος) means filled full, glutted. You should make a collection of such words denoting divine love and divine madness. You cannot have enough of them. Yes, love towards Christ is never enough. The more you love Him, the more you believe that you don't love Him and the more you desire to love Him. At the same time, however, your soul is flooded by His presence and your joy in the Lord is inalienable. You don't want then to desire anything. Abba Isaac the Syrian writes similarly:

'The joy that is in God is stronger than this present life. And he who finds this joy, not only will he not pay attention to the passions, but he will not even give a thought to his own life, nor will he have awareness of anything else, if his experience of this joy is true. Love is sweeter than life. And the concord with God from which love is born is sweeter than honey and the honeycomb. It does not seem grievous to Love to undergo a bitter death for the sake of her beloved… And to the heart which has received this joy every sweetness of this world seems superfluous. For there is nothing which can be likened to the sweetness of the knowledge of God.'†

And in the *Soliloquies* of Saint Augustine we read:

'I love You, Lord my God, and I desire to love You ever more intensely. For You are truly sweeter than any honey, more wholesome than any milk and brighter than any light; for me You are infinitely

* Sung at his feast on 22nd January (3rd *troparion* of the 4th Ode).

† Isaac the Syrian, *Ἀσκητικά*, Homily 38. Cf. *The Ascetical Homilies of St Isaac the Syrian*, Holy Transfiguration Monastery, 1984, p. 297.

more precious than gold or silver or precious stones... O love that is ever boiling over and never cooled! Consume me with your heat! I shall love You, Lord, because You first loved me. And where shall I find words sufficient to describe all the signs of Your greatest love for me?... You flooded me with the light of Your countenance and set Your glory as a sign above the door of my heart...'*

With divine love everything becomes Christ, everything becomes Paradise

The poetic canon in honour of Saint Pachomios written by Theophanes speaks very beautifully about divine love:†

> *By passionate love of impassion possessed,*
> *the material roots of the passions*
> *you caused to waste away,*
> *and winged on love you attained,*
> *most blessed father Pachomios,*
> *all the welling splendour of the godhead.*
>
> *In the love of God you conversed with the Spirit's teachings,*
> *and illumined by these, you attained the height of virtue,*
> *having rid your soul of the passions.*
>
> *Punctured by longing for the Master,*
> *through self-restraint you extinguished*
> *the susceptibility of the flesh to the passions,*
> *and the whole of your life, O Pachomios,*
> *you offered as a sacrifice most fragrant.*

Ah, that's a real treasure. These words are very precious. Theophanes is a great poet. The 'height of virtue' is the love of God which is perfect and absolute. 'Punctured': when our soul is 'punctured', when she is wounded by divine longing, the susceptibility of the flesh to the passions withers away. Divine craving defeats every pain, and so every pain is transformed and becomes love of Christ. Love Christ and He will love you. All pains will pass away, they will be defeated and transformed. Then everything becomes Christ, Paradise. But in order to live in Paradise, we must first die — die to everything and be as if dead. Then we

* (Pseudo-)Augustine, *Soliloquia*, Chapter 19 (*Patrologia Latina* 40. 880–81).
† Sung on his feast on 15th May (*troparia* from the 1st, 5th and 4th Odes). Theophanes the Branded, Hymnographer and Confessor (775–845).

will live truly; we will live in Paradise. If we do not first die to our old self nothing happens.

I'm very fond of the poem by Veritis called 'In company with Christ':

I longed to live in company with Christ,
His warming love enclosed within my breast,
To open up the strictures of my heart,
*That loving more, it never love enough.**

That the heart may never love enough! The more wine you drink, the more you want to drink. The more you give yourself to the love of Christ, the more you want to give yourself. We must love Him with all our soul, heart, strength, power and mind. We must plug our heart into His love and be united with Him. That is what the Lord demands, not for Himself out of selfishness, but for us, so that He can give us everything — joy and happiness.

The poet achieved this. He loved Christ and was loved by Him. He had discovered the secret of divine love. It's not difficult. On the contrary, it's very easy to discover it. It depends on our preparation and the way we approach Him. It requires an Orthodox spirit.

This love, this passion and this enthusiasm lead even to martyrdom. They make you sacrifice yourself and disregard all else. You fear nothing and may retreat far from the world into caves and holes in the earth. The saint who inspired me, Saint John the Hut-dweller, had this divine madness. And the saints and martyrs who were filled with this divine madness didn't hold back before any impediment, they rushed with joy and enthusiasm to martyrdom. He who loves little, gives little. He who loves more, gives more. And he who loves beyond measure, what has he to give? He gives himself!

On account of their love for Christ the saints did not feel the pains of martyrdom, however intense they were. Recall the Three Youths in the fiery furnace. As they sang hymns and praises to God, they were cooled in the midst of the furnace. Remember Saint Demetrios, Saint George, Saint Catherine, Saint Barbara, Saint Paraskevi, and the Forty Martyrs in the frozen lake. *A cloud of witnesses* as Saint Paul the Apostle says.

Cf. Dan. 3:50 [Song of the Three Youths v. 27 DC]

Heb. 12:1

All these saints and martyrs, just as they did on earth, so now, and much more, sing hymns and praises to the Lord in heaven. They are in Paradise and behold the countenance of God *face to face*. And that is everything. How do the Prayers of Thanksgiving after Holy Communion

1 Cor. 13:12

* G. Veritis, *Ἡ Ὠδὴ τοῦ Ἀγαπητοῦ* (*The Ode of the Loved One*), Athens, 1947, p. 11.

put it? Don't they mention at one point, 'those who behold the ineffable beauty of Your countenance'? Paradise is for one to see forever the face of God. It is an experience higher than the sight of flowers and exotic birds, of clear gurgling water and roses and of all the beauties that exist on earth, and higher than all lesser loves.

When you love Christ, in spite of all your weaknesses and your consciousness of them, you have the certainty that you have overcome death, because you are in communion with the love of Christ. These are the things I struggle for — may God have mercy on me! These are the things I devote myself to day and night. That's what happens when you love Christ — you want to suffer for Christ.

Let us pray that God will grant us to see the face of the Lord, even here while we are on earth.

Christ is our friend

We should regard Christ as our friend. He is our friend. He asserts this
John 15:14 Himself when he says, *you are my friends...* Let us stretch out to Him
and approach Him as a friend. Do we fall? Do we sin? With familiarity, love and trust let us run to Him — not with fear that He will punish us, but with the confidence which we derive from the sense of being with a friend. We can say to Him, 'I have fallen, forgive me.' At the same time, however, let us have the sense that He loves us and that He receives us with tenderness and love and forgives us. Don't let sin separate us from Christ. When we believe that He loves us and we love Him, we don't feel strangers and distanced from Him, even when we sin. We have secured His love, and however we behave, we know that He loves us.

If we love Christ truly, there is no fear that we will lose our respect for Him. Here those words of Saint Paul the Apostle hold good: *Who shall separate us from the love of Christ? Tribulation or distress...for I am per-*
Rom. 8:35, *suaded that neither death nor life...nor height nor depth...shall be able to*
38–9 *separate us from the love of God, which is in Christ Jesus our Lord.* The
relation of the soul to God is a higher, unique relationship which nothing can sever and which nothing can threaten or shake.

Cf. Matt. Certainly the Gospel tells us in a symbolic language that the unjust
8:12 & man will find himself in a place where there is 'grinding and gnashing of
13:42 teeth' — because that is what it is like far from God. And among the Fa-
thers of the Church, who teach vigilance and prayer, there are many who speak about the fear of death and hell. They say, 'Have constant remembrance of death.' If we explore these words deeply, they create in us the

fear of hell. In our attempt to avoid sin, we invoke these thoughts so that our soul will be filled with fear of death, hell and the devil.

Everything has its meaning, its time and its place. The concept of fear is good in the initial stages. It is for beginners, those in whom our ancestral fallen nature lives on. The beginner, whose sensibility has not yet been refined, is held back from evil by fear. And fear is essential since we are men of flesh and blood and earth-bound. But that is a stage, a low level of relationship to the divine. We think in terms of a business deal in order to win Paradise or escape hell. But if we examine the matter more closely we see that it is governed by self-interest. That's not something that appeals to me. When someone progresses and enters into the love of God, what need does he have of fear? Whatever he does, he does out of love, and that is of infinitely greater value. For someone to become good out of fear of God and not out of love is not of such value.

As we progress, the Gospel leads us to understand that Christ is joy and truth, that Christ is Paradise. Saint John the Evangelist says, *There is no fear in love, but perfect love casts out fear, because fear involves torment. The person who fears is not perfected in love.* As we exert ourselves 1 John 4:18
out of fear, we gradually enter into the love of God. Then the torment of hell, fear and death all disappear. We are interested only in the love of God. We do everything for this love, as the bridegroom does for the bride.

If we wish to follow Him, then this life, too, with Christ, is joy, even amid difficulties. As Saint Paul says, *I rejoice in my sufferings.* This is our Col. 1:24
religion, and that's the direction we must move in. It is not the outward formalities that count; it is living with Christ that matters. When you achieve this, what else do you want? You have gained everything. You live in Christ and Christ lives in you. Thereafter everything is easy: obedience, humility and peace.

Christ is the Bridegroom of the soul

The Song of Songs by Solomon the Wise grew out of this adoration for Christ. This book cultivates divine craving, divine love, adoration and vigilance in relation to the heavenly Bridegroom. What wonderful words — erotic, full of love and passion, divine *eros*! They appear like human words, but they are divine. 'For I have been wounded by your love'* says

* These words appear in a hymn which is frequently sung at the commemoration of women martyrs, e.g. Saint Euphemia (16th September and 11th July), Saint Kyriaki (7th July) and Saint Marina (17th July). The words of the hymn are as follows: (*see overleaf*)

one of the hymns. That is, 'I suffer, I am pained, my soul desires You, she longs for You who are my light, my life, my God, my Lord and my God.'

More than anywhere else, in the Song of Songs we see Christ as the Bridegroom. Christ is the Bridegroom of our soul. Our soul is His bride, and follows Him in everything — even to martyrdom, to Golgotha and the Crucifixion, but also to the Resurrection. When we attain to this love, Christ will stoop over us and pervade our soul.

Fix your gaze unwaveringly upwards towards Christ. Become familiar with Christ. Work with Christ. Live with Christ. Breathe with Christ. Suffer with Christ. Rejoice with Christ. Let Christ be everything for you. Let your soul long for and cry out to her Bridegroom, 'I crave for You, O my Bridegroom…'* Christ is the Bridegroom, He is the Father, He is everything. There is nothing higher in life than love for Christ. Whatever we desire we find in Christ. Christ is everything: all joy, all gladness, all Paradise. When we have Christ within us, we possess all magnificence. The soul that is in love with Christ is always joyful and happy, however much pain and sacrifice this may cost.

No one can deny that Christ is the fullness of life. Those who deny this truth are soul-sick and possessed by an evil spirit. They deny that which they are lacking. And so the devil finds their soul empty and enters in. And just as a child is deeply traumatized if he is deprived of his father and mother in his life, so too, and much more so, is the person who is deprived of Christ and His Holy Mother.

In the Song of Songs the bride says of Christ the Bridegroom, *I sleep,*
S. of S. 5:2 *but my heart awakes. The voice of my beloved knocks at the door.*

The bride stays awake and dreams of Him. Even if she sleeps, her soul turns towards Him. Thus she expresses her love and complete devotion. She has Him constantly in her mind and in her heart, even when she is asleep. She adores and worships Him. Do you understand? Worship must spring from the whole soul and whole heart. What does that mean? Your only thought must be God. But the thought of God is unlike other thoughts. It is different. It is a kind of worship of Christ. This is the thought that beguiles and delights. It is not something that is done under

* Words from a dismissal hymn commonly sung at the commemoration of women martyrs.

At the right hand of the Saviour stood the virgin, victor and martyr, arrayed in the invincibility of the virtues, coloured with the oil of purity and the blood of contest, and with lighted torch crying out to Him in rejoicing: I have run to the fragrance of your myrrh, O Christ God, for I have been wounded by your love; do not part from me, O heavenly Bridegroom. Through her supplications, send, almighty Saviour, your mercies on us.'

duress. You feel a spiritual delight and pleasure. It's not like the homework a child does for school. It is like the passionate love between two people, but higher and spiritual.

And as a woman in childbirth draws near the time of delivery and in her pain cries out, so have we been towards Your Beloved on account of Your fear, O Lord. We have conceived, we have been in travail and we have brought forth, says the Prophet Isaiah. Isa. 26:17–18

Thus our soul cries out to God on account of the pain she feels when she craves for Him. And she makes an effort; she strains herself. What do the effort and tears of the '*woman in childbirth*' mean? Is it not the pain and travail until Christ enters us. This pain is the greatest of all. Those who have experienced it know what it is. It is an unbearable torment…

Whoever wants to become a Christian must first become a poet

The soul of the Christian needs to be refined and sensitive, to have sensibility and wings, to be constantly in flight and to live in dreams, to fly through infinity, among the stars, amidst the greatness of God, amid silence.

Whoever wants to become a Christian must first become a poet. That's what it is! You must suffer. You must love and suffer — suffer for the one you love. Love makes effort for the loved one. She runs all through the night; she stays awake; she stains her feet with blood in order to meet her beloved. She makes sacrifices and disregards all impediments, threats and difficulties for the sake of the loved one. Love towards Christ is something even higher, infinitely higher.

And when we say 'love', we don't mean the virtues that we will acquire, but the heart that is pervaded by love towards Christ and others. We need to turn everything in this direction. Do we see a mother with her child in her arms and bending to give the child a kiss, her heart overflowing with emotion? Do we notice how her face lights up as she holds her little angel? These things do not escape a person with love of God. He sees them and is impressed by them and he says, 'If only I had those emotions towards my God, towards my Holy Lady and our saints!' Look, that's how we must love Christ our God. You desire it, you want it, and with the grace of God you acquire it.

But are we inflamed by love for Christ? Do we run to the Beloved when we are exhausted to find rest in prayer, or do we do it as a burdensome duty and say, 'Now I have to do my prayers and prostrations…?' What's missing when we feel like this? Divine *eros* is what's missing.

Prayer of this kind is not worth the saying. Indeed it could even be harmful.

If the soul is disfigured and becomes unworthy of Christ's love, Christ suspends the relationship, because Christ does not wish 'uncouth' souls in His proximity. The soul needs to regain her composure in order to become worthy of Christ. She needs to repent, *even unto seventy times*
Matt. 18:22 *seven*. True repentance will bring sanctification with it. You mustn't say,
'all my years have been wasted; I'm not worthy,' etc. Instead you can say, 'I remember all the empty days when I didn't live close to God...'. And in my own life there will have been such empty days. I was twelve years old when I left to go the Holy Mountain. Don't these count as years? I may have been a small boy, but nevertheless I lived for twelve years far from God. So many years!

Listen to what Ignatius Brianchaninov says in his book, *On the Prayer of Jesus*:*

'Every physical and spiritual task which does not involve pain, toil and trouble never bears fruit for the person who engages in it, for the
Matt. 11:12 Kingdom of Heaven is taken by violence and *the violent lay hold of it*' —
'violence' here meaning the laborious exercise of the body in everything.'

When you love Christ you exert yourself, but in blessed exertions. You suffer, but with joy. You make prostrations and pray because these are things you crave for with divine craving. They are at once pain and longing, passion and yearning and exaltation and joy and love. Prostrations and vigils and fasting are exertions which are made for the Beloved, exertions in order to experience Christ. But this exertion is not made under duress; you don't protest and rebel. Whatever you do under compulsion is very harmful both to you and to the work you are doing. The pressure and coercion provoke opposition. Exertion for Christ, true de-
Ps. 83:3 sire for Christ, is love, sacrifice and dissolution of self. This is also how
[84:3] David felt: *My soul longs and faints for the courts of the Lord.* My soul
longs with craving and melts away out of love for God.

It requires care and effort in order to understand the words one reads and take them to heart. This is the effort you need to make. Then you will enter into compunction, ardour and tears without effort. They follow as a gift from God. Does passionate love require effort? When you understand the words of the hymns, poetic canons and Scripture you are drawn

* Bishop Ignatius Brianchaninov, *On the Prayer of Jesus*, tr. Archimandrite Lazarus Moore, St John of Kronstadt Press, 1995.

towards God with a sense of joy, you enter into truth joyfully. *You have given joy to my heart*, as David says. You enter into a state of compunction spontaneously, without bloodshed. Do you understand? Ps. 4:8 [4:7]

I, poor wretch, long to hear the words of the Fathers and of the ascetics, and the words of the Old and New Testaments. These are the things my heart wishes to devote itself to and take delight in. These are the things that cultivate divine *eros*. I desire them fervently and try, but I am unable. I have fallen ill; the *spirit is willing, but the flesh is weak*. I am unable to make prostrations. Not one. I long passionately to be on the Holy Mountain, to make prostrations, to pray, to celebrate the Divine Liturgy and to be with another hermit. It's better when there are two together. Christ himself said so: *Wherever two or three are gathered together in my name, there am I in the midst of them.* Matt. 26:41 Matt. 18:20

Humility and selflessness in the worship of God

Christ stands outside the door of our soul and knocks for us to open to Him, but He doesn't enter. He doesn't want to violate the freedom which He Himself gave us. The Book of Revelation says this in so many words: *Behold, I stand at the door and knock. If anyone will hear my voice and open the door, I will come in to him, and I will dine with him, and he with me.* Christ is courteous. He stands outside the door of our soul and knocks gently. If we open to Him, He will enter us and give us everything — Himself — secretly and silently. Rev. 3:20

We will not be able to know Christ unless He knows us. I can't explain these things very precisely; they are mysterious. Listen to what Saint Paul says, *Now that you have known God, or rather are known by God…* Nor can we love Him unless He loves us. Christ will not love us if we are not worthy for Him to love us. In order for Him to love us, He must discover something special in us. You may desire, demand, struggle and entreat, but you receive nothing. You prepare yourself to acquire those things which Christ desires in order for divine grace to enter you, but it cannot enter when that special ingredient you require is lacking. What is that? It is humility. Without humility, we cannot love Christ…humility and selflessness in the worship of God… *Do not let your left hand know what your right hand is doing.* Gal. 4:9 Matt. 6:3

No one must see you; no one must understand the motions of your worship towards the divinity. All these things must be hidden and secret, as with the hermits. Do you remember what I told you about the nightingale? It sings in the middle of the forest, amid the silence. Can

you say that anyone hears it or applauds it? Not a soul. Such breathtakingly beautiful singing in the midst of the wilds! Have you seen how its throat puffs up? That's what happens also to the person who falls in love with Christ. If he starts to love, his throat swells, he is overcome, his tongue moves incessantly. He finds a cave, a hidden dell, and lives with
Rom. 8:26 God secretly, *with groanings that cannot be uttered.* This is a sign that he is living with God 'in whom all things live and move',* because *in him we*
Acts 17:28 *live and move and have our being.*

When you arrive at such a degree of humility and you compel the grace of God to dwell within you, then you have gained everything. When you have attained humility, when you have become a captive of God — a captive in the good sense, that is, a vessel of divine grace — then you can say along with Saint Paul, *it is no longer I who live; Christ lives in me.*
Gal. 2:20 It is very easy for this to happen, that is, for us to do what God wants. Not simply easy, but extremely easy. It suffices for us to make the opening. When we make the opening to receive the divine, we become worthy of God, for Christ to condescend to enter us. And if Christ stoops within us, He grants us freedom. Where can you find words to describe those mysteries! The whole secret is love, passionate love for Christ, *eros*, abandonment to the spiritual world. You don't feel loneliness, or anything else. You live in another world, in a place where the soul rejoices, where it is glad and where it is never sated.

Holy Scripture and the Fathers cultivate divine eros

Everything proceeds from Holy Scripture. You must read it continually in order to learn the secrets of spiritual struggle. In the ninth chapter of my beloved Wisdom of Solomon it says:

O God of my fathers and Lord of mercy, who made all things by your word, and by your wisdom formed man to have dominion over the creatures you have made, and to rule the world in holiness and righteousness, and to pronounce judgment in uprightness of soul, give me the wisdom that sits by your thrones, and do not reject me from among your servants.
Wisd. 9:1–5 *For I am your slave and the son of your maidservant, a man who is weak*
[DC] *and short-lived, with little understanding of judgment and laws.*

We see here how the wise Solomon asks God in such a humble way for His wisdom. And God gave it to him in abundance. All these wise things that he writes are not his own. They are inspired by the same

* First Antiphon of the Hymns of Ascent from Sunday Matins, Tone 3.

Spirit which inspired the words of the poetic canons written by the hymnographers of the Church. That's why I love them so much. Read them, study them and delight in them. That's how you will acquire divine *eros*. Listen to some of the words of one of the Trinitarian canons:

Three divinely reigning hypostases we hymn,
of one single nature, an unchanging form,
a good God and lover of mankind,
*who for our transgressions grants atonement to us.**

Tell me, how do I know all this? I have an obsession, an intoxication, a divine inebriation. I cannot have enough of it all. The first prayer of thanksgiving after Holy Communion says:

'And thus setting aside this earthly sojourn in hope of life eternal, I shall attain to everlasting rest, in that place where there is the unceasing sound of festal joy and the boundless pleasure of those who behold the ineffable beauty of your countenance. For you are the true desire and inexpressible delight of those who love you, O Christ our God, and all creation hymns you unto the ages.'

It is one great festivity, and the focus of all the delight is the person of Christ. What it is exactly, we cannot ultimately understand, because God is infinite; God is a mystery; God is silence. God is infinitely hidden, but everywhere existent. We live in God, we breathe God, but we cannot sense His greatness, His providence. He frequently conceals the actions of His divine providence. But when we acquire holy humility, then we see everything and experience everything. We experience God openly and manifestly and we sense His mysteries. Then we cannot but start to love Him. And that is something which He asks for. It is the first thing which He demands for our own happiness, as He says, *You shall love the Lord your God with all your heart and all your soul and all your mind; this is the first and great commandment.* Matt. 22:37–8

Such was the love the saints had. Such was the love possessed by the saint whose name I bear, Saint Porphyrios of Gaza. One of the hymns sung on his feast day says:

The dart of your true desire attained its mark,
For through continence you humbled the passions
And you advanced towards God in rejoicing,

* From the Sunday Midnight Office (Tone 6, 1st *troparion* of the 1st Ode).

And now you stand with the highest of all you crave, Porphyrios,
*Most perfect model and yardstick for bishops and shepherds.**

'The dart of your true desire attained its mark...and you advanced towards God in rejoicing...': from the object of craving up to the very highest; you loved the 'summit of desire'. The summit of desire is God, Father, Son and Holy Spirit. All three persons are one among themselves and one also with the Church.

O Christ, you are my love!

I don't think about death. Whatever the Lord desires. I want to think about Christ. And you too, open your arms and throw yourselves into Christ's embrace. Then He lives within you. And you constantly think that you don't love Him very much and you want even more to come close to Him and be with Him. Show disdain for the passions and don't concern yourselves with the devil. Turn to Christ. For all this to happen it is necessary for grace to come: 'The divine grace which ever makes good what is weak and supplies what is lacking.'†

* Sung on 26th February (1st *troparion* of the 6th Ode).
† Words from a prayer spoken at services of Ordination.

ON PRAYER

Pray to God with fervour and love in a calm state of mind, with meekness and gentleness, without forcing yourself

The Lord Himself will teach us how to pray

Man seeks joy and happiness in heaven. He seeks what is eternal far from everyone and everything. He seeks to find joy in God. God is a mystery. He is silence. He is infinite. He is everything. Everyone possesses this inclination of the soul for heaven. All people seek something heavenly. All beings turn towards Him, albeit unconsciously.

Turn your mind towards Him continually. Learn to love prayer, familiar converse with the Lord. What counts above all is love, passionate love for the Lord, for Christ the Bridegroom. Become worthy of Christ's love. In order not to live in darkness, turn on the switch of prayer so that divine light may flood your soul. Christ will appear in the depths of your being. There, in the deepest and most inward part, is the Kingdom of God. *The Kingdom of God is within you.* Luke 17:21

Prayer is made only with the Holy Spirit. It teaches the soul how to pray. *For we know not what to pray for as we ought, but the Spirit itself makes intercession for us with groanings that cannot be uttered.* It's not Rom. 8:26 necessary for us to make any effort. We should address ourselves to God in the manner of a humble servant with a voice of entreaty and supplication. Then our prayer will be well-pleasing to God. Let us stand devoutly before the Cross of Christ and say: 'Lord Jesus Christ, have mercy on me.' That says everything. When the mind moves in prayer, divine grace comes in a split second. The person then becomes full of grace and sees everything with different eyes. The important thing is to love Christ, prayer and meditation on His words. In prayer human effort represents only a tiny millionth part.

Before we pray the soul must prepare itself with prayer. Prayer for prayer. Listen to the prayer which the priest recites secretly during the Divine Liturgy while the Apostle is being read:

'Shine in our hearts, O loving Master, the pure light of your divine knowledge and open the eyes of our mind to understand the proclamations of your Gospel. Instill within us fear of your blessed commandments, so that trampling down all fleshly desires we may lead a spiritual life, thinking and doing everything with a view to pleasing you. For you are the illumination of our souls and bodies, O Christ our God, and to you we ascribe glory, along with your Father who is without beginning and your all-holy and good and life-giving Spirit, now and for ever and unto the ages of ages.'*

We enter into prayer without realizing it. We need to find ourselves in appropriate surroundings. Converse with Christ, conversation, the reading of Scripture, the singing of psalms, the light of the oil lamp and
Wisd. 1:13 the fragrance of incense all create the appropriate atmosphere so that
[DC] everything happens naturally, *in simplicity of heart*. As we read the divine offices with love, we are sanctified without being aware of it. The divine words fill our hearts with gladness. This gladness of heart, this joy is our own effort so that we enter easily into the atmosphere of prayer — it's our warm-up, as you might say. We may call to mind beautiful images from landscapes we have seen. This effort is gentle, without bloodshed. But don't let us forget what the Lord said, *Without me you*
John 15:5 *can do nothing.*

The Lord Himself will teach us how to pray. We won't learn prayer on our own, nor will anyone else teach us it. Don't let's say to ourselves, 'I have made such-and-such a number of prostrations, so now I have secured divine grace', but rather let us make entreaty for the pure light of divine knowledge to shine within us and open our spiritual eyes so that we may understand His divine words.

In this way, without realizing it, we love God without contorting ourselves and without exertion and struggle. What is difficult for man is easy for God. We will love God suddenly when grace overshadows us. If we love Christ very much, the prayer will say itself. Christ will be continually in our mind and in our heart.

If, however, we are to remain in this state and not to lose it, we require divine *eros*, divine, burning love for Christ. *Eros* directs itself to a higher being. The Lover, God, desires the beloved, and the beloved strives to reach the Lover. The Lover loves His beloved with a divine and perfect love. God, who loves mankind, is selfless.

Love towards God is a higher love when it is expressed as thanksgiving. It is necessary for us to love not as a duty, but just in the way that it is necessary for us to eat. Often we approach God out of necessity to lean on Him because we find no repose in all the things around us and we feel deserted.

* This prayer is read by the priest in preparation for his reading the Gospel.

Divine grace teaches us our own obligation. In order to attract this grace we need love and craving. The grace of God requires divine *eros*. Love is sufficient to bring us into a suitable frame of mind for prayer. Christ will come on His own and He will stoop over our soul as long as he finds certain little things which gratify Him: good intention, humility and love. Without these things we cannot pray the words, 'Lord Jesus Christ, have mercy on me.'

Let's assume, for example, that we have a radio. When we turn the aerial to 'position one', in the direction of the greatest number of transmitters, we hear the programme loud and clear. At 'position two' there aren't so many transmitters, and so the signal is somewhat less clear. At 'position three' the programme is virtually inaudible. The same is true for our communication with God. When our soul is turned facing 'direction one', communication is excellent. And that is due, of course, to two basic prerequisites: love and humility. With those prerequisites, the soul communicates with God, hears His voice and accepts His word. It receives strength and divine grace and is transfigured. It turns towards God in a natural way and feels compunction. When there is less love and humility — our 'position two' — we have a correspondingly inferior communication with God. When our soul assumes 'position three', communication breaks down almost completely, because we are filled with passions, hatreds and enmities and our soul cannot ascend.

For Christ to enter within us when we invoke Him with the words 'Lord Jesus Christ', our heart must be pure and free from all impediments. It must be devoid of hatred, egotism and malice. We must love Him and He must love us. If, however, our heart does harbour some thought of censure or ill will, there is still something we can do about it. The secret is to ask forgiveness or to make confession. But that, of course, as we said, requires humility. If you put the words of God into practice and are not troubled by pricks of conscience, you are calm and do good works, then you enter naturally into prayer without realizing it. Then you simply wait patiently until grace comes.

On every occasion when something happens to you, place the blame on yourself. Pray with humility and don't seek to justify yourself. If, for example, you find yourself the object of enmity, pray with love so that you pour love over the enmity. If you hear a slander against you, then Wisd. 1:10
pray and be careful, because *the noise of murmurings shall not be hidden.* [DC]
The slightest murmuring against your neighbour affects your soul and

you are unable to pray. When the Holy Spirit finds the soul in this state it does not dare to approach.

Let us ask of God for His will to be done in our life

Our prayers are not heard because we are not worthy. You must become worthy in order to pray. We are not worthy because we do not love our neighbour as our self. Christ says so Himself: *If you bring your gift to the altar and there you remember that your brother holds something against*
Matt. *you, leave there your gift before the altar and go first be reconciled with*
5:23–4 *your brother and then come and offer your gift.* Go first to be reconciled with your brother and receive forgiveness in order to become worthy. If that is not done, you will be unable to pray. If you are not worthy, you can do nothing. Once you have set in order all your unsettled business and prepared yourself, then go and offer your gift.

Those who desire and crave to belong to Christ and who abandon themselves to the will of God become worthy. It's a great thing, all-important, to have no will. The slave has no will of his own. And it is possible for us to have no will of our own in a very simple manner: through love for Christ and the keeping of His commandments. *He who has my commandments and keeps them, he is the one who loves me; and he who loves me shall be loved by my Father and I will love*
John 14:21 *him and will manifest myself to him.* Effort is required. For we have to
Eph. 6:12 wrestle against the *rulers of the darkness of this age.* We have to wres-
1 Pet. 5:8 tle with the *roaring lion.* We cannot allow the devious enemy to prevail in the struggle.

This presupposes tears, repentance, prayer, almsgiving and entreaties
Matt. 8:26 in conjunction with trust in Christ and not being of *little faith.* Only Christ can free us from the shackles of solitude. Prayer, repentance and almsgiving: give at least a glass of water if you don't have money. And you may know that the more you are sanctified, the more your prayers are heard.

We shouldn't blackmail God with our prayers. We shouldn't ask God to release us from something, from an illness, for example, or to solve our problems, but we should ask for strength and support from Him to bear what we have to bear. Just as He knocks discretely at the door of our soul, so we should ask discretely for what we desire and if the Lord does not respond, we should cease to ask. When God does not give us something that we ask for insistently, then He has His reasons. God, too, has His 'secrets'. Since we believe in His good providence, since we believe that

He knows everything about our lives and that He always desires what is good, why should we not trust Him? Let us pray naturally and gently, without forcing ourself and without passion. We know that past present and future are all known, '*open and laid bare*' before God. As Saint Paul says, *Before him no creature is hidden, but all are open and laid bare to*
His eyes. We should not insist; such persistence does harm instead of Heb. 4:13
good. We shouldn't continue relentlessly in order to acquire what we want; rather we should leave things to the will of God. Because the more we pursue something, the more it runs away from us. So what is required is patience, faith and composure. And if we forget it, the Lord never forgets; and if it is for our good, He will give us what we require when we require it.

In our prayer we should ask only for the salvation of our soul. Didn't
the Lord say, *Seek first the Kingdom of God, and all these things will be* Matt. 6:33 &
added to you? Easily, without the slightest difficulty, Christ can give us Luke 12:31
what we want. And remember the secret. The secret is not to think about asking for the specific thing at all. The secret is to ask for your union with Christ with utter selflessness, without saying 'give me this' or 'give me that'. It suffices to say, 'Lord Jesus Christ, have mercy on me.' God has no need to be informed by us about our various needs. He knows them all incomparably better than we do and He gives us His love. What is important is for us to respond to this love with prayer and with the keeping of His commandments. We should ask for the will of God to be done. That is what is in our best interest and the safest thing for us and for those for whom we pray. Christ will give us everything abundantly. When there is even a trace of egotism, nothing happens.

We must go on our own to God in simplicity and artlessness of heart

When we have a relationship of absolute trust with Christ, we are happy and joyful. We possess the joy of Paradise. This is the secret. Then
we can exclaim with Saint Paul, *For me to live is Christ and to die is gain* Phil. 1:21
and, *It is no longer I who live; Christ lives in me*. Such marvellous words! Gal. 2:20
Delightful! All things must be done simply and gently.

We must go on our own to God in simplicity and artlessness of heart. What does wise Solomon have to say? He says that we need simplicity. *Be mindful of the Lord in goodness and seek Him in simplicity of heart;*
for He is found with those who do not tempt Him, and appears to those Wisd. 1:1–2
who are not unfaithful to Him. Simplicity is holy humility, that is, ab- [DC]
solute trust in Christ, when we give our whole life to Christ. In the

Divine Liturgy we say, 'we commend our whole life to Christ our God,'[*] and at another point, 'To You, O loving Master, we commend our whole life and hope, and we entreat You and pray and supplicate.'[†]

Some time ago a bishop came to see me. We were speaking about prayer and I asked him:

'What is meant by praying "in simplicity of heart and artlessness?"'

'Praying with simplicity,' he replied.

'And do you understand what that means, Your Eminence,' I said.

'Yes, I do,' he responded.

'Well, I don't,' I said. 'It's a mystery. It's something that happens only with divine grace.'

'You're quite right,' he said. 'I don't understand either. And I'm grateful to you for reminding me that simplicity and artlessness can only be understood and achieved through divine grace.'

So that's how you should engage in your spiritual struggle: simply, gently and without force. Simplicity and gentleness are a very saintly mode of spiritual life, but you cannot learn this in an external way. It must suffuse itself mystically within you, so that your soul embraces this mode of life through the grace of God. But very often, in spite of our desire to acquire this simplicity, our enemy recognizes the fact and impedes us. Put into practice the advice, *Do not let your left hand know what your*
Matt. 6:3 *right hand is doing.* When you desire something and try to force God, it
Cf. Matt. doesn't come. It will come 'on a day when you do not expect and at an
24:50 & hour you do not know'. This is where the mystery lies. I can't explain it
Luke 12:46 to you. Just as happened to me on Patmos.[§]

When you lose the divine grace, don't do anything. Continue your life and your struggle simply and normally until, without anxiety, you will be filled again with love and longing for Christ. And then everything will be fine. And then grace will fill you and give you joy. One secret is to be found in the divine offices. Abandon yourself to these and the grace of God will overtake you mystically.

The key to the spiritual life is the Jesus Prayer

Pray to God with open arms. This is the secret of the saints. As soon as they opened their arms, they were visited by divine grace.

[*] Words with which the deacon regularly concludes his intentions for prayer throughout the Divine Liturgy.

[†] Prayer read by the priest before the Lord's Prayer.

[§] See pp. 245–7 below.

As the most effective prayer the Church Fathers use the short phrase, 'Lord Jesus Christ, have mercy on me.' This prayer is the key to the spiritual life. It is a prayer that cannot be taught either by books, or by spiritual fathers or by anyone else. Its sole teacher is divine grace.

If I tell you honey is sweet and runny, or this and that, you won't understand unless you taste it. The same is true of prayer. If I say, 'this is what it's like' or 'this is how you'll feel', you won't understand, nor will
you pray *except in the Holy Spirit.* 1 Cor. 12:3

Only the Holy Spirit, only the grace of God, can inspire the Jesus Prayer. It's not difficult to repeat the words, but you cannot pray it properly because your old fallen self rebuffs it. Unless you enter into the atmosphere of grace, you will not be able to say the prayer. As soon as you hear an offensive word are you grieved? And as soon as you hear something complimentary are you pleased? That shows that you are not ready, that you do not yet have what is required. For divine grace to come you must acquire the prerequisites: love and humility. Otherwise it provokes rebuff and rejection. To enter into this 'frame of mind', start with obedience. You must submit first to obedience in order for humility to come. When He sees humility, the Lord sends divine grace and then prayer supervenes on its own, effortlessly. If you don't submit to obedience and don't have humility, the prayer doesn't come and there is a danger of being led into error and delusion. Prepare yourself gradually and gently and repeat the prayer in your mind. Whatever is in our mind is also in our heart.

When grace comes, you say the name 'Christ' and your mind and hear are flooded

Only through divine grace can you pray. No prayer can occur without divine grace. Remember the Wisdom of Sirach: *In wisdom praise shall be* Sir. 15:10
spoken, and the Lord will give it favourable progress. That is, only the per- [DC]
son who possesses divine wisdom can praise God truly. And the Lord alone gives grace for this end. When grace comes, when love comes, you say the name 'Christ' and your mind and heart are flooded. This love, this craving, also has degrees. When you experience this love, you desire to acquire spiritual things, not only when you are awake, but even in your dreams you see the same things. You desire to do everything within the embrace of this love, to move within this love. You wish to engage in effort, in every effort, out of love for God. You feel love and gratitude towards God, without having in mind to achieve anything specific. What is of value is to repeat

the Jesus Prayer with tenderness of soul, with love, with longing, and then it doesn't appear at all as a chore to you. It's like when you say, 'my mother…my father', and you feel perfect consolation.

Force, therefore, is not the way to acquire prayer. You don't say, 'I'll struggle hard to acquire prayer and gain entrance to Paradise.' Don't think that you will be repaid a hundredfold in heaven. Pray without calculations, without ulterior motives, not in order to gain anything. And if you make a thousand prostrations in order to gain entrance to Paradise, they are worthless. Make prostrations out of love, and if God wishes to put you in hell, let Him do as He wishes. That's what selflessness means. There is no point in making a hundred prostrations if they leave you unmoved. Make only twenty or fifteen, but with fervour and love for the Lord and in conformity with His divine commandments. In this way our passions gradually subside, our sins abate, and gently, without forcing ourselves, we enter into prayer. If you are empty — something which signifies that you are lacking in love — however much you make prostrations and pray, you achieve nothing. And when for whatever reason you enter into a state of compunction, do not miss the opportunity to say the Jesus Prayer, and thus it gradually becomes second nature. When you progress, it's not the thought of the prayer that is heard in your mind, but something else. It is something you feel within you, but without your making any effort. That 'something' is the divine grace which Christ is bestowing on you.

Compunction is a sacred suffering; you suffer without straining yourself. I explain everything through Holy Scripture: *But one of the soldiers punctured* (ἔνυξε) *his side with a spear, and immediately there came forth*
John 19:34 *blood and water.* The soldier pierced his side with the spearhead and made a wound. The root of the word *κατάνυξις*, 'compunction', is the verb *νύττω*, 'to puncture or pierce', *κατανύττω*, 'to stab or wound repeatedly'. And when the word is used in relation to the soul, 'to feel compunction' means that I am wounded over and over again by the love of God. Another verb meaning 'to wound' is κατατιτρώσκω, as in the hymn which says: 'I have been wounded (τέτρωμαι) by your love.'* And in the Song of Songs we read: *I have charged you, O daughters of Jerusalem, by the powers and the virtues of the field: if you should find my Beloved, what shall you say to*
S. of S. 5:8 *him? That I am wounded* (τετρωμένη) *with love.* That is, the bride who is looking to find Christ the Bridegroom says, 'I am deeply wounded by my love for Him. How can I forget Him? How shall I live without Him? I

* See footnote on pp. 105–6 above.

suffer deeply when He is distant from me.' Compunction, therefore, is a deep pain, a sacred suffering.

Let us take an image from human love. The person who is in love cannot live apart from his loved one. Heart and mind are one: as soon as he sees the girl he loves, his heart leaps, but when they are apart and he thinks of her, again his heart leaps. He doesn't require to make any effort. The same happens with Christ, although here, of course, everything is divine — divine *eros*, divine love, not carnal love. It is serene, but more intense, more profound. And just as in human love, when you do not see your beloved you suffer, so here, too, you suffer. But also just as when you are near your beloved you suffer out of love and shed tears, so too here you suffer out of love and, without being aware of it, you break down in tears of love, of compunction and joy. That is what compunction is. Tears, however, are not always the sign of compunction. They can often be a sign of womanly weakness.

Let us bring Christ into our mind in an unforced manner by repeating the Jesus Prayer

Prayer of the heart is prayed only by a person who has attracted the grace of God. It mustn't be done with the thought, 'I'll learn it, I'll do it, I'll acquire it', because in this way we may be led to egotism and pride. Not only experience and genuine desire, but also wisdom, care and prudence are required if our prayer is to be pure and pleasing to God. A single seductive thought, 'I have really made progress', for example, brings everything to naught. Why should we be proud? We have nothing that is our own. These are very delicate matters.

Pray without forming images in your mind. Don't try to imagine Christ. The Fathers emphasized the need for prayer to be free of images. With an image, the focus of prayer is easily lost, because one image can easily be displaced by another. And the evil one may intrude images and we lose the grace.

Prayer should be interior, prayed with the mind and not with the lips, so as not to cause distraction with the mind wandering here and there. Let us bring Christ into our mind in an unforced manner by repeating very gently, 'Lord Jesus Christ, have mercy on me'. Don't think anything except the words, 'Lord Jesus Christ, have mercy on me'. Nothing else. Nothing at all. Calmly, with open eyes, so that you are not in danger of succumbing to fantasies and delusions, and with care and devotion, turn towards Christ. Repeat the prayer in an unforced manner and not continually, but when there is the disposition and an atmosphere of compunction, which is a gift of divine grace. Without grace you fall into a state of self-hypnotism and you can end up seeing lights and delusions and become mentally deranged.

The prayer should not be said as a chore. Coercion may provoke a reaction within us and be harmful. Many people have become ill as a result of the prayer because they coerced themselves. Something happens, of course, even when you do it as a chore, but it is not healthy. Nor should you employ diverse techniques. You don't need to sit on a low stool, nor do you need to bow down your head, nor to close your eyes. Many say, 'Sit on a low stool, hunch yourself up, gather yourself up tightly and concentrate.' But on what? Try and see. It's not necessary to concentrate particularly to say the prayer. And you don't need any effort when you're filled with divine love. You can say the prayer, 'Lord Jesus Christ, have mercy on me', gently, without straining and without contortion wherever you happen to be — on a stool, on a chair, in a car, walking along the road, at school, in the office or at work. Don't tie yourself down to a specific place. What is all-important is love for Christ. If your soul repeats with worship and adoration the seven words, 'Lord Jesus Christ, have mercy on me', it never can have enough. They are insatiable words! Repeat them all your life. There is such life-giving sap hidden within them!

Have your mind on God and your heart will leap for joy spontaneously

Listen and I'll tell you about something that happened to me a few days ago. A monk who practices the Jesus Prayer came here from the Holy Mountain and he asked me:

'How do you say the Jesus Prayer? Do you sit on a low stool? Do you lower your head and concentrate?'

'No,' I replied. 'I say, "Lord Jesus Christ..." clearly in my mind giving attention to the words. "Lord Jesus Christ, have mercy on me... Lord Jesus..." That's how I do it in my mind and pay attention only to the words.'

'That's not right at all, Elder,' he said. 'The way you describe it is quite erroneous, not to say deluded. The mind needs to be in the heart. That's why it's called "prayer of the heart".'

'I'll tell you something else,' I said to him. 'Sometimes when I would be facing some temptation, I would bring into my mind the image of Christ on the cross with his transfixed hands and feet dripping blood and with the crown of thorns piercing his brow and with myself kneeling before him and saying to Him, "Lord Jesus Christ, have mercy on me".'

'And you didn't bring your mind into your heart?' he interrupted.

'No,' I replied.

'You are deluded,' he said to me. 'The mind must be in the heart. That's why it's called "prayer of the heart". Delusion!'

He got up to leave.

'Elder!' I said to him. 'Listen and I'll tell you something. When I am repeating the prayer in my mind, sometimes my joy becomes more and more intense. And when my joy becomes ever stronger with the words, "Lord Jesus Christ…", I feel my mind leaping within me along with my heart. That is, I feel my mind plummeting into my heart and there I experience all this joy as I say the prayer. I begin with the mind and then my mind moves on its own when joy comes.'

'So that's how you pray! That indeed is the way!' he said to me. 'Forgive me for saying "delusion".'

It is the mind that thinks. The heart doesn't think. Have your mind on God and your heart will leap for joy spontaneously. It will feel compunction. For Christ to enter your heart you must love Him. In order to love Him, He must first love you. God must first know you and then you Him. He will stoop to you, if you first seek Him. In order for Him to love you, you must be worthy. In order to be worthy, you must prepare yourself.

First of all, you must shun all self-interest. Prayer must be entirely selfless. Everything must happen mystically and without self-interest. That is, don't think that if you concentrate with your mind then grace will come into your heart also and you will experience that leap of joy. Don't pray with that motive, but with simplicity and humility. Aspire always to the glory of God. What did I tell you about the nightingale? It sings without anyone seeing. Be like that — selfless. Give yourself over to the worship of God in secret.

But be careful! As we said, *Don't let your left hand know what your right hand is doing.* Don't let your malicious self know what's going on. Matt. 6:3
Live in Paradise and don't let your evil self know and envy it. Don't forget that there exists the envy of the evil one.

Preparation is also to learn to keep the commandments of God. To expel the passions — condemnation, anger, etc. — in a subtle way. That is, do not strike at the evil directly, but, disdaining the passion, turn with love to God. Occupy yourself with singing hymns, the triumphant hymns of the saints and martyrs and the Psalms of David. Study Holy Scripture and the Church Fathers. In this way your soul will be softened, sanctified and assimilated to God. It will be ready to hear the disclosures of God.

Gradually grace will visit you. You will enter into joy. You will begin to live in peace and then you will become stronger by virtue of the divine grace. You will not become angry, or irritated, you will not be offended, you will not judge others, but rather receive everyone with love. You will have that which Saint Paul describes: *love does not boast…it does not behave in an unseemly manner…it does not rejoice in injustice, but rejoices*
1 Cor. *in truth; it covers and protects all things, it believes all things, hopes all*
13:4–8 *things, endures all things. Love never fails.* The prayer purifies the soul and keeps the mind in check. The most perfect work is done in the depths of the human soul, which is hermetically sealed and known only to God. And so we witness something extraordinary: people who are transformed into children of God, even though they had reached the very depths of their self-destructiveness.

And I, too, wretched and crocked-up fellow that I am, make this effort. I don't give myself over openly in prayer, but secretly I pray. Do you understand? The grace of God comes and overshadows you too. It brings a freshness and joy to you also as we live together, eat together, talk and pray and simply keep company with one another. Do you understand? Only someone who is thoughtless, someone who is 'thick-skinned' and
Ps. 50:6 cannot be moved by prayer, remains a stranger to grace. Pray for God to
[51:6] reveal to you the 'unseen' things. There is much that we do not know. Say to Christ, 'Whatever You want. Whatever Your love desires.' He will lead you. Look to Him.

Prayer of the heart is impossible without a spiritual guide

If you are going to occupy yourself with prayer of the heart exclusively you must have the guidance of a spiritual father. Prayer of the heart is impossible without a spiritual guide. There is a danger of the soul being deluded. Care is needed. Your spiritual guide will teach you how to get into the right order for prayer, because if you don't get into the right order, there's a danger of your seeing the luciferic light, of living in delusion and being plunged into darkness, and then one becomes aggressive and changes character and so on. This is the splitting of the personality. Do you see how delusion is created? If, however, you progress in prayer with the counsels of a spiritual father, you will see the true light.

The spiritual guide must be experienced in prayer of the heart. If he prays mechanically and has not experienced prayer with the grace of God, he is unable to tell someone else how to pray. Certainly, he will be able to say what he has read in books and what the Fathers say. Whole books have been written which talk about prayer. And so many people read them and none knows how to pray. 'But', you will object, 'we read these books, we learn the method of prayer, we prepare ourselves and God gives His blessing and sends us His grace and we understand them.' That's all very well, but it is a mystery. Prayer is a mystery, and above all prayer of the heart is a mystery.

The most dreadful delusion can be created by spiritual prayer. Other prayers are prayed to a large extent by our mind. We simply say them and our ears hear them. They are said in a different way. But spiritual prayer is something else. And if in this spiritual dimension desire is enkindled, not by your good self, but by the other self, the egotistical self, then undoubtedly you will begin to see lights, but not the light of Christ, and undoubtedly you will begin to experience a pseudo-joy. But in your outward life, in your relations with other people, you will be ever more aggressive and irascible, more quick-tempered and fretful. These are the signs of the person who is deluded. The person who is deluded does not accept that he is suffering from delusion. He is fanatical and does harm. This is what happens with zealots, those who act with a zeal that is not tempered by divine knowledge. Listen to an example of this:

Saint Makarios, the famous Desert Father, had decided to go to a church festival along with the monk who was subservient to him. The young monk had gone on ahead. He was a beginner and had a beginner's zeal. As he was walking along he met an idolater, a priest of a pagan temple. He spoke harshly to him and said:

'Where are you off to, you deluded soul?'

The priest was enraged and attacked the novice, leaving him virtually unconscious.

A short time later the priest met the elder. When Abba Makarios, blessed as he was by divine grace, saw the man in a state of shock and aggravation, he said to him:

'Good man of God, where are you going to?'

As soon as the priest heard these words his heart softened, he stopped in his tracks, and said:

'Your words have calmed me down.'

'Yes,' said Abba Makarios. 'I see you're in a hurry, only you don't know where you're hurrying to.'

But he said it in a humble and brotherly tone of love.

'When you speak,' said the idolater, 'your words open my heart, but a short time ago another monk spoke to me in a very different way and I gave him a good beating.'

Abba Makarios spoke to him in such an inspired way, that the idolater gradually changed his beliefs, became a monk and was saved. With his good words and manners he communicated the good spirit. He communicated the uncreated energy and entered the soul of the idolater. The novice, on the contrary, communicated a spirit of anger and aggression from the spirit he had within him.*

Do you see what delusion means? When you have a spiritual guide you are not in danger of delusion. When you have a good, God-inspired elder you learn the secrets of prayer. You pray with your elder and you gradually begin to enter into the spiritual life and to learn how the elder prays. He is not able to tell you, 'Do this or do that.' But you do what you see him do. When you go to your elder, certainly, he tells you about the prayer of the heart. You need to know, however, that if he does not experience the prayer of the heart himself, he will not be able to communicate anything. But when the elder has experienced and experiences the prayer of the heart, something mysterious takes place. The mystery is that the novice hears his words, but more importantly, he sees the way his heart opens and how he speaks to God in his heart. His soul watches him. And not only this, but soul communicates with soul and the one soul senses the other. The novice feels how the whole 'frame of mind' is created, how this state is created through divine grace.

This is not a simple matter. This is the teaching. We say that prayer cannot be taught, but in point of fact it can be taught when you live with someone who truly prays. When you take a book about prayer and read it, it may be that you don't understand anything. But when you have an elder next to you who prays, whatever he tells you about prayer you understand and take to heart. You enter into his prayer, and you pray too without realizing it. You communicate. It's not the book or the knowledge, it's the sensation, it's the manner, it's the opening of the heart, it's the embrace of prayer.

And is not what we are doing now as I am speaking to you, is this too not a prayer? Am I not speaking from my heart and do we not feel that leaping sensation of joy and impellent desire? If this is not prayer, how can it be explained that we have such a sense of strong desire?

The flood of divine love fills the soul with joy and exultation

Let us love Christ. Then the name of Christ will burst forth from within us with impellent desire, with fervour, with divine *eros*. We will shout His

* Abba Makarios in the *Wisdom of the Desert Fathers*.

name secretly, without spoken words. Let us stand before God in adoration, humbly, and in the footsteps of Christ — that Christ may free us from every trace of our fallen nature. Let us ask for tears to be given to us before prayer. But be careful! *Do not let your right hand know what the left is doing.* Pray with contrition: 'Am I worthy for You to give such grace, O Christ?' And then these tears become tears of gratitude. I am deeply moved; I have not done the will of God, but I ask for His mercy. Matt. 6:3

Pray to God with love and yearning, in tranquility, with meekness, gently and without forcing yourself. And when you repeat the prayer, 'Lord Jesus Christ, have mercy on me', say it slowly, humbly, gently and with divine love. Pronounce the name of Christ with sweetness. Say the words one at a time: 'Lord…Jesus…Christ…have mercy on me', smoothly, tenderly, affectionately, silently, secretly, mystically, but with exaltation, with longing, with passion, without tension, force or unbecoming emphasis, without compulsion and pressure. In the way a mother speaks to the child she loves: 'my little boy…my darling girl…my little Johnny…my wee Mary!' With longing. Yes, longing. That's the whole secret. Here the heart is speaking: 'My little child, my joy!' 'My Lord, my Jesus, my Jesus, my Jesus!' What you have in your heart and in your mind, that is what you express *with all your heart and with all your soul and with all your strength and with all your mind.* Luke 10:27

Sometimes it is good to say the prayer, 'Lord Jesus Christ, have mercy on me', out loud so that you hear it with your ears. We are body and soul and there is interaction between the two.

But when you have fallen in love with Christ you prefer silence and spiritual prayer. Then words cease. It is inner silence that precedes, accompanies and follows the divine visitation, the divine union and co-mingling of the soul with the divine. When you find yourself in this state, words are not needed. This is something you experience, something that cannot be explained. Only the person who experiences this state understands it. The sense of love floods through you and unites you with Christ. You are filled with joy and exultation which shows that you have the divine, perfect love within you. Divine love is selfless, simple and true.

The most perfect form of prayer is silent prayer. Silence. 'Let all mortal flesh keep silence.'* Amid the mystery of silence the assimilation to God takes place. It is here too that truest worship takes place. To

* Words sung at the Vesperal Liturgy on the eve of Easter Day during the procession bearing the Bread and Wine to the Holy Table.

experience this, however, you have to attain to a certain level. Then words fall silent. Remember: 'Let all mortal flesh keep silence.' This manner of silence is the most perfect. This is how you are assimilated to God. You enter into the mysteries of God. We must not speak much, but leave grace to speak.

I repeated the prayer, 'Lord Jesus Christ, have mercy on me', and new horizons would open up. Tears of joy and gladness would flow from my eyes on account of Christ's love and His sacrifice on the Cross. Insuperable longing! In this the whole greatness is concealed, Paradise itself. Because you love Christ, you repeat this prayer, these seven words, with craving and with your heart. And gradually the words are lost. The heart is so replete that it suffices to say two words, 'My Jesus!', and ultimately no words at all. Love is better expressed without words. But when a soul truly falls in love with the Lord, it prefers silence and spiritual prayer. The flood of divine love fills the soul with joy and exultation.

This soul has previously progressed though, and exercised itself day by day in the Psalter and the service books of the Church. Now words have come to an end. The soul experiences divine humility very profoundly. Christ has descended into it and it senses the divine voice. It is both in the world and out of the world. It is in Paradise, that is, in the Church, in the uncreated Paradise. Ignatius Brianchaninov says:

'Prayer of the heart is highly desirable. It is highly desirable to live in the most remote desert, because these circumstances are especially favourable for prayer of the heart and silence of the heart.'*

'Silence of the heart' is for nothing to distract you — to live alone for God alone.

God is everywhere present and fills all things. I try to take wings to infinity and fly amidst the stars. My mind is lost in the magnificence of God's omnipotence as I contemplate the distances of millions of light years. I feel this omnipotent God before me and I open my arms and I open my soul to be united with Him, to participate in the Godhead...

In prayer what is important is the intensity

In prayer what is important is not the duration but the intensity. Pray albeit for five minutes, but abandoning yourself to God with love and longing. One person may pray all night long and another person only for

* Brianchaninov, *On the Prayer of Jesus*, tr. Archimandrite Lazarus Moore, St. John of Kronstadt Press, 1995.

five minutes and yet the five-minute prayer may be superior. This is a mysterious matter, of course, but that's the way it is. Listen, and I'll give you an example.

A monk was walking in the desert one day and there he met another monk. He greeted him saying:

'Where have you come from?'

'From that village over there.'

'And how are things there?'

'We're suffering from a dreadful drought and we're at our wits' end.'

'What have you done about it? Have you prayed?'

'Yes, we have.'

'And did it rain?'

'Not a drop.'

'It seems then that you haven't been praying intensely enough. Let's pray to God here and now to ask for His help.'

And so they started to pray. And at once a little cloud appeared which grew bigger and bigger and darker and darker and drew lower and lower until, Bang! It started to rain in buckets.

What happened here? What happened was earnest prayer. A little prayer brought rain. But what was important was its intensity.

'With labour and with intensity' was what Abba Makarios used to say. Saint Makarios prayed intensely with all his soul and with all his heart and with all his mind. He gave himself over entirely in soul and body to worship. In this state he would raise up his arms and remain stiff and motionless on account of the profound intensity of his prayer. In the same way someone who raises his arms to pronounce a curse against someone can communicate evil.

Someone said to me:

'We want you to make a prayer for us.'

I replied to him saying:

'I'll pray with my heart and with humility to the Lord. I'll pray with understanding.'

'What do you mean by "with understanding"?' he asked.

'I mean prayer that is done consciously and with the mind concentrated. Listen and you'll see what I mean. Once people had assembled in a public square demanding that the prophet David speak to them because a great event had occurred and everyone was shouting. The prophet appeared and said to them: *Sing praises to God, sing praises; sing praises to our King, sing praises. For God is King of all the earth; sing praises with understanding.*

'Where's that to be found in Holy Scripture?' he asked. 'Which psalm is it? I want to go and find it.'

'I think,' I said, 'it's the psalm that begins, *O clap your hands, all you*
Ps. 46 [47] *nations, shout to God in a voice of exultation…*'

The person who belongs to Christ turns everything into prayer

We should refer all our problems, whatever they are, to God, just as we say in the Divine Liturgy that we 'commend our whole life to Christ our God'. We leave everything to You, O Lord. Whatever You will. *Let Your*
Matt. 6:10 *will be done on earth as it is in heaven.*

The person who belongs to Christ turns everything into prayer. He makes both difficulties and tribulations into prayer. Whatever happens to him, he begins, 'Lord Jesus Christ…'. Prayer is beneficial for everything, even for the simplest of things. For example, if you are suffering from insomnia, don't think about sleep. Get up and leave your bedroom and then come back in and lie down on your bed as if for the first time, without thinking about whether you will sleep or not. Then concentrate your mind, recite the doxology and then repeat the prayer, 'Lord Jesus Christ…', three times over and that way you will fall asleep.

All matters are sorted out with prayer. But your prayer must be endued with love and fire. You mustn't have anxiety, but trust in God's love and providence. All things are embraced in spiritual life. All things are sanctified, both the good things and the difficult things, the material and the spiritual, and whatever you do, do for the glory of God. Saint Paul says, *Whether you eat or whether you drink, whatever you do, do for*
1 Cor. 10:31 *the glory of God.* When you are at prayer, all things happen as they should. For example, you wash the dishes and you don't break any. The grace of God enters within you. When you have the grace of God, everything is done with joy and without pain.

When we pray continually, God will enlighten us as to what we must do in each situation, even the most difficult. God will speak in our heart. He will find ways. Of course, we can combine prayer with fasting. That is, when we are faced with a serious problem or dilemma, we should approach it with much prayer and fasting. That's how I have dealt with things often.

When we want to ask things for other people, we should ask for them
Matt. 6:6 secretly, with prayer which is *in secret* and does not appear outwardly. Worry and distraction do not help prayer. Forget about telephone calls, communications and long conversations with people. If the Lord

doesn't assist, what will our own efforts achieve? So what is required is prayer, prayer with love. It is preferable for us to help people from a distance with prayer. In that way we help them in the best and most perfect manner.

When we pray for other people we should say, 'Lord Jesus Christ, have mercy on me'

Pray for the Church, for the world, for everyone. The whole of Christendom is contained in prayer. If we pray only for ourselves, that conceals self-interest. But when you pray for the Church, you also are embraced within the Church. In the Church is Christ, united with the Church and with the Father and with the Holy Spirit. The Holy Trinity and the Church are one. Your desire must be for this: for the world to be sanctified and for everything to belong to Christ. Then you enter into the Church and you live in the joy of Paradise. You live with God, because the whole fullness of divinity dwells in the Church. Cf. Col. 2:9

We are all one body with Christ as the head. We all constitute the Church. Our religion has this magnificent quality of uniting the world spiritually. The power of prayer is great, very great, especially when done by many together. All are united in common prayer. We feel that our neighbour is as our self. This is our life, our exaltation and our treasure. All things are easy in Christ. Christ is the centre; all move towards the centre and are united in one spirit and one heart. Something like this happened at Pentecost. When we all hear the Psalter and the readings at the same time and in the same place, we are united in hearing by the grace of God, because what the reader says is heard by everyone and we all participate in it. The power of the many individuals is multiplied — as when they see something beautiful and they all admire it together with profound desire. Their vision, which converges on that beautiful object, unites them. The freeing of Saint Peter the Apostle from prison is an example of this: *Prayer was made by the Church without ceasing.* This Acts 12:5
prayer released Peter from the fetters of prison.

Love, worship of God, desire, union with God and union with the Church constitute Paradise on earth. If we acquire divine grace, all things are easy, joyful and a blessing from God. Come now and find me a religion that makes man perfect and happy! And what a pity we don't comprehend this extraordinary quality in our religion!

When we or someone else are facing some problem, let us ask others for their prayers and let us all entreat God with faith and love. Be sure that God is pleased with these prayers and intervenes with miracles. This is something we haven't understood properly. We say, 'Say a prayer for me', but without realizing the power of common prayer.

Pray for others more than for yourself. Say, 'Lord Jesus Christ, have mercy on me', and you will always have others in your mind. We are all children of the same Father; we are all one. And so, when we pray for others, we say, 'Lord Jesus Christ, have mercy on me', and not, 'have mercy on them'. In this way we make them one with ourselves.

Prayer for others which is made gently and with deep love is selfless and has great spiritual benefit. It brings grace to the person who prays and also to the person for whom he is praying. When you have great love and this love moves you to prayer, then the waves of love are transmitted and affect the person for whom you are praying and you create around him a shield of protection and you influence him, you lead him towards what is good. When He sees your efforts, God bestows His grace abundantly on both you and on the person you are praying for. But we must die to ourselves. Do you understand?

You get upset when others are unwell, whereas what you should do is devote yourself to prayer so that what is desired comes about through the grace of God. With your own wisdom, you tell others what should be done, when that is not necessarily the best thing. The secret is to be found elsewhere, and not in what we say or suggest to others. The secret lies in our devotion, our prayer to God for what is best for our brethren to come about through the grace of God. That is the best. What we are unable to do will be done through His grace.

In my life, prayer occupies the first place. I do not fear hell and I don't think of Paradise. I ask only for God to have mercy on the whole world and on me. If I repeat 'Lord Jesus Christ, have mercy on me' with intensity, even when I have people around me, I am not distracted from the prayer. It is just the same as when I am on my own. I pray, I receive everyone in the Spirit of Christ, and I am eager to pray for all the people. I try to love Christ. That is my aim. Because of my many illnesses, I'm not able to speak much. But prayer helps more than words.

I pray for the matters that are occupying you, but that is not enough. My prayer must find a response from you. God, who sends His grace on us, must find our arms open to receive it. And whatever He permits will be for the benefit of our soul. Nothing is achieved, however, if we are praying and you are sleeping!

Ps. 37:14 People often make accusations against me, but *I am like a deaf man*
[38:13] *that does not hear, and like a dumb man that does not open his mouth.*

Pray for those who make accusations against you. Say, 'Lord Jesus Christ, have mercy on me', not 'have mercy on him', and your accuser will be embraced in this prayer. Does someone say something to you that upsets you? God knows it. What you have to do is open your arms and say, 'Lord Jesus Christ, have mercy on me', and make your accuser one with yourself. And God knows what is torturing your accuser deep inside him and, seeing your love, he hastens to help. He searches the desires of hearts. What is it that Saint Paul says in his Epistle to the Romans? *He who searches the hearts knows what the mind of the Spirit is, because in accord with God He makes intercession for the saints.* Rom. 8:27

Pray for the purification of each and every person so that you may imitate the prayer of the angels in your life. Yes, the angels don't pray for themselves. This is how I pray for people, for the Church and for the body of the Church. The moment you pray for the Church, you are released from your passions. The moment you glorify God, your soul is calmed and sanctified by divine grace. This is the art I want you to learn.

God wants us to become like the angels. The angels only glorify God. This is their prayer, glorification of God and nothing else. The glorification of God is a very subtle matter; it eludes human criteria. We are very material and earth-bound, and for that reason we pray to God in a self-interested manner. We ask Him to order our affairs, to help our businesses do well, to protect our health and to safeguard our children. But we pray in a human way and with self-interest. Doxology is prayer without self-interest. The angels do not pray in order to receive something; they are selfless. God also gave to us the possibility for our prayer to be an unending doxology, an angelic prayer. This is where the great secret lies. When we enter into this prayer, we will glorify God continually, leaving everything to Him, just as our Church prays: 'We commend our whole life to Christ our God.'* This is the 'higher mathematics' of our religion!

* See footnote to p. 118 above.

ON SPIRITUAL STRUGGLE

What makes a person holy is love, the adoration of Christ

When Christ enters our soul, everything within us will be altered

Man is a mystery. We carry within us an age-old inheritance — all the good and precious experience of the prophets, the saints, the martyrs, the apostles and above all of our Lord Jesus Christ; but we also carry within us the inheritance of the evil that exists in the world from Adam until the present. All this is within us, instincts and everything, and all demand satisfaction. If we don't satisfy them, they will take revenge at some time, unless, that is, we divert them elsewhere, to something higher, to God.

That is why we must die to our ancestral humanity and enrobe ourselves in the new humanity. This is what we confess in the sacrament of baptism. With baptism we enter into the joy of Christ. *As many as are*
Gal. 2:27 *baptized in Christ, have put on Christ.* Confession is a second baptism in
which we are purified of our passions, in which our passions are benumbed. Thus divine grace comes through the sacraments.

Cf. John The Lord said to his disciples, 'When the Holy Spirit will come, it will
14:26 teach you all things.' The Holy Spirit teaches us everything. It sanctifies us. It assimilates us to God. When we have the Spirit of God, we become incapable of all sin, incapable of sinning. When we have the Holy Spirit, we cannot do evil. We cannot be filled with anger or hate or speak evil.

We must become filled, replete with the Holy Spirit. This is where the essence of spiritual life lies. This is an art — the art of arts. Let us open our arms and throw ourselves into Christ's embrace. When Christ comes, we will have gained everything. Christ will alter everything within us. He will bring peace, joy, humility, love, prayer and the uplifting of our soul. The grace of Christ will renew us. If we turn to Him with intense longing and desire, with devotion and love, Christ will give us everything.

Without Christ it is impossible to correct ourselves. We will not be able to detach ourselves from our passions. On our own we cannot be-
John 15:5 come good. *Without me, you can do nothing.* However much we try, we
will achieve nothing. There is one thing we must do, and that is turn to

Him and love Him *with all our soul*. Love for Christ: this is the best and sole remedy for the passions. Mark 12:30

God has placed a power in man's soul. But it is up to him how he channels it — for good or for evil. If we imagine the good as a garden full of flowers, trees and plants and the evil as weeds and thorns and the power as water, then what can happen is as follows: when the water is directed towards the flower-garden, then all the plants grow, blossom and bear fruit; and at the same time, the weeds and thorns, because they are not being watered, wither and die. And the opposite, of course, can also happen.

It is not necessary, therefore, to concern yourselves with the weeds. Don't occupy yourself with rooting out evil. Christ does not wish us to occupy ourselves with the passions, but with the opposite. Channel the water, that is, all the strength of your soul, to the flowers and you will enjoy their beauty, their fragrance and their freshness.

You won't become saints by hounding after evil. Ignore evil. Look towards Christ and He will save you. Instead of standing outside the door shooing the evil one away, treat him with disdain. If evil approaches from one direction, then calmly turn in the opposite direction. If evil comes to assault you, turn all your inner strength to good, to Christ. Pray, 'Lord Jesus Christ, have mercy on me.' He knows how and in what way to have mercy on you. And when you have filled yourself with good, don't turn any more towards evil. In this way you become good on your own, with the grace of God. Where can evil then find a foothold? It disappears!

All things are possible with Christ. Where is the pain and effort for you to become good? Things are simple. You will invoke God and He will transform things into good. If you give your heart to Him, there will be no room for the other things. When you 'put on' Christ, you will not need any effort to attain virtue. He will give it to you. Are you engulfed by fear and disenchantment? Turn to Christ. Love Him simply and humbly, without any demand, and He Himself will free you. Turn to Christ and say with humility and hope like Saint Paul, *Who shall deliver me from the body of this death?* Turn towards Christ, therefore, and He will come im- Rom. 7:24
mediately. His grace will act at once.

In the spiritual life engage in your daily contest simply, easily and without force

Our religion is perfectly and profoundly conceived. What is simple is also what is most precious. Accordingly, in your spiritual life engage in your daily contest simply, easily and without force. The soul is sanctified and purified through the study of the words of the Fathers, through the memorization of the psalms and of portions of Scripture, through the singing of hymns and through the repetition of the Jesus Prayer.

Devote your efforts, therefore, to these spiritual things and ignore all the other things. We can attain to the worship of God easily and bloodlessly. There are two paths that lead to God: the hard and debilitating path with fierce assaults against evil and the easy path with love. There are many who chose the hard path and 'shed blood in order to receive Spirit'* until they attained great virtue. I find that the shorter and safer route is the path with love. This is the path that you, too, should follow.

That is, you can make a different kind of effort: to study and pray and have as your aim to advance in the love of God and of the Church. Do not fight to expel the darkness from the chamber of your soul. Open a tiny aperture for light to enter, and the darkness will disappear. The same holds for our passions and our weaknesses. Do not fight them, but transform them into strengths by showing disdain for evil. Occupy yourself with hymns of praise, with the poetic canons, with the worship of God and with divine *eros*. All the holy books of our Church — the Book of the Eight Tones, the Book of the Hours, the Psalter, the books with the Offices for the Feasts and Saint-day Commemorations — contain holy, loving words addressed to Christ. Read them with joy and love and exaltation. When you devote yourself to this effort with intense desire, your soul will be sanctified in a gentle and mystical way without your even being aware of it.

The lives of the saints, and especially the life of Saint John the Hut-dweller, made a profound impression on me. The saints are friends of God. All day long one can meditate on and take delight in their achievements and imitate their way of life. The saints gave themselves entirely to Christ.

By reading these books you will gradually acquire meekness, humility and love, and your soul will be made good. Do not choose negative methods to correct yourselves. There is no need to fear the devil, hell or anything else. These things provoke a negative reaction. I, myself, have some little experience in these matters. The object is not to sit and afflict and constrict yourself in order to improve. The object is to live, to study, to pray and to advance in love — in love for Christ and for the Church.

What is holy and beautiful and what gladdens the heart and frees the soul from every evil is the effort to unite yourself to Christ, to love

* Cf. *Wisdom of the Desert Fathers*, Abba Longinos.

Christ, to crave for Christ and to live in Christ, just as Saint Paul said, *It is no longer I who live; Christ lives in me*. This should be your aim. Let Gal. 2:20
all other efforts be secret and hidden. What must dominate is love for Christ. Let this be in your head, your thought, your imagination, your heart and your will. Your most intense effort should be how you will encounter Christ, how you will be united to Him and how you will keep Him in your heart.

Forget about all your weaknesses so that the adverse spirit does not realize what is going on and grab you and pin you down and cause you grief. Make no effort to free yourself from these weaknesses. Make your struggle with calmness and simplicity, without contortion and anxiety. Don't say: 'Now I'll force myself and I'll pray to acquire love and become good.' It is not profitable to afflict yourself to become good. In this way your negative response will be worse. Everything should be done in a natural way, calmly and freely. Nor should you pray, 'O God free me from my anger, my sorrow, etc.' It is not good to pray about or think about the specific passion; something happens in our soul and we become even more enmeshed in the passion. Attack your passion head on, and you'll see how strongly it will entwine you and grip you and you won't be able to do anything.

Don't struggle directly with temptation, don't pray for it to go away, don't say, 'Take it from me, O God!' Then you are acknowledging the strength of the temptation and it takes hold of you. Because, although you are saying 'Take it from me, O God', basically you are bringing it to mind and fomenting it even more. Your desire to be free of the passion will, of course, be there, but it will exist in a hidden and discreet way, without appearing outwardly. Remember what Scripture says: *Don't let your left hand know what your right hand is doing*. Let all your strength Matt. 6:3
be turned to love for God, worship of God and adhesion to God. In this way your release from evil and from your weaknesses will happen in a mystical manner, without your being aware of it and without exertion.

This is the kind of effort I make. I have found that the bloodless mode is the best mode of sanctification. It is better, that is, to devote ourselves to love through the study of the hymns and psalms. This study and preoccupation directs my mind to Christ and refreshes my heart without my realizing it. At the same time I pray, opening my arms in longing, love and joy, and the Lord takes me up into His love. That is our aim — to attain to that love. What do you say? Isn't this way bloodless?

There are many other ways, for example through remembrance of death, of hell and of the devil. Thus you avoid evil out of fear and through counting the cost. In my own life, I have never employed those methods which are exhausting, cause a negative reaction and often produce the opposite of the desired effect. The soul, especially when it is sensitive, is filled with gladness and enthusiasm through love; it is strengthened and transforms, alters and transfigures all the negative and ugly things.

For this reason I prefer the 'easy path', that is, the way that leads through the meditation on the poetic canons of the saints. In these canons we will discover the means employed by the saints, the ascetics and the martyrs. It is good to 'steal' their wisdom, that is, for us to do what they did. They cast themselves on Christ's love. They gave their hearts. We must steal their method.

The spiritual labour which you carry out in the depths of your soul should never be discerned

The spiritual labour which you carry out in the depths of your soul should be done in secret and never be discerned, not only by others, but not even by yourselves. What is done by our good self should not be discerned by
Matt. 6:3 our evil self: *Don't let your left hand know what your right hand is doing.* The 'left hand' is our contrary self, which, when it recognizes what is happening, will undo everything. 'Contrary self' I use as a euphemism for our evil self. Our new self is our selfhood in Christ, whereas the other self is the 'old' self. Art is required to prevent our old self from recognizing what is going on. Art and, above all, the grace of God are required.

There are some secrets here. The Gospel and Christ Himself admonish us on how we can avoid certain things which will hinder us in our struggle. This is why He says, *Don't let your left hand know what your right hand is doing.* Do you, for example, wish to taste some joy from God? What is the secret here? Even if you believe and you ask for this joy and you say, 'There is no way God will not give me this joy', nevertheless, He does not give it. You yourselves are the cause of this. It is not that God does not wish to give us this joy, but the whole secret lies in our own simplicity and meekness. When simplicity is lacking and you say, 'I'll do this, that and the other, and God will give me what I ask for', then nothing happens. Yes, indeed, I should do this, that and the other, but with such secrecy and such simplicity and such meekness, that even I who ask for the thing am unconscious of it.

Do everything simply and meekly. Do nothing with an ulterior motive. Don't say 'I'll do this in order to have that result', but do it naturally, without taking cognizance of it. That is, pray simply and don't think about what God will bestow on your soul. Don't make any calculations. You know, of course, what God bestows when you enter into communion with Him, but it is as if you don't know. Don't discuss the matter even with yourself. So when you repeat the prayer 'Lord Jesus Christ, have mercy on me', say it simply and ingenuously and think of nothing other than the prayer. These are very delicate matters and the intervention of the grace of God is required.

Your heart must be simple and not divided and dishonest, sincere and not devious and self-seeking. All people desire to find a good and simple soul; they feel comfortable with such a person and they approach him without fear and without suspicion. And such a person lives with inner peace and has good relations with everyone and with all creation.

The good-hearted person who has no devious thoughts attracts the grace of God. Above all, good-heartedness and simplicity attract the grace of God; they are the pre-conditions for God to come and *make His abode* in us. But the good-hearted person must be aware of the schem- John 14:23
ings of the devil and of men, because he will be sorely tormented. Otherwise he would have to live in a society of angels.

In Holy Scripture, the word of God speaks to us unambiguously about simplicity and tenderness of heart:

Love righteousness, you that judge the earth: be mindful of the Lord in goodness and seek Him in simplicity of heart; for He is found with those who do not tempt Him, and appears to those who are not unfaithful to Him; devious thoughts separate from God, and His power, when it is tested, reproves the unwise; for wisdom shall not enter into an evil-crafted Wisd. 1:1–4
soul, nor dwell in a body that is mortgaged to sin.' [DC]

Simplicity and goodness: that is everything if you want to acquire divine grace. How many secrets are contained in Holy Scripture! An '*evil-crafted soul*' is a poorly constructed and badly made soul and one which crafts evil. Divine Wisdom does not enter and much less does it dwell in such a soul. Where there is corruption and cunning the grace of God does not enter.

'The people that sat in darkness saw great light'

I have said this to you many times: devote yourselves to the study of Holy Scripture, the psalms and the writings of the Fathers, and study them with divine *eros*. Look up every word in the dictionary and read clearly and correctly and with attention to the meaning and every last detail of punctuation. Find out how many times a word such as, for

example, 'simplicity' occurs in Holy Scripture. The light of Christ will flood your soul. In this way the prophecy quoted by Saint Matthew will be fulfilled: *The people that sat in darkness saw great light; and light*
Matt. 4:16 *dawned on those that sat in the land and shadow of death.*

This light is the uncreated light of Christ. If we acquire this light we will know the truth. And God is truth. God knows everything. For Him all things are known and luminous. The world is the work of God. God illuminates this world with His uncreated light. God Himself is light. He is light because He knows Himself. We do not know ourselves, and that is why we are in darkness. When we allow the light to flood over us, we have communion with God. If this does not happen, we have other lights, thousands of lights, but we do not have *the* light. When we are united to Him, Christ makes us luminous. He offers the 'great light' to each of us. If only we would receive it! Then we acquire deeper faith and what hap-
Wisd. 1:1–4 pens is what the Wisdom of Solomon says: *He appears to those who are*
[DC] *not unfaithful to Him.*

To those who are distrustful, who doubt and dispute and use only the faculty of reason and are not open to God, God does not show Himself. God does not enter locked souls; He does not force an entrance. On the contrary, to those who have a simple and steadfast faith, God shows Himself and bestows on them His uncreated light. He accords it to them abundantly in this life and very much more in the next.

Do not imagine, however, that everyone here sees the light of truth with the same clarity. Each person sees according to the state of his soul, his spirit and his education. Everyone, for example, may see the same picture, but not everyone who sees it has the same emotions. This is also true of the divine light. The true light does not shine in all human hearts in the same way. Natural sunlight shines the same everywhere, but the rays of light do not penetrate far into a house that has dirty windows. The same happens with the uncreated light. If our windows are dirty and our heart is not pure then the blackness does not allow the rays to penetrate.

The same happened even to our saints and to the prophets. Even they experienced the divine light according to their purity. Does this not agree with what theology says?

Vigilance is passionate love for God

Be mindful always of God. That is how our mind will acquire agility. Agility of mind comes from vigilance. Vigilance is passionate love for

God. It is always having your heart and mind focused on Christ, even if you are engaged in other tasks. Vigilance requires love and yearning for Christ. You will acquire remembrance of God through the prayer 'Lord Jesus Christ…', through the prayers of the Church, through the hymns and through bringing to mind the acts of God and recalling passages from Holy Scripture and from other spiritual books. This, of course, all requires good intention. It can't be done by force and comes about primarily through divine grace. But divine grace requires in turn its preconditions: love and humility.

If you live in the embrace of divine grace, evil will not harm you. If you do not live with divinity, evil will encircle you and you will be overtaken by indolence and you will be afflicted. If you see someone who is indolent, then the person is sick in the soul. Often when we see a quiet, discreet and circumspect person, we say, 'A very fine and saintly person.' And yet he may be indolent. The indolent, sluggard and lazy are not acceptable in the eyes of God. Laziness is a very bad thing. Indolence is an illness; it is a sin. God does not want us to be indolent. Can you live in idleness and ill-discipline? You say, 'I forgot to close the door on leaving the room', for example. What does 'I forgot' mean? You should remember and pay attention! On the contrary, constant effort, movement, work and activity are a virtue. Physical exertion is a struggle, a spiritual struggle. The more thoughtless you are, the more you are tormented. On the contrary, the more scrupulous and careful you are, the happier you are.

In the cell I have on the Holy Mountain there is an old latch on the door. In order to open the door you have to press it and then it makes a very loud noise. Every time someone would come and press it down, the latch would go 'cra-aa-a-ck'. The noise could be heard a hundred yards away. No one could open it without making a noise, even though it was easy and I showed them how to do it. But when they tried again, again they made a noise.

These things appear very simple, but they are connected with our whole way of life. The more you approach God, the more careful you are — without trying to be — in all things, including spiritual things. As you pay attention to your soul, with the grace of God, you become more vigilant. Have you ever in your life worked without distracting thoughts? You don't make mistakes. The grace of God protects you.

A Christian mustn't be indolent; he mustn't sleep. Wherever he is and wherever he goes, he should be taking wings with his prayer and with his imagination. And indeed it is possible for a Christian who loves God to fly with his imagination; to soar among the stars, in infinity, in the mystery and eternity, in God; to be a high-flyer; to pray and feel that he too becomes God by grace; to become all wings and fly with his thought. And his thought is not pure imagination. When we say 'fly', we are not talking about something imaginary, but something real. A Christian does not live 'in the clouds' as the saying goes. He understands reality and experiences it. What he reads in the Gospel and in the Fathers, he takes to heart and experiences; he goes into the details and delves deeply into the meaning and makes it his life. He becomes a sensitive receiver of signals from God.

When you become a captive of good, sin ceases and Christ lives

Inside us we have two worlds: the world of good and the world of evil. And both of these draw power from one source. This power is like the battery. If evil inserts its plug into the battery, it leads us to destruction. But if good connects with the battery, then everything in our life is beautiful, serene and divine. But the same source supplies power to our good and our 'contrary' self. At all times we are captive to one of the two, to good or to evil. We must try to be captive to good.

Let me give you another example. All around us are the radio waves of the Greek Radio station, but we are not aware of them. As soon as we switch on our radio receiver, then we become aware of them and we hear and sense them.

The same happens when we enter the spiritual world. We experience Christ and we take off! We feel great joy and have wondrous spiritual experiences. Then we gradually become captives of good, captives of Christ. And when you become captive of good, you cannot speak evil, you cannot hate and you cannot tell lies. You are unable to, even if you want to. How can the evil one approach to bring despair, disenchantment, indolence and suchlike? Divine grace fills you and these things have no power to enter. They cannot enter when your room is full of your aether-borne spiritual friends — I mean the angels, the saints, the martyrs and above all Christ. The opposite occurs when you become captive to the old self. Then you are dominated by the evil spirit and you cannot do good; you are filled with malice, condemnation and anger.

When evil assaults you, you must be agile and turn at once to the good. Turn, transform and transfigure every evil into good. This transformation comes about only through grace. Water, for example, becomes wine at the Wedding in Cana. He who is above nature is well pleased… This is supernatural. Of course, it can also be transformed into wine or butter with chemical elements and become exactly like the genuine product. But this does not have in it authenticity. True transformation is made by divine grace. For this to happen, a person must have given himself to Christ *with all his soul and with all his heart.* Mark 12:30

Remember Stephen the first martyr. He was possessed by God and, even while he was being persecuted and stoned, he prayed for his persecutors, saying, *Lord, do not count this sin against them.* Why did Saint Acts 7:60
Stephen behave in this way? Quite simply, because he could behave no differently. He was a captive of good. Do you think that it is easy to have a hailstorm of stones thrown at you? Try having one stone thrown at you! All very well, but when the stone hits you, you'll start to shout and swear. That shows that we are overtaken by the evil spirit. And in this situation, how can Christ come and where can he find a place to remain within us? Every space within us is occupied. But as soon as we enter into the spiritual life, as soon as we enter into Christ, everything changes. If you are a thief, you stop stealing; if you are a murderer, you stop murdering; if you are resentful, you cease to think with malice… Everything ceases. Sin ceases and Christ lives in you. It is what Saint Paul said: *It is no longer I who live; Christ lives in me.* Gal. 2:20

Freedom cannot be achieved unless we free our inner self from confusions and passions. And this, of course, can only be done with Christ. Joy is found in Christ. Christ transforms the passion into joy.

This is our Church, this is our joy, this is everything for us. And this is what people today are looking for. They take poisons and drugs in order to be transported into worlds of joy, but of false joy. They sense something for a moment, but the next day they are broken and exhausted. The one wears people down, consumes, exhausts and torments them, while the other — abandonment to Christ, I mean — gives them life and joy and makes them rejoice in living and gives them a sense of strength and magnificence.

This is our religion: sublimity, magnificence, grace, joy and exultation! How very intensely the prophet David experienced all this! He said, Ps. 83:3
My soul longs and faints for the courts of the Lord. How marvellous! [84:2]

A person can become a saint anywhere

It is a great art to succeed in having your soul sanctified. A person can become a saint anywhere. He can become a saint in Omonia Square,* if he

* Omonia Square: the commercial centre of Athens, also synonymous with vice and corruption.

wants. At your work, whatever it may be, you can become saints — through meekness, patience and love. Make a new start every day, with new resolution, with enthusiasm and love, prayer and silence — not with anxiety so that you get a pain in the chest.

If it happens, for example, that you are given tasks to do that fall outside the remit of your duties it is not right for you to protest and become irritated and complain. Such vexations do you harm. Look on all things as opportunities to be sanctified. And there is a further gain. When you are assigned many tasks, you learn how to do everything in your area of work and you become more responsible. You learn things that perhaps will be required later. If the tasks you are assigned are beyond your abilities, however, you can always say politely, 'Excuse me, but I am unable to do this task.' But equally you can say nothing, and all the effort you make will be for your good.

That's what I did, as I've told you, when I was little. My father went to America to work on the Panama Canal. I was little and my parents were poor. My mother sent me to a shop in Chalkida. There were two other boys there. They were constantly bossing me around. I did whatever they told me to do without thinking it was unfair. And that turned out for my good. One day when I was sweeping the shop there were some unground coffee beans that had spilled on the floor, I bent down and picked them up in my hand to put them back in the sack. The boss was in his office and saw me and he realized what I was about to do and he called me over. He also called the other boys and gave them a lesson. Great wastage went on in that shop and I made a good impression on him. From that day we shared out the jobs and introduced some order into the shop.* I worked at everything conscientiously and without objection. Did it do me any harm?

Work with vigilance, simply and naturally, without anxiety, with joy and happiness, with a good disposition. And then divine grace will come.

Deal with all situations with love, kindness, meekness, patience and humility

Certain people often become overwhelmingly distressed about the state of the world. They are vexed when they see that the will of God is not done today by others and by themselves and they suffer with the physical and psychological pain of others. This sensitivity is a gift of God. We find it more frequently among women. Souls with this sensitivity are

* See p. 1 above.

especially receptive to the will of God. These sensitive souls have the ability to advance greatly in the life in Christ, because they love God and do not wish to cause Him vexation. They do, however, run a danger. If they do not entrust their life fully to Christ, it is possible for the evil spirit to exploit their sensitivity and to lead them to depression and despair.

Sensitivity cannot be corrected. It can only be transformed, altered and transfigured so as to become love, joy and worship. How? By turning upwards. By turning every sorrow into knowledge of Christ, love of Christ and worship of Christ. And Christ, who constantly waits with eagerness to help us, will give you His grace and His strength to transform sorrow into joy, into love for our fellows and worship of Him. Thus darkness will flee. Remember Saint Paul. What did he say? *Now I rejoice in my sufferings.* Col. 1:24

Let your soul devote itself to the prayer 'Lord Jesus Christ, have mercy on me' in all your worries, for everything and for everyone. Don't look at what's happening to you, look at the light, at Christ, just as the child looks to its mother when something happens to it. See everything without anxiety, without depression, without strain and without stress. There is no need to exert yourselves and strain yourselves. Let all your effort be directed towards the light and towards acquiring the light, so that instead of devoting yourselves to thoughts of despair, which do not come from the Spirit of God, you devote yourselves to the praise of God.

All the unpleasant things which are within your soul and cause you anxiety can become occasions for the glorification of God and cease to torment you. Have trust in God. Then you will forget your worries and become His instruments. Distress shows that we are not entrusting our life to Christ. Doesn't Saint Paul say, *We are afflicted on every side, but not distressed*? 2 Cor. 4:8

Deal with everything with love, kindness, meekness, patience and humility. Be rocks. Let all the waves break over you and turn back leaving you untroubled. You'll say, 'That sounds fine, but is it possible?' The answer is, 'Yes, always — with the grace of God.' If we look at things in human terms, of course, it is impossible. But instead of affecting you adversely, all these things can be of benefit to you, increasing your patience and your faith. Because all the difficulties that surround us represent a kind of gymnastics for us. We exercise ourselves in patience and endurance. Listen and I'll give you an example.

A man once came to me and started to recount all his grievances with his wife. When he had finished I said to him:

'Are you really so stupid?'

'What's so stupid about what I've been saying?' he asked.

'Everything,' I replied. 'This wife of yours loves you deeply.'

'I know,' he said, 'but look at all the things that she does to me…'

'She does all these things to you to sanctify you, but you're too dim-witted to realize it. Instead of being sanctified, you are infuriated and you make your life hell.'

If only he had had patience and humility, he wouldn't have missed those opportunities for sanctification.

Patience is a great thing, a great virtue. Christ said that if you don't
Cf. Luke have patience, you will lose your souls, and in order to gain your souls
21:19 you must have patience. Patience is love, and without love you can't have patience. But it's a matter of faith. In reality, we are without faith, because we don't know how God works and frees us from difficulties and vexations. Make petition to our Holy Lady:

Turn now my lamentation to joy
And into gladness change my mourning and sorrowing,
My grieving and pain convert to mirth, into festal delight,
*O Most Blessed Virgin who gave birth to God.**

Our disposition to love God also contains within it a certain pain. When we wish to live spiritually we suffer pain because we need to sever every bond that links us to matter. But when we wish to satisfy ourselves or others, what we expend is love, an energy, a power of our soul. We need to take care about how and for whom we expend that energy.

The sorrow which we have in our love for God contains within it joy, and on account of this joy we persevere and do not give way to soul-destroying depression. Where there is humility, there is no depression. An egotist is vexed at the slightest thing. A humble person is free and independent from everyone and everything. This comes about only through union with Christ. All our senses function in accordance with the law of our Lord. You are ready to empty yourself to anyone whomsoever. This is freedom. Where there is love, there is freedom. When you live in the love of God, you live in freedom.

With eager longing for Christ the power of the soul eludes the snares of the enemy

Many people, Christians included, refuse to accept the existence of the devil. The demonic, however, is something that cannot be denied.

* Canon to the Holy Theotokos from the *Theotokarion* edited by Saint Nikodemos (Tone 5, Tuesday Vespers).

I believe that the devil exists and, indeed, that if we remove from the Gospel belief in the existence of the devil, the whole of the Gospel falls to the ground. *For this purpose the Son of God was manifested, that he might destroy the works of the devil.* And elsewhere Scripture says *the demons* 1 John 3:8
also believe, and tremble, and that Christ was incarnate *so that through* Jas. 2:19
death he might destroy him who had the power of death, that is the devil. Heb. 2:14
What do these passages reveal? Don't they speak about the nullification of the devil by Christ Himself? We cannot ignore the existence of the devil whose works Christ came to set at naught.

But I tell you always that instead of concerning yourselves with the devil and his knaveries, and instead of paying attention to your passions, you should turn to the love of Christ. Look how the poet expresses this in the Canon for Saint Onesimos:

> *By the robustness of your mind, Onesimos,*
> *You cast down the machinations of deception,*
> *And with instruments of piety, wrought in wisdom divine,*
> *You set them all at naught.**

Look here at each word in this finely structured verse: 'machinations of deception'. The evil one set up snares and traps and Saint Onesimos put him to flight with the robustness of his mind. With his robust mind he defeated all comers. He worshipped and craved for Christ. That's how it's done.

Satan contrives machinations of deception. Without our being aware of it, the evil one sets snares. With eager longing for Christ, the power of the soul escapes from the traps and runs to Christ. This is a marvellous thing — a more elegant approach. To enter into the fray with your enemy means getting involved in the hurly-burly of battle. In the love of Christ, however, the confusions and pressures of combat are avoided. Here the power of the soul is transfigured without effort. You mustn't respond with the same means. Show indifference! This indifference towards one's enemy is a great art — the art of arts. It is achieved only through divine grace. The contest with evil through the grace of God is carried out without bloodshed and without exertion, without pressure and without strain.

What have we said? Haven't we said that the devil has many wiles? The machinations of the devil are wicked. Terrible! So we in turn must contrive pious mechanisms of defense, devoid of wickedness, in order

*Sung on his feast day on 15th February (2nd *troparion* of the 7th Ode).

to destroy the power of his snares. Didn't Saint Paul say something of this sort in his epistle to the Ephesians? *For our struggle is not against flesh and blood, but against principalities, against powers, against the rulers of the darkness of this world, against the spirits of wickedness in the*
Eph. *heavens; therefore put on the whole armour of God so that you may be*
6:12–13 *able to resist in the evil day and stand firm having done everything.* When we put on the whole armour of God we will achieve all things — and indeed very easily. All things are easy once we enter the grace of God. For then we are freer and stronger. Divine grace protects us. If we fight the good fight and fall in love with Christ, then we acquire divine grace. And once we are armed with divine grace, we are in no danger and the devil sees us and takes flight.

This is how I, in my own poor efforts, have approached matters since I was a boy and I've acquired some experience in all this. I didn't want to think about the snares; I was indifferent to them. To begin with, it is true, I set out on a different tack. I laid down and said that I was dead. I chastised myself with the chastisement of death. Demons would come and, for all my fear, I would still say, 'Maintain constant remembrance of death and of hell.' But I gave up this approach. I had experience of those things, and they are all right for beginners. But *he who fears is not*
1 John 4:18 *made perfect in love.*

Saint Augustine writes: 'Meditations preoccupy me and I am caught up in disputations.'* You see, here the old, fallen self has entered into dialogue with the new self in Christ. It has become engaged in discussion. I don't like to converse with the 'old' self. That is, it grabs me from behind, by the cassock, but at once I open my arms to Christ and so, with divine grace, I show contempt for it and cease to think about it. I act like the little child who opens his arms and falls into his mother's embrace. It's a mystery and I don't know if you understand just how fine a matter it is. When you try to escape from the old self without the gift of grace, you are drawn into it and experience that old self. But with the gift of grace, however, it no longer concerns you. It continues to exist deep down. All things remain within us, ugly things included; they do not disappear. But with grace, however, they are transubstantiated, altered and transformed. Isn't this what Saint Basil's prayer of the Ninth Hour says: '...so that setting aside the old man, we may put on the new man and live with You our Master?'

Christ wishes us to unite ourselves to Him and He waits outside the

* (Pseudo-)Augustine, *Soliloquia*, Chapter 2 (*Patrologia Latina* 40. 866).

door of our soul. It is up to us to accept the divine grace. Only divine grace can change us. On our own we can do nothing. Grace will give us everything. For our part, we should attempt to reduce our egotism and self-centeredness and to have humility. If we give ourselves to Christ, all the negative reactions of body and soul go away.

Remember Saint Paul who said, *O wretched man that I am! Who shall deliver me from the body of this death?* He said this because, when he was Rom. 7:24
still at the beginning, he felt that his soul was incapable of doing good. He did the evil that he didn't want, and so he confessed, *I do not do what I want, but I do the very thing I hate.* The spirit of evil came to draw him Rom. 7:15
away from his struggle. It came and instilled fear into him, saying, 'You will die.' But when the grace of God entered his soul, all the difficulties disappeared and he exclaimed enthusiastically, 'It is no longer I who live; Christ lives in me...for me to live is Christ, and to die is gain.' Here, you Cf. Gal. 2:20
see, there is neither death, nor hell, nor the devil! Whereas he was pre- & Phil. 1:21
viously incapable of doing good, he later became incapable of doing evil. He was unable to and had no will to. His soul had been permeated by God, filled by Christ, and he was unable to think of anything else or contain anything else within him.

With divine grace all things are possible. With divine grace the martyrs of Christ did not feel the pains of their martyrdom. With divine grace all things become painless. Employ this gentle method. Don't struggle to expel darkness and evil. You achieve nothing by flailing at darkness. Are you in darkness and do you want to escape? Then what do you do? You assault darkness with all your might, but it doesn't go away. Do you wish light? Open a little hole and a ray of sunlight will enter and light will come. Instead of expelling darkness and instead of fighting the enemy to prevent him entering into you, open your arms to Christ's embrace. This is the most perfect way. That is, don't wage war on evil directly, but love Christ and His light, and evil will then retreat.

Treat every attack by the evil one with contempt

The most important weapon to use against the devil is the Holy Cross, of which he is terrified. But make the sign of the cross correctly: with the three fingers of the right hand joined together, touch your forehead, your abdomen, your right shoulder and finally you left shoulder. The sign of the cross may be made in conjunction with prostrations.

Communication with Christ, when it takes place simply and naturally and without force, makes the devil flee. Satan does not go away with force and coercion. He is sent away with meekness and prayer. He retreats when he sees the soul showing contempt for him and turning in love towards Christ. Contempt is something he is unable to bear because he is arrogant. But when you apply force to yourself, the evil spirit becomes aware of the fact and starts to fight you. Do not concern yourself with the devil, nor pray for him to leave. The more you pray for him to leave, the more tightly he embraces you. Show contempt for the devil. Don't meet him head on. When you struggle against the devil with obstinacy, he flies at you like a tiger or a wild cat. When you shoot a bullet at him, he lobs a hand-grenade at you. And when you throw a bomb at him, he launches a rocket against you. Don't look at evil. Turn your eyes to God's embrace and fall into His arms and continue on your way. Abandon yourself to Him; love Christ; live in vigilance. Vigilance is essential for the person who loves God.

Things are simple and easy in the spiritual life, in the life in Christ, as long as you possess discernment. When something bothers you — a seductive thought, a temptation, an assault — ignore all these things, and turn your attention, your eyes, to Christ. He will then take over the task of raising you up. He will take you by the hand and will give you His divine grace abundantly. All you need to do is make a tiny little effort. The human contribution in all this represents only a millionth of a millionth part — a slight inclination, that is. Take a step in God's direction, and in a split second divine grace will come. As soon as you think of it, the Holy Spirit will come. You don't do anything. You just move in that direction, and divine grace comes immediately. As soon as you let out a groan, it comes and acts. What is it Saint Paul says? *The Holy Spirit makes inter-*
Rom. 8:26 *cession for us with groanings which cannot be uttered.* Great wisdom! These are not simply words, but the living Word of God.

When you see the contrary spirit approaching to take hold of you, do not be afraid; neither look at it nor attempt to expel it from within you. What do you do? The best thing is contempt. Open your arms to Christ like the little child that sees a wild beast approaching and is not afraid because his father is at his side and he throws himself into his father's embrace. That is how to deal with every attack by the evil one and with every evil thought — with contempt.

At the moment when your soul is in danger and you are struggling, cry out, 'Lord Jesus Christ, have mercy on me.' Beat off everything with timely prayer. This is the great secret. At the moment of temptation, just as you are about to show contempt for it, the evil one grabs you, pins you down and throttles you and does what he wishes and not what you wish.

You must make your move towards God in time. But for you to succeed in this, divine grace must illuminate you. If this isn't done at once, then the evil one will grab hold of you, and in spite of your efforts to throw him off, he will already have you in his power. Let me give you an example.

I once asked someone to do something for me, but he refused saying that it wasn't in accord with scientific principles. I insisted, but he remained adamant. I began to feel exasperation, but then I realized what was happening, and at once I turned to Christ and managed to prevent evil gaining a hold.

This is our method. We will raise our arms to Christ and He will give us His grace.

Listen to another example.

Once I was on a road in the Tourkovounia area of Athens where I was living. The road was very steep with a slope running down for about two hundred yards. At the top of the road the ground leveled out. Nikos's mother was up there talking to two other women from the neighbourhood. At the bottom of the road her child, Nikos, was playing with other children. Suddenly, I saw Nikos running up the hill and as soon as he got to the top he rushed and buried his face in his mother's lap and burst into tears.

'What's the matter?' she asked.

'Manolya's boy punched me,' he said.

His tears stopped at once, as soon as he found his mother.

What do I mean by this? At the moment of temptation, the easiest thing to do is to turn to your loved one, to God, and to look to Him steadfastly and expectantly and you will be filled with strength at once. As soon as you see evil coming to get you, ignore it and run to God's embrace. Turn to Him in time. And so when you go towards good, you cease to remember evil. This is the secret: show contempt for evil. But you are unable to do this unless you turn to Christ. We say, 'Show contempt for evil!' It's an easy thing to say, but it is not easy to do. This contempt is a great art.

Contempt for the evil spirit is possible only with the grace of God. Turn to Christ, run to Christ, open your arms to Christ, try to get to know Christ, to love Christ and to feel Christ. And through this effort, when your motives are pure and sincere, grace opens your soul and says to you:
Sleeper awake and rise from the dead and Christ will shine on you. And Eph. 5:14
there in the divine light we will live forever, provided our soul loves and yearns for God. So, with Christ's grace, all things are easy and Christ's
words are true when He says, *My yoke is easy, and my burden is light.* Matt. 11:30

Some people see the devil appearing to them in various forms — making noises and attacking them and so on. These things, in most cases, happen to people who are deeply confused. The great Fathers of the Church, such as Saint John Chrysostom, Saint Basil the Great and the others, don't tell us about the devil and about how he appears or any such thing. They followed the path we have been describing, namely love for Christ. Satan appears according to the kind of person you are. If someone has not set out on the spiritual life in a normal manner, or if he is burdened by something hereditary, he sees Satan appearing before him and causing mayhem and so on. Sometimes a person can even end up with schizophrenia. The schizophrenic is affected by the experiences of the fallen life of his forebears.

And something else. Don't give any rights of access to the devil. I don't allow even one resentful thought to remain within me, not a single flash of egotism, in case the devil finds an open window. An open window is a right of access. When you distance yourself from God, you put yourself in danger, because Satan finds you on your own and takes dominion over you. Pay heed to what I say, because I have some experience of these things.

Holy humility is complete trust in God

Complete trust in God — that's what holy humility is. Complete obedience to God, without protest, without reaction, even when some things seem difficult and unreasonable. Abandonment to the hands of God. The words we repeat during the Divine Liturgy say it all: 'Let us commend our whole life to Christ our God.' The secret prayer of the priest says the same thing: 'We commend our whole life and hope to You, O loving Master, and we entreat You and beseech You and supplicate You...'* To You, O Lord, we leave everything. That is what trust in God is. This is holy humility. This is what transfigures a person and makes him a 'God-man'.

The humble person is conscious of his inner state and, however unsightly it is, he does not lose his personality. He knows he is sinful and is grieved by the fact, but he does not despair and does not annihilate himself. The person who possesses holy humility does not speak at all, that is, he doesn't react. He accepts to be criticized and rebuked by others, without getting angry and defending himself. He does not lose his equilibrium. The opposite happens with the egotist, the person who has a sense of inferiority. To begin with he seems to be humble, but if

* Prayer read by the priest before the Lord's Prayer.

he is goaded a little, he immediately loses his calm and is irritated and upset.

The humble person believes that all things depend on Christ and that Christ gives His grace and in that way he makes progress. The person who possesses holy humility lives even now in the earthly uncreated Church. He always has the joy of Christ, even in the most displeasing circumstances. We see this in the lives of the saints. What was Saint Paul? He was a man like us. But what happened? He became an instrument of God,
a *chosen vessel*. His words bear witness to this: 'It is no longer I who live; Acts 9:15
Christ lives in me...for me to live is Christ, and to die is gain.' He was Cf. Gal. 2:20
consumed by burning love for Christ. His humility raised him up to that & Phil. 1:21
state. To burn for God — that is everything!

If you have love for your neighbour and for God, God will give you humility and He will bestow on you sanctification. If you do not have love for God and for your neighbour, and if you are indolent, Satan will tyrannize you, your old self will take revenge on you, and you will find fault with everyone and everything and be forever complaining. You will think that your work and responsibilities or your exhaustion are to blame. You will say, 'How on earth did I end up in this state, why am I behaving in this way?' without being aware of what induced this state. This state, however, is the revenge of your instincts.

When a person lives without God, without serenity, without trust, and with anxiety, worry, depression and despair, he develops physical and mental illnesses. Mental illness, neurosis and split personality are demonic states. Feigned humility is also demonic. It's what's called an inferiority complex. True humility doesn't speak and doesn't make a show of humility. It doesn't say, for example, 'I am a sinner and unworthy and the very least of men...'. The humble person fears that such words may lead him to fall into vanity. The grace of God does not approach here. On the contrary, the grace of God is to be found where there is true humility, divine humility, perfect trust in God, total dependence on Him.

It is a priceless thing to be led by God and to have no will of your own. The slave has no will of his own. He does his master's will. The faithful servant of God does the same. Become His slave, and in God you will find freedom. This is true freedom — to burn for God. This is everything. We have said this time and again. If you are defeated by God, you are enslaved to Him and you live in the freedom enjoyed by the children of God. *For by whomsoever a person is defeated, by the same he is led in*
bondage. This also happens, however, in the case of the monk who 2 Pet. 2:19
lives in total obedience to his elder and God bestows on him His

grace. Remember the prophet Elisha. He took the cloak and struck the
waters and they did not part in two as they had done for the prophet Elijah, because he did what he did with egotism and not with humility. Once
Cf. 4 Kings he was humiliated and saw that on his own he achieved nothing, he
[2 Kings] humbly sought the help of his elder, the prophet Elijah, and he received
2:8–15 the grace. The waters parted and a path opened for him to cross.

A little effort, of course, is required, but profound humility is not acquired only by struggle and exertion. It is a gift of grace. I say this from
Ps. 126:1 my own experience: what I have, I have by grace. *Except the Lord build*
[127:1] *the house, they labour in vain that build it.* Christ gives everything.

We must all be humble: in thought, in word and in behaviour. We will never go before God and say, 'I have virtues.' God does not want our virtues. Always appear before God as a sinner, not with despair, but 'trusting in the mercy of His compassion'.* Suffice it that we find the secret.

The secret is love for Christ and humility. Christ will give us the humility. We with our weaknesses are unable to love Him. Let Him love us. Let us entreat Him earnestly to love us and to give us the zeal for us to love Him too.

If you want to philosophize about it, place all blame on your evil self and you will be humbled continually. It is humility to believe that all people are good, and if you hear something negative about someone, not to believe it; to love everyone and not think badly of anyone and to pray for everyone. No other philosophy is needed. The heart of a vain person cannot be humbled. When he is corrected or rebuked, he reacts angrily, and when he is praised and flattered he behaves unbecomingly. Whatever you say to him, he takes in such a way as to become even more swollen with pride. His whole world centres on himself. On the contrary, the sinner who repents and makes confession transcends himself. When he has made confession, he does not turn back.

The vain person alienates his soul from eternal life. In the final analysis, conceit is straightforward stupidity! Vanity makes us void and empty. When we do something for show, we end up empty in soul. What we do, we should do as thanksgiving to God — selflessly, without vanity, without pride, without egotism, without, without, without… Be like a singer in a church or monastery who sings to God with an angelic voice, but without being aware of all the people who are listening to him, that is, without giving it any thought. Is it possible? It's not easy. It's difficult. And that's why many singers have been led astray. As a rule, all good

* Words from one of the *troparia* sung after Psalm 50 [51] in Sunday Matins during Lent.

singers have a great conceit. Not all, certainly, but the majority. But when you have humility, even if you sing and read well, you are not affected by those who are listening to you. You'll ask me, 'And what about if you sing and read well and your elder is listening?' That's of no importance, if you have humility.

We must, at all costs, become good. That's what I, poor wretch, try to do. But on the one hand I get worn out, and on the other my illness weighs me down, and I am unable to do anything. Nevertheless, I try. I wish to become better, I wish to worship God with love and yearning, and I dream about it and try my best, but nothing happens. But the thing that gives me joy and satisfaction is that finally I am attempting to love Christ. I haven't succeeded, but it is something I desire strongly.

Those who 'tempt' God are those who doubt

Solomon the Wise says that Christ *is to be found with those who do not* Wisd. 1:2
tempt Him. Those who 'tempt' God are those who doubt, hesitate or, even [DC]
worse, resist His omnipotence and wisdom. Our soul mustn't resist and say, 'Why did God make things in this way and not that, could He not have made things differently?' All these things reveal an inner meanness of spirit and reaction. They reveal the great idea we have of ourselves, our pride and our great conceit. People are greatly tormented by these 'whys'. They cause what people generally call 'complexes'. 'Why am I so tall?' for example. Or the opposite: 'Why am I so small?' These questions do not go away. The person may pray and hold vigils, but the outcome is the opposite of the desired. And the person suffers and protests to no avail. With Christ, however, and with grace, all these torments disappear. There remains 'something' deep down, the 'why' is still there, but the grace of God overshadows the person and, while the root is the 'complex', above ground what grows is a rose bush with beautiful roses. And the more it is watered by faith, love, patience and humility, the more evil ceases to have any power and ceases to exist. That is, it is not made to disappear, it simply withers away. On the other hand, the more the rose bush is not watered, the more it withers, dries up and is lost, whereas the thorns at once sprout up.

It is not only our resistance and our 'whys' that show that we are tempting God. We tempt God when we ask something from Him while our life is far removed from Him. We tempt Him when we ask for something, but our life is not in concord with His will. On the one hand we are filled with things opposed to God — anxiety and worry — and on the other hand we make petition to Him.

'A fat belly does not make for a refined mind'

You don't become holy by fighting evil. Let evil be. Look towards Christ and that will save you. What makes a person saintly is love — the adoration of Christ which cannot be expressed, which is beyond expression, which is beyond... And such a person attempts to undertake ascetic exercises and to do things to cause himself to suffer for the love of God.

No monk became holy without ascetic exercises. No one can ascend to spirituality without exercising himself. These things must be done. Ascetic exercises are such things as prostrations, vigils and so on, but done without force. All are done with joy. What is important is not the prostrations we will make or the prayers, but the act of self-giving, the passionate love for Christ and for spiritual things. There are many people who do these things, not for God, but for the sake of exercise, in order to reap physical benefit. But spiritual people do them in order to reap spiritual benefit; they do them for God. At the same time, however, the body is greatly benefited and doesn't fall ill. Many good things flow from them.

Among the various ascetic exercises, prostrations, vigils and other deprivations, is fasting. 'A fat belly does not make for a refined mind', as I know the Fathers like to say.* All the books of the Fathers speak of fasting. They emphasize that we should not eat foods that are difficult to digest, or that are rich and fatty, because they are bad for the body and for the soul. They say that a lamb eats only grass and that is why it is so placid. That's why we say someone 'is like a lamb'. The dog or cat and all the carnivorous animals are all fierce animals. Meat is bad for people. Fruit and vegetables are good. That's why the Fathers speak about fasting and condemn overeating and the pleasure one feels when one eats rich foods. Let our food be more simple, and don't let's occupy ourselves so much with it.

It is not food or good conditions of life which secure good health. It is a saintly life, the life of Christ. I know hermits who fasted with the greatest austerity and were never ill. You're not in danger of coming to any harm by fasting. No one has become ill by fasting. People who eat meat and eggs and milk-products are much more likely to become ill than those who adopt a meagre diet. This is an established fact and endorsed by medical science. Indeed, this is what doctors recommend. Not only do those who fast not come to any harm, but they are cured of illnesses.

To do this, however, you need to have faith. Otherwise you will feel

* See, for example, Gregory the Theologian (*PG* 37. 723) and John Chrysostom (*PG* 62. 569).

empty and nauseous and have a craving for food. Fasting is also a matter of faith. It does you no harm when you digest your food properly. The hermits transform air into albumen and fasting doesn't affect them. When you have love for things divine, you can fast with pleasure and everything is easy; otherwise everything would seem impossibly difficult. All those who have given their heart to Christ and pray with fervent love have managed to overcome and control their craving for food and lack of continence.

There are many people today who were unable to fast for a single day and now live as vegetarians, not for religious reasons, but simply because they believed it would be good for their health. But you have to believe that you won't come to any harm by not eating meat. When someone is ill, however, there is no sin in his eating meat, eggs and dairy products to restore his health.

Salt is required by the human body. It is often heard that salt is harmful, but this is not true. It is an element that is necessary. Indeed, there are some people who have great need of it. For others it is not so necessary and some for whom it is harmful. It's a matter of the trace elements in the body. Tests are required.

I have a great dream! — for the Holy Mountain, that is. We used to order wheat to mill for brown bread. And now I am thinking of taking various pulses and grinding them and mixing them up: wheat with rice, with soya, soya flour with lentils, etc. And then we have the marrows and the tomatoes and the potatoes and all the vegetables. Father Hesychios and I used to day-dream together. We said we would go and become hermits somewhere and sow wheat and then soak it in water and eat it. Isn't that what Saint Basil did in the desert? But nowadays it seems very austere to us.

ON THE MONASTIC LIFE

In the monastery all things are sanctified: there are so many souls praying, engaging in ascetic exercises and living the life of God

The monastic life transcends the common human lot

The monastic life is a great thing! Very great. It is a great and exalted life, a divine and poetic life. It is a life which transcends the common human lot. The monk may live on earth, but he journeys in the heavens among the stars and in infinity. He experiences God and heaven in imagination. He lives an extraordinary life. They call it an angelic life, and such it truly is.

For the monk to live this life properly, however, he needs to have a monastic consciousness. He gains this consciousness by turning with all his being towards God and towards the aim he has set himself. He lives in silence, with prayer of the heart, with asceticism and in obedience. He must die to everything in order to live in Christ. He wakes up full of zeal, completes his rule of private prayer and runs eagerly to the church services and to his various duties. He has one object alone in mind — how to be pleasing to God, how to serve God and how to become an occasion for God's name to be glorified. He constantly remembers the vows he made before God when he became a monk. This is why he frequently reads the Service of Monastic Tonsure with care. He does not disrupt the order and rule of life in the monastery. He observes all the regulations.

If a monk is to make progress in a monastery, he needs to engage willingly in spiritual struggle without pressure from anyone else. He needs to do everything with joy and eagerness and not as a chore. A monk is not a person who is forced to do something mechanically and reluctantly. Whatever he does, he does solely out of love for the heavenly Bridegroom, out of divine *eros*. He doesn't bring thoughts of hell or death into his mind. Monasticism mustn't be a negative flight from the world, but a flight of divine love and divine worship.

The whole secret is prayer, self-giving and love directed towards Christ. Monastic life is carefree and joyous. A monk must taste the sweetness of prayer and be attracted by divine love. He will not be able to endure the monastic life if he does not know the sweetness of prayer. Without this he will not be able to stay in the monastery.

But what keeps him in the monastery along with prayer is his work and his handicraft. Work is not one thing and prayer another. Work does not prevent prayer, on the contrary, it reinforces it and makes it better. It's a matter of love. Work, indeed, is like praying, like making prostrations. Work is a blessing. That's why we see that Christ called his disciples and indeed his prophets while they were working, for example, while one was fishing and another was tending his sheep.

A monk's joy is to enter into the love of God, to enter into the Church, the Holy Trinity and into Christ. He is united with Christ and his heart leaps for joy and is filled with grace. Christ is his joy, his enthusiasm, his hope and his love. What can I say? When I, by the grace of God, went to the Holy Mountain, what a life I led — such love, such devotion, such desire, such obedience, such prayer. How we felt one for another with a smile and with acts of kindness. Truly it is a heavenly way of life!

The hermit who goes into the desert sacrifices everything, even his sleep, provided he can find a way to sense the grace of God and feel Christ's warmth and embrace; if only he can be united with God and sense God's company, his union with God; if only he can become one with others, just as the Three Persons of the Holy Trinity are one. So he leaves this world not with a sense of despair, but with a great sense of comfort and in company with a large retinue. His retinue is the whole of nature, the birds and the animals, all the saints, the martyrs and the angels. Above all he is in the company of our All-holy Lady and her Son.

The monastic life flows from Holy Scripture

All things have their foundation in the eternal book, in Holy Scripture. The monastic life flows from Holy Scripture, from the Gospel. What does the Old Testament say? *Leave your country and your kindred and your
father's house, and come to the land which I will show you.* And what Gen. 12:1
does Christ say? *He who loves father or mother more than me is not worthy of me, and he who loves son or daughter more than me is not worthy
of me; and he who does not take up his cross and follow after me is not* Matt.
worthy of me. 10:37–8

Equally, all that the holy Fathers have to say about monasticism is inspired by Holy Scripture. It's impossible to reject any one of the Fathers. If you reject Saint Symeon the New Theologian then you will be obliged to reject Saint Paul also, because what Saint Symeon said and experienced was said by Saint Paul.

It's particularly important for someone to recognize his calling

Someone who wants to enter the monastic life must see all the possibilities open before him and make a free choice, with divine love as his sole incentive and without any selfish motivation. It's not good to brood morosely and afflict yourself in order to become a monk. Make a different kind of effort: read and pray, and have as your sole aim to advance in the love of God and of the Church. And so, as you live within the love of God, you will live in freedom, because where there is love there is freedom. Move only within the realm of divine love.

In the eyes of God, the married and the unmarried person are the same, provided they live in accordance with the commandments of God and provided they live the life of God. Chastity, lack of possessions and poverty, which are the virtues of the monk, are to be found in a person's heart. Someone may be a virgin as far as the body is concerned, but be like an inveterate whore as far as the soul is concerned on account of his malice and passions. Someone may own a dozen houses and yet in his soul be liberated from material things and live like someone who owns nothing. On the other hand, someone may be poor in an external sense, but not be free of possessions internally. It is not the quantity of possessions that makes someone propertied or unpropertied, but the attachment of the heart.

It is particularly important for someone to recognize his or her calling. Some people wish to enter the monastic life as a reaction to something. Let me tell you a story.

A girl went to live in a convent. Her parents protested loudly and bewailed the fact, but in response the girl became all the more adamant. The parents came to me and I advised them not to behave in that way, but to leave the girl free to do as she liked. I suggested they go to the services at the convent and shower their best wishes on everyone and speak kindly to the Mother of the community and so on. And so in this way the reaction evaporated. After a short time the young girl asked the Mother of the community for permission to study for a theology degree at the university. And this she did. She lived in the monastery and went to the university to sit the exams at the end of each semester until she got her degree. As soon as she got her degree, she left the monastery.

The life of the monk is life in an alien land

The life of a monk is life in an alien land. This is embroidered into the monastic 'schema' or breast-cloth worn by the monk. A large letter Ξ is joined to the letter Z, standing for Ξένη Ζωή, which means 'Alien Life'. I have experienced this living in an alien land, far from everyone and everything. You work and you pray and only God sees you. I loved the desert very much. Even now I continue to love the desert. The best thing would be if I were able to go to Kavsokalyvia on the Holy Mountain. I am always filled with joy when I go to Kavsokalyvia.

It's truly marvellous for a hermit to live along with two or three like-minded people, so that what the one desires the others desire. If one makes spiritual progress, then the others also make progress. They all engage in ascetic exercise together and experience the spiritual joy given by Christ. They have died to the whole world. In this way a hermit is not harmed. On the contrary, he is invigorated.

What the hermit has chosen is the most magnificent, the most sacred and the most holy way of life — provided he keeps in mind to love Christ. If he loves Him, then he will give himself conscientiously to Christ, he will progress in order to offer himself to Him with all his soul. If he is not able to do this, however, it's not bad for him to work in the Church in a different way.

I felt that my obedience to my elders was like Paradise

It's possible for everything in a monastery to be well ordered, but for there to be no monastic life. The monastery must place obedience and the confessor's stole above all else. Every time that I made confession I was filled with an immense joy and I devoted myself to prayer. Not only then, but even now, when I make confession I feel joy and at once all burdens are lifted from my soul. I have invested great faith in the sacrament of confession. I believe all guidance should be given through the sacrament of confession. All things should be done in obedience and in sanctification.

Obedience is a great and wise thing. It is the secret of spiritual life. We are unable to comprehend it. But, with the grace of our Lord, I have experienced it. I know how delightful it is and how perfect and carefree it is to obey God, to devote yourself to the worship of God and to obey your elder. Obedience is very important. It is a great virtue and is the same as humility. Obedience with joy and willingness — even if what your elder demands is wrong-headed. Obedience as such is of great value. Such obedience is touching to God: *I love those who love me, and those who seek me shall find grace.* Prov. 8:17

With obedience you are transformed in everything. You become quick, clever, stronger and rejuvenated in everything. Christ loved me and gave me the grace to be obedient. And I sensed this grace a little, and what I have, I have as a result of obedience. I felt that my obedience to my elders was like Paradise. And indeed I wanted them to be even more severe towards me. I was not satisfied. Now, however, in my old age, I see that they were in fact very strict. At the time I didn't realize it.

Obedience, especially to a spiritual father, is a great capital. When you live with a saint, you too are sanctified. You assume something of his saintly habits from his words and from his silence. His prayer affects you. Even when you don't speak, something takes place, something holy and divine is transmitted to you without your realizing it. Saint Prochoros and Saint Proclos and others lived with holy teachers and were inspired by them and became saints themselves. The same is true of Saint Symeon the New Theologian and Saint Gregory Palamas and many more.

Our elder plays a very important role in our lives. The elder guides our footsteps. He is not simply an educated man who has become an elder because he has studied theology. We need to recognize what an elder is. An elder may be quite uneducated and have little worldly knowledge; he may be lacking in eloquence and have read little, but nevertheless he may be superior to the educated person when he has lived in obedience and has received the grace of God. Such an elder is able to benefit those under him immensely, if they are obedient to him.

Of course it's true that what your elder says is also said in books. But it's not the same thing. The elder who experiences these spiritual things and who doesn't say to you, 'this Father says this, and that book says that', but who himself experiences the life of Christ and who will speak to you out of his own experience, will transmit these spiritual experiences to you and will imprint them in your soul and you will learn from him how to attract the grace of God.

When you have an elder and you live close to him, you will love him. And when the elder loves you in turn and you are like-minded, then you become one. *Where two or three are gathered together in my name, there*
Matt. 18:20 *am I in the midst of them.* Christ is there. In this state distance is abolished. Wherever we may be, we are united in Christ and we pray; and thus the grace of God visits us and invigorates us continually. In this way we experience unity in the Church. We have the sense of 'oneness', that is, that we are all one. That is how elders and the monks subject to them used to live.

These are not fairy-tales. I have seen these things many times. When

I went to the Holy Mountain, all things were left behind — 'the world and the rulers of the world',* my family and relatives — they all became obedience to my elder, they became prayer, they became joy. As I walked around Kavsokalyvia they became heaven. But whenever I started to feel a little tired of it all, immediately my regard for my parents and for the world would weigh down on me again.

Obedience to an elder is a great virtue, a great advantage. It is everything. You must pass through obedience to be a complete person, in order to face the difficulties of human life. Without humility and without obedience, you do not have the grace of God. If you do not pass through humility and therefore through obedience you have a very hard time. Lack of obedience is due to egotism and self-love. Egotism and pride engendered the disobedience which ejected us from Paradise. A proud person can never be obedient. He always wants to examine and question what he is told in order to see if it's right or wrong and to respond accordingly. Or else he does it, but with protestations and objections, believing that in this way he is demonstrating his freedom. But in obedience a person discovers true freedom, whereas slavery is that which compels him not to obey. When he obeys, he enters into the freedom of the children of God.

Even those who live in a cave experience these things. It is the process of assimilation to God — *theosis* — which embraces everything. They are united with God. They cultivate the spirit and this cultivation is endless and insatiable. God is the height of perfection, the highest good. Union with God has everything. Full satisfaction is achieved by this union. No other pleasure is higher than the pleasure given by union with God. It is the pleasure which passes all understanding. It is the pleasure of those who have given themselves to God. This all happens with divine help. Where grace is effective, things are supernatural.

Pray that God may grant us to sense and experience these magnificent things, albeit to a small degree.

By studying the words of God you can become saints without very great effort

Devote yourselves to the Scriptures. Love reading and studying them. The more I hear the Psalter and the poetic canons, the more I want to hear them. They are so close-to-life and engaging that I cannot have enough of them. Read clearly and distinctly, word by word. Read the

* Cf. the *doxastikon* at Vespers of the feast of Saint Basil, 1st January.

words aloud and listen to them; that's a great help. And where you come across a particularly meaty passage, read it again to understand it better. What can I say! I listen to the words again and again with an unquenchable thirst. They sweeten the soul. That's what is important.

And so since you will thirst for the words of the poetic canons, of the Psalter and of all the church service books, and since you will desire to read, hear and take them to heart, as soon as the *simantron* sounds, you will run at once with love and eagerness to hear the first words of the daily cycle of prayer, 'On rising from sleep, we fall down before You, Good Lord.' That's the way to achieve the object of your desire. The soul then reverts to its original luster, to its primeval state, to its ancient beauty. What does God say? 'On whom shall I look, if not on the meek
Cf. Isa. 66 : 2 and peaceful man who fears my words?' Christ gives grace to the person who loves His words and all good things come easily to him.

As you see, we struggle without warfare and without bloody contests. Our soul is gladdened and our hearing is sweetened as we hear the hymns and something happens within us. This pleasure brings divine enthusiasm and our soul becomes worthy to receive the grace of God and God Himself sanctifies the soul. We cannot be sanctified without divine grace, however much we try. Whereas by meditating on the words of Scripture we can become saints, simply and without great effort.

I also liked, and I still like, the books written by the holy Fathers of the Church — John Chrysostom, Basil the Great, Gregory the Theologian, Gregory of Nyssa, Gregory Palamas and so on. But, to be quite honest, I haven't studied them closely. Nevertheless, I know all these blessed fathers...

On the Holy Mountain they didn't use to allow you to read *The Philokalia** and the other ascetic fathers — only Holy Scripture and the lives of the saints. Don't misunderstand me on this. To read these books you have to have a spiritual father who has experience of these things, otherwise there is a high likelihood that you will be confused. And this is because they must be accompanied by obedience. Without obedience, you come to harm. These books write about very exalted matters, divine illuminations, which the evil spirit can exploit if there is not obedience to a spiritual father. And what is required is pure obedience — not egotistical obedience or obedience designed solely to please the spiritual father — but simple, selfless obedience.

That's why I want you to devote yourselves more to the study of the

* A five-volume collection of writings on prayer and the spiritual life; see fn. to p. 250 below.

Old and New Testament and to the hymns and poetic canons. Read the Church Fathers with the same zeal that you would read the hymns and the poetic canons, but first of all read Holy Scripture. Read the Gospel and the Old Testament. This is the treasure-house, because all the Fathers drew on this wealth. It is the source and the foundation. It is inexhaustible and you can never weary of it. You will undoubtedly feel Ps. 118:103
too what the Psalmist says: *Your words are above honey to my mouth.* [119:103]
He doesn't say 'like honey', but *'above honey to my mouth'*, in order to indicate the exceptional sweetness of the words of God.

The divine services in the church should always be celebrated with eros

The divine services of the Church are words in which we converse and speak to God with our worship and with our love. The hours spent closest to Paradise are the hours spent in the church together with all our brethren when we celebrate the Divine Liturgy, when we sing and when we receive Holy Communion. Together we all follow the divine services — the words of our Lord. With the Gospel, the Epistles, the hymns of the Book of the Eight Tones, of the Lenten Triodion, and of the Offices of the Saints, we achieve our union with Christ.

But the snares of Satan are many for those who worship God. Temptation manages very successfully to ensure that we pay no attention to the worship. We go to church frequently, only to continue our sleep. As soon as we hear the readings and the hymns, we close our eyes. We enter into a state of languidity and we are unable to follow the words of the hymns. It is a satanic thing, this soporific state, and very obviously so.

Think what we are missing when we are in church in this thoughtless state! Although before you go to church you say to yourself, 'I'll pay attention, I won't doze off again, I'll be alert', yet you don't succeed. All these exhortations, 'I'll pay attention', and so on, are attempts to compel ourselves which provoke a negative reaction within us. And with compulsion we achieve nothing. On the contrary, the state of sloth overtakes us and ridicules us: 'Concentrate hard now, force yourself, do what you like, but I, your old self, have you in my hand and I'll keep a tight hold on you, and now, if you can, let me see you make your spiritual progress!'

Whatever you do under compulsion and whatever causes your soul to kick instinctively and protest, causes you harm. This is something I've said many times. I have seen monks and lay people of every age leaving the Church and abandoning God entirely, because they are unable to bear the inner pressure and the pressure from other people. Pressure causes a person not only to react negatively against the Church, but not to want the Church at all. It does not have a positive effect. It bears no fruit. He does whatever it is, albeit reluctantly, because his elder or spiritual father told him to. He says to himself, for example, 'Now I must go to Compline.' Yes, he does the thing, but whatever is done in a mechanical way is harmful and not beneficial.

You are often forced to do what is good. But it mustn't be done under duress; it's not beneficial, it's not spiritually edifying. Take, for example, the Jesus Prayer. If you force yourself to say it, after a time you will weary of it and you will throw it away; and then what happens? If you do it as a chore, the pressure builds up inside you until it bursts out in some evil. Pressure of this kind can even make you not want to go to church at all. Go to church in a different spirit, not with pushing and shoving, but with pleasure and joy. For this to happen, you must pay attention and take pleasure and joy in the services, in the hymns, the readings and the prayers. Listen to each word and follow the meanings. Do you see? This is where the joy comes from.

There is, however, another great danger. If we don't pay attention, we may listen to and sing everything mechanically. We read the words and hear them because we must. For example, the monk goes to Vespers and hears the words: *How lovely are Your dwelling places, O Lord of*
Ps. 83 [84] *Hosts; my soul longs and faints for the courts of the Lord....* We hear it today, we hear it tomorrow, we hear it the day after and all the year round.* The same thing again and again. When a person hears it without participating, he wearies of it, he dozes off, he doesn't enter more deeply into the words, he becomes bored and then reaction sets in. Thereafter he finds no benefit and no joy. Despair sets in and the devil doesn't miss the opportunity to work harm.

The divine services are a very great affair. They are everything. I have experienced this. The precondition is for everything to be done with *eros*, with interest and with a sincere disposition to worship Christ — not as a chore and not perfunctorily, but with *eros* and divine enthusiasm. If we do not feel like this, the services are without value. Not only are they valueless, but they are harmful. 'Then,' you will say, 'let's stop doing them.' No, not at all. But as far as you can, avoid simply following the book and look to the substance of the matter. That is, take pleasure in prayer and in conversation with God. Boredom is disaster for the monk.

For my own part, I am never bored. I have always enjoyed the services.

* This psalm is read daily at the Ninth Hour.

I didn't put any pressure on myself and I never did anything as a bounden duty. On the contrary, if possible I want to hear the same things today and every day. Over and over again. That's what's of value. I cannot be satisfied even if I repeat the words all day long. And I believe that all these things benefit us greatly. There is so much juice to be extracted which refreshes and nourishes our soul. You, too, should in this way give yourselves with all your heart to Christ.

When I read the prayer of the Ninth Hour before the Cross on Good Friday in the Polyclinic once, I read it and it became a living reality for me: 'Master, Lord Jesus Christ our God, long-suffering...'*

The next day the consultant said to me in front of the student doctors:

'Father, how marvellous that prayer was yesterday! You must be a saint.'

'I'm no saint,' I replied. 'But because I want to become a saint, I asked for God's mercy to sanctify me and my soul was touched. I am very sinful and that was a sign from Christ.'

That prayer is a masterpiece, isn't it? And so, I say, read it over and over again.

The liturgical prayers which seem perfunctory become your own when they are said with meaning and care. When even the most sinful person reads the Prayers of Preparation for Communion he is greatly sanctified.

In this way the soul is cultivated without our realizing. Bloodlessly. That is, the old self is rendered useless. It is rendered useless without a fight. It is not provoked, but it is rendered useless and the new man grows and develops.

Prayer at night is best

Choose physical exhaustion. Make this an aim in order for body and soul to be exercised. Our life depends on our will. We can experience whatever and however we want. The person who makes greater effort for Christ — something which of course is a product of divine *eros* — attracts more grace. And when we say effort, we mean, apart from everything else, prayer during the night. It is of great benefit to get up during the night for prayer. Prayer at night is best. We hear the
prophet Isaiah saying, *From night my spirit holds vigil towards You, O* Isa. 26:9
God, and David says, *I kept vigil and I became as a sparrow alone on a* Ps. 101:8
rooftop... Hear my prayer in the morning... '*You shall hear my voice in* [102:7]

* The Prayer of Saint Basil the Great at the end of the Ninth Hour.

Ps. 5:4 *the morning, in the morning I shall stand before You and You shall*
Ps. 62:2 *watch over me… O God, my God, I hold vigil towards You.* How mar-
[63:1] velously David expresses it! He doesn't say it, he lives it and rejoices
in it. He has the grace of God. The Holy Spirit.

Many on the Holy Mountain pray day and night. And when you pray from evening until morning you are not aware of the time passing. In the love of God time flies at a different speed. You cannot imagine what happens on the Holy Mountain at night! Fragrance, incense, angels, prayers… The angels take the prayers of the saints and bring them before God. A mystery!

On the Holy Mountain we woke up without an alarm clock. When the time came we got up immediately. Even if you were tired from the day before and hadn't gone to bed until late, you still leapt up when the time came. It is a matter of habit to jump out of bed as soon as you wake up. Of course, you can equally well just turn over on your other side and sleep until mid-day. A very bad habit! As soon as you wake up, get up at once. Choose the night-time hours. You enter into prayer more easily. Even if you just happen to wake up during the night, don't go back to sleep at once. God is giving you an opportunity to pray as much as you can in the stillness and quiet.

Apart from the stillness, there is something else which happens at night. I have noticed a strange thing. During the twenty-four hour cycle there is a difference among the hours and the way they affect the human organism. For example, whereas a wound remains in the same state, the temperature of the body fluctuates. In the morning the temperature drops and in the evening and at night it rises more and at midnight it changes. This depends on the movement of the earth. Just as the body is affected by the times of day and night, so is the soul.

The person who stays up praying during the night is able to work better the following day because God gives him grace and his spirit is renewed. On the contrary, the person who is not disposed to make sacrifices for the love of Christ excludes himself from grace.

Body and soul participate in the worship of God

Bodily exertion causes the body to protest and complain and react, but it is unable to make the soul lax in prayer. You simply turn the radio up louder, you listen to the music, you enjoy it and you don't hear the complaints. I mean that by intensifying the prayer, the prayer neutralizes the weariness. Before complaining about your bodily exhaustion, start praying, because when you complain grace departs and you are left with your own strength. If you say 'Lord Jesus Christ, have mercy on me' three times, you continue joyfully. God sees you and stretches out His hand to help you. From that moment on, true communion with Him commences.

When bodily exertion — prostrations, vigils and sacrifices — takes place with love, with passionate *eros*, the body is not harmed. When this effort is made freely and with love towards the loved one, towards Christ, you show how much you love Him. No one takes account of exertion and fatigue for the person he loves. For example, a monk climbs up a mountain, he struggles and sweats and tires himself out. 'Why did you do it?' people ask him. 'For the person I love,' he replies. 'Because I knew that I would make him happy.' The person with faith displays his love, his devotion and his adoration of Christ in tangible ways. That's why bodily exertion is made. That's why we make prostrations. Not to gain anything, but because your love for Christ doesn't allow you to do otherwise.

Perhaps someone will say, 'I have love in my heart.' That's all very well, but prostrations and all the other exercises are still required, because, although they are external forms, through those formal actions we are able to penetrate to the substance. If we don't penetrate to the heart of the matter, all is a waste of time. Should I turn somersaults now for God to see and be pleased? God takes no delight in these things. Nor do we add anything to Christ with the worship which we offer Him. It is we who receive the fruits of our efforts; we have need of those things. There are a thousand heresies about and you see the kind of torments they subject the body to. They have gymnastic exercises where you stick your feet up and your head down. They have the most incredible bodily contortions and they attempt in this way to affect the soul. We are not suggesting anything of that sort. But when prostrations are made for Christ, grace works directly on the soul and brings penitence, serenity, peace and joy. But these things come with divine grace and then the body is benefited also.

There used to be rulers and slaves. In order to demonstrate their subjection and respect towards their rulers, the slaves would bow down before their masters. Thus with our prostrations we demonstrate that we are humble servants of God. We acknowledge our lowliness and display our respect in a tangible way. With prostrations the Christian is humbled, and this helps for the grace of God to come upon him. When grace comes, his heart is set on fire. The fire of love makes sacrifices. Prostrations are a sacrifice and offering — an offering of love and worship. And the whole person participates in the worship, body and soul.

Don't take pity on your body. Chastise it. You can't understand what the fire of love is. You need to make sacrifice, exercise — spiritual and bodily exercise. Without exercise nothing is achieved. Subject yourself to a spiritual programme, for example, a rule of prayer, a cycle of church services, and so on, and do not diverge from it. Don't put off for tomorrow. Don't abandon it even on account of illness, only for mortal illness. When I was young I did three thousand prostrations a day and I didn't get tired, I was inured to it. I chastised myself and disregarded the exhaustion. I came back from the mountain worn out after collecting wood, and my elders would set me to dig the garden. I chastised and disdained my body, and yet I was very strong. But I had such fire within me! Such fire!

I'll show you how I did the prostrations. I did them rhythmically and quickly without touching my knees on the ground. First I made the sign of the cross, striking my fingers on my forehead, then on my knees and then on each of my shoulders. Then I touched the ground with my hands and rose up swiftly. Then I would rest my knees briefly on the ground each time. Do you see how body and soul participate in the worship of God? Mind and heart are with Christ and the body too is with Christ. Make the prostrations with piety and love and don't count them. It's better to make ten good prostrations rather than a large number without zeal, without worship and without divine *eros*. Make as many as you can, depending on your disposition, but not pseudo-prostrations and pseudo-prayers. Don't offer external forms to God. God demands that what we do for Him be done 'with all the soul and all the heart'.

Cf. Mark 12:30, 33 & Luke 10:27

Prayer should be said all day with love — prayer, hymns and prostrations in turn. And the prostrations which we make to our Holy Lady are directed to Christ, because Our Lady carries Christ within her. Christ is the Saviour of our soul and our Holy Lady is our mother, our great intercessor.

Prostrations are also gymnastics. And — even though we shouldn't think of this at all — there is no better gymnastics for the abdomen, the bowels, the chest, the heart and the spinal column. It is highly beneficial, so why shouldn't we do it? When this exercise is done for the worship of God and the soul achieves this worship, it is filled with joy and becomes calm and peaceful. This is everything. At the same time, of course, it also benefits the body. The body follows and is benefited in turn. Do you see? Peace and calm come to the soul and good functioning is ensured for all our bodily systems — circulatory, digestive, respiratory and endocrine — all of which have a direct relation with our soul.

The effect of prayer is miraculous

When you enter your monastery, let your soul open to the love of God. There all things are sanctified: there are so many souls praying, engaging in ascetic exercises and living the life of God. Sanctified souls are the splendour of the monastery. The soul has tremendous powers that are reflected in the environment. Thus places that are sanctified affect us and elevate us. When I find myself in such places, before I even start to pray, the sanctified place elevates me to a heavenly state, as for example, on Patmos and on the Holy Mountain.

To many people the monk seems remote and unsociable. It seems that he is concerned only with his own soul and that he offers nothing to the Church or to the world. That is not the case. If the Church has been preserved for so many years, this is due to monasticism. The person who enters a monastery and offers everything to Christ enters into the Church. Perhaps someone will ask, 'Do those who live alone in a cave help the Church?' The answer is 'yes'. The cave-dwellers help the Church in a mystical way. A monk who lives in a cave may not cultivate trees and vegetable gardens, he may not write books and do other things that help towards spiritual life and progress, but there he creates and develops and is assimilated to God. Hermits stay in caves so that no one distracts them from the spiritual life. With their fervent and pure life and above all with their prayer they help the Church. I'll say something that will seem grossly excessive to you. But I want you to believe it. It is about the contribution of a monk's prayer. Listen to me carefully.

Let us assume that there are seven educated preachers who live holy lives. Their rhetorical skill is unparalleled. Each has a parish with ten thousand parishioners. Every day their words are heard by seventy thousand people. Thousands who hear them are moved to repentance and return to Christ. Whole families are saved. Nevertheless, one monk whom no one sees and who sits in a cave somewhere has a much greater effect with his humble prayer. One produces a greater effect than seven. That is what I see. I am sure of it. That is how important a monk's prayer is. He is on his own in his cell, but the reverberations of his prayer reach everyone, even if they are far off. With his prayer, the monk participates in all the problems which people face and works miracles. His contribution, accordingly, is greater than that of the most gifted and worthy preacher.

'You shall love the Lord your God with all your heart...'

Pray for your relatives without worrying about their salvation, because in that way you lose your communion with Christ and display little faith. Entrust everything in confidence to the love and providence of God. The best is for you to give yourself over to the love of God and to cut yourself off from the world and from your relatives and from your parents and your brothers and sisters. All the things that are experienced by hermits are written in the Order of Monastic Tonsure. It says:

You who, as is written, would come follow after me
Readily renounce all worldly ties,
The parents who gave you birth,
Both children and wives, brothers, sisters and friends,
Money and homes, relatives and servants,
And receive the rank of my Apostles.

Listen to what happened to a hermit in the *Wisdom of the Desert Fathers.*

An only son of rich parents went into the Nitria desert and there he made great progress. The years passed. His parents died. There was no heir and so some of his fellow townsmen came to find him. The inheritance was very great. They said to him, 'We came to tell you to come, if you wish, to take over the property of your parents who have died.'

He bowed his head and after a short pause he said, 'I died to the world before they did, how is it possible for the dead to inherit the dead?'

If we do not die to the world, nothing happens. We must love Christ and He will love us. All pains will pass; they will be conquered and transformed. Saint Symeon the New Theologian writes in one of his hymns:

...children of God, as is written,
and gods according to grace...children of light...
as many as shall renounce the vain and delusive world
*as many as shall unhatingly hate parents and brethren...**

What a marvellous thing this is! The great secret lies in the 'expenditure'. The monk also possesses maternal and paternal affection, and if he is not careful, the 'expenditure' is made in that direction. If you have within you five units of love and you spend two on your parents and two on your brothers and sisters, what is left for God? Whereas in God are found all the loves of the world. If you love God, you love everything, because all things are contained within God, and that is how God wishes you to love Him. He says so Himself: *You shall love the Lord your God with all your heart and with all*
Mark 12:30 *your soul and with all your mind and with all your strength.*

These are the 'Higher Mathematics' of the Christian religion. No other religion has conceived these ideas, because they are not human excogitations. God revealed them to us.

* Hymn 8, lines 12–15 (Sources Chrétiennes 156, 214).

ON THE MYSTERY OF REPENTANCE

True repentance will bring sanctification

'Come to me all you who labour and are heavy laden...'

There is nothing higher than what is called repentance and confession. This sacrament is the offering of God's love to mankind. In this perfect way a person is freed of evil. We go and confess and we sense our reconciliation with God; joy enters us and guilt departs. In the Orthodox Church there is no impasse. There is no impasse because of the existence of the confessor who has the gift of grace to forgive. To be a confessor is a great thing.

I had the habit from the time I was a boy — and it's a habit I still have — that whenever I sinned I went and confessed and everything went away. I would jump for joy. I am sinful and weak. I resort to God's compassion and I am saved, I become calm and I forget everything. Every day I think that I sin, but I desire that whatever happens to me I turn it into prayer and I don't keep it locked within me.

Sin makes a person very confused psychologically. The confusion doesn't dissipate whatever you do. Only with the light of Christ does the confusion depart. Christ makes the first move, *Come to me all you who labour and are heavy laden...* Thereafter we accept this light in our good Matt. 11:28
will, which we express with our love towards Him, with our prayer and with the sacraments.

For the soul to repent it must first awake. It is in this awakening that the miracle of repentance occurs. This is where human will plays its role. The awakening, however, is not something that rests only with the individual man or woman. The individual on his own is unable to bring it about. God intervenes. Then divine grace comes. Without grace a person cannot repent. The love of God does everything. He may use something — an illness, or something else, it depends — in order to bring a person to repentance. Accordingly repentance is achieved through divine grace. We simply make a move towards God and from then onwards grace supervenes.

You may say to me, 'If that is so, all things are done by grace.' This is a fine point. Here, too, we have a case of what I say, namely, that we cannot love God if God does not love us. Saint Paul puts it very well: *Now*

Gal. 4:9 *having known God, or rather having been known by God…* The same happens with repentance. We cannot repent unless the Lord gives us repentance. And this holds for everything. It is a case of the scriptural
John 15:5 principle, *Without me you can do nothing.* If there are not the preconditions for Christ to enter into us, repentance does not come. The preconditions are humility, love, prayer, prostrations and labour for Christ. If the sentiment is not pure, if there is no simplicity and if the soul is moved by self-interest, then divine grace does not come. In that case we go and confess, but we don't feel relief.

Repentance is a very delicate matter. True repentance will bring sanctification. Repentance will sanctify us.

When a person makes confession, grace frees him from his psychological wounds

Man is not solely responsible for his transgressions. The mistakes, sins and passions are not only personal experiences of the person who comes to confession. Every person has incorporated into himself the experiences of his parents and especially of his mother, that is, how his mother lived when she was carrying him in her womb — if she was anxious, if her nervous system was exhausted, if she was happy, if she was sad, if she was depressed. In other words, her whole nervous system affected the nervous system of the embryo. So that when the child is born and grows up, it assumes also the experiences of its mother, that is, of another person. A state is created in a person's soul on account of his parents, which he carries with him all through his life. It leaves its marks within him and many things that happen to him during his life are a consequence of this state. The way he behaves has a direct relation to the state of his parents. He grows up, is educated, but is not remedied. This is where a large part of the responsibility for the spiritual state of a person is to be found.

There is, however, a secret. There is a way for a person to be freed from this evil. This way is a general confession, which takes place through the grace of God. Your spiritual father might say to you, 'How much I wish that we could be in a quiet place and that I could be free of all other duties so that you could tell me about your life from the beginning, from the time you first had consciousness of your self, about all the events you remember and how you reacted to them, not only the unpleasant memories, but also the pleasant ones, not only your sins, but also the good things, your successes and failures. Everything. Everything that goes to make up your life.'

I have often used this general confession and I have seen miracles worked through it. The moment you relate these things to your confessor, divine grace comes and frees you from all the unpleasant experiences and wounds, the psychological traumas and feelings of guilt, because while you are talking, your spiritual father is praying fervently to the Lord for you to be liberated from all these things.

Some time ago a woman came to me and made a confession of this kind and she was greatly benefited. Her psychological state improved, because something had been tormenting her. Now this woman sent a friend of hers to me and we went out and sat on the rock outside the monastery at Kallisia and she started to talk. I said to her, 'Tell me whatever you feel you need to. If I ask you about something, then tell me. If I don't ask you, then continue talking, just as you feel you need to.'

I listened to all that she was telling me, not simply with attention, but I observed the effect of prayer on her psychological world. I looked inside her soul and I saw that grace was entering her, just as I saw her before me. Because in the confessor there is grace and in the priest there is grace. Do you understand what I am saying? When someone is making confession, the priest is praying for him. At the same time grace comes and frees him from the traumas in his soul, which have been tormenting him for years without his being aware of what caused them. Yes indeed, I believe very strongly in all this!

You can speak to your confessor just as you feel, but that's not as important as it is that, as he prays, the priest looks into your soul and sees how you are and transmits to you the grace of God. It has been proved that this looking into the soul is a spiritual radiation, which relieves you and cures you. Don't imagine that these are natural rays. These things are true. And what happened with Christ? He took hold of the hand of the woman with an issue of blood and said, *I felt power leaving me.* You'll say, 'Yes, but He was Luke 8:46
God.' Christ, of course, was God, but did not the Apostles do the same?

All spiritual fathers and confessors have this grace and when they pray they transmit it as conductors. For example, if we want to switch on an electric heater in this room then we need to take the cable and plug it in, otherwise it won't work. As soon as the cable is plugged in, however, the current passes through the cable. These are spiritual matters of our religion. We may speak about cables, but in reality this is 'divine psychoanalysis'.

God forgives everything with confession

Don't let's turn back to sins we have confessed. The recollection of sins is harmful. Have we asked for forgiveness? Then the matter is closed.

God forgives everything with confession. We mustn't turn back and enmesh ourselves in despair. We need to be humble servants before God and have a sense of gratitude for the forgiveness of our sins.

It is not healthy to be excessively downcast on account of your sins and to turn with such revulsion against your evil self that you end up in despair. Despondency is the worst thing. It is a snare set by Satan to make a person lose his appetite for spiritual things and to bring him into a state of despair, inactivity and negligence. In this state a person is unable to do anything and rendered useless. The person says, 'I am sinful and wretched, I am this, I am that, I didn't do this, I didn't do that...I should have done that then, now it's too late, nothing can be done...I've wasted my life, I am unworthy...' He is brought into a sense of inferiority and consumed by fruitless self-reproach. Do you know what a destructive thing that is? It is pseudo-humility.

All these things are symptoms of a person in despair whom Satan has brought under his sway. Such a person reaches the point where he doesn't even want to receive Communion because he regards himself as unworthy of everything. He attempts to negate everything about himself and is rendered useless. This is a snare set by Satan so that a person will lose his hope in God's love. All this is quite terrible and contrary to the Spirit of God.

I, too, think that I am sinful and that I am not living as I should. Nevertheless, I make whatever distresses me into prayer. I do not shut it up inside myself. I go to my spiritual father and confess it and it is finished and done with. Don't let's go back and recriminate and say what we didn't do. What is important is what we will do now, from this moment onwards — as Saint Paul says, *forgetting the things that are behind and*
Phil. 3:14 *stretching forward to the things that are before us.*

The spirit of cowardice attempted to sever Saint Paul's zeal for Christ, but he took courage and said, *It is no longer I who live; Christ lives in me.*
Gal. 2:20 And also, *Who shall separate us from the love of Christ? Shall tribulation*
or distress, or persecution, or famine, or nakedness, or peril or sword? As
it is written, for Your sake we are killed all the day long; we are accounted
Rom. 8:35–6 *as sheep for the slaughter.* And David the prophet and king said, *I shall*
Ps. 117:17 *not die, but live, and declare the works of the Lord.* Read the Scriptures.
[118:17] Remember the fine words, *I love those who love me, and those who seek*
Prov. 8:17 *me shall find grace.*

In Christ is found all that is beautiful and all that is healthy

If we love Christ, all is easy. I have not yet succeeded in this, but now I am trying to love Him. In Christ there is everything — all that is beautiful

and all that is healthy. The healthy soul experiences the gifts of the Holy
Spirit which are *love, joy, peace, long-suffering, gentleness, goodness, faith,*
meekness, continence. The man of God experiences also the things men- Gal. 5:22–3
tioned by Saint Paul in his hymn to love: *Love is long-suffering and is*
kind…it does not think any evil…it covers and protects all things and be- 1 Cor.
lieves all things…love never fails. 13:4–8

Do you possess these things? Then you possess happiness, Christ, Paradise. And even the body functions smoothly, without irregularities. The grace of God changes a person; it transfigures him in soul and in body. All illnesses then disappear — no colitis, no thyroid or stomach problems, or anything. Everything functions normally. It is good to walk, work and go about your business enjoying good health. But first of all you should have health of soul. The foundation is health of soul; health of body follows. Almost all illnesses come from lack of faith in God and this creates the anxiety. The abolition of the religious sentiment creates anxiety. If you don't have love for Christ and if you don't occupy yourself with holy matters, you will certainly be filled with melancholy and evil. What happens in the world, however? Listen and I'll give you an example.

A girl went to a doctor and he prescribed hormones for her. I said to her:

'Don't take them, my child! I'm not a doctor, and I don't want you to act on my say-so, but I know that you shouldn't take them. At least go to see an endocrinologist first. The problem is more a matter for an endocrinologist. It's because of your worries.'

'It's true,' she said, 'I've had a lot of worries.'

'Well then, that's what it is. Calm down, be at peace, make confession and receive Communion and all will be well.'

Well, she went to an endocrinologist and explained her problem. The doctor told her:

'On no account should you take this medicine. Throw it away. It will do you a great deal of harm.'

She telephoned me afterwards and said:

'The doctor told me exactly the same thing as you did.'

You see then what happens in the world? Whereas with confession and Holy Communion many people have been cured.

When someone is empty of Christ then a thousand and one other things come to fill his soul: jealousies, hatreds, boredom, melancholy, negativity, a worldly frame of mind and worldly pleasures. Try to fill your soul with Christ so as not to have it empty. Your soul is like a cistern full of water. If you channel the water to the flowers, that is, to the virtues, you will experience true joy and all the thorns of evil will wither away.

But if you channel the water to the weeds, these will grow and choke you and all the flowers will wither.

Raise everything up to Christ. That's how you will experience joy with
Phil. 4:13 the grace of God. *I can do all things through Christ who strengthens me…*
Don't say that you will achieve something. Never imagine such a thing.
John 15:5 The Lord said, *Without me you can do nothing.* There is no other way.
Never should a person trust in his own powers, but rather in the mercy and compassion of God. He will make a little effort, but Christ will crown that effort. It is a delusion to believe that you achieved something on your own. The more someone progresses and approaches towards Christ, the
Cf. Luke more he feels that he is imperfect. The Pharisee, on the contrary, who says,
18:10–14 'Look at me! I am good, I do this and I do that…', is deluded.

Prayer and worship gradually transform depression and turn it into joy

Nowadays people often feel sadness, despair, lethargy, laziness, apathy and all things satanic. They are downcast, discontent and melancholy. They disregard their families, spend vast sums on psychoanalysts and take anti-depressants. People explain this as 'insecurity'. Our religion believes that these states derive from satanic temptation.

Pain is a psychological power which God implanted in us with a view to doing us good and leading us to love, joy and prayer. Instead of this, the devil succeeds in taking this power from the battery of our soul and using it for evil. He transforms it into depression and brings the soul into a state of lethargy and apathy. He torments us, takes us captive and makes us psychologically ill.

There is a secret. Turn the satanic energy into good energy. This is difficult and requires some preparation. The requisite preparation is humility. With humility you attract the grace of God. You surrender yourself to the love of God, to worship and to prayer. But even if you do all in the world, you achieve nothing if you haven't acquired humility. All the evil feelings, insecurity, despair and disenchantment, which come to take control of the soul, disappear with humility. The person who lacks humility, the egotist, doesn't want you to get in the way of his desires, to make any criticism of him or tell him what to do. He gets upset, irritated and reacts violently and is overcome by depression.

This state is cured by grace. The soul must turn to God's love. The cure will come when we start to love God passionately. Many of our saints transformed depression into joy with their love for Christ. That is, they took this power of the soul which the devil wished to crush and gave it to God and they transformed it into joy and exultation. Prayer and worship gradually transform depression and turn it into joy, because the grace of God takes effect. Here you need to have the strength to attract the grace of God which will help you to be united with Him. Art is required. When you give yourself to God and become one with Him, you will forget the evil spirit which drags at you from behind, and this spirit, when it is disdained, will leave. And the more you devote yourself to the Spirit of God, the less you will look behind to see the spirit that is dragging at you. When grace attracts you, you will be united with God. And when you unite yourself to God and abandon yourself to Him, everything else disappears and is forgotten and you are saved. The great art, the great secret, in order to rid yourself of depression and all that is negative is to give yourself over to the love of God.

Something which can help a person who is depressed is work, interest in life. The garden, plants, flowers, trees, the countryside, a walk in the open air — all these things tear a person away from a state of inactivity and awake other interests. They act like a medicine. To occupy oneself with the arts, with music and so on, is very beneficial. The thing that I place top of the list, however, is interest in the Church, in reading Holy Scripture and attending services. As you study the words of God you are cured without being aware of it.

Let me tell you about a girl who came to me. She was suffering from dreadful depression. Drugs had had no effect. She had given up everything — her work, her home, her interests. I told her about what I knew. I told her about the love of Christ which takes the soul captive because the grace of God fills the soul and changes it. I explained to her that the force which takes over the soul and transforms the power of the soul into depression is demonic. It throws the soul to the ground, torments it and renders it useless. I advised her to devote herself to things like music which she had formerly enjoyed. I emphasized, however, most of all her need to turn to Christ with love. I told her, moreover, that in our Church a cure is to be found through love for God and prayer, provided this is done with all her heart.

This is the secret of the remedy. That is what our Church believes.

ON LOVE FOR ONE'S NEIGHBOUR

Love for God and for one's neighbour, they go together and cannot be divorced

Love towards one's brother cultivates love towards God

One thing is needful in our life — love, adoration of Christ and love towards our fellow men. What is required is for us all to be one, with Christ as the head. This is the only way in which we will acquire grace, heaven and eternal life.

Love towards one's brother cultivates love towards God. We are happy when we secretly love all people. Then we will feel that everyone loves us. No one can attain to God unless he first passes through his fellow men. *For the person who does not love his brother whom he has seen,*
1 John 4:20 *how can he love God whom he has not seen?* We need to love and sacrifice
ourselves selflessly for everyone without seeking recompense. A love that seeks something in return is selfish. It is not genuine, pure and sincere.

Love and have compassion for everyone. *And if one member suffers,*
1 Cor. *all the members suffer with it... For you are members of Christ and par-*
12:26–7 *ticular members of His body.* This is the Church: I, you, and the others all
feel that we are members of Christ, that we are one. Love of self is egotism. Don't let's ask of God that 'I' may remain steadfast and that 'I' may go to Paradise, but rather let us feel this love for everyone. Do you understand? This is humility.

In this way, if we live in unity we will be happy and we will live in Par-
Cf. Eph. 5:30 adise. Our every neighbour is 'flesh of our flesh'. Can I be indifferent
towards him? Can I cause him distress? Can I hate him? This is the greatest mystery of our Church: that we all become one in God. If we do this we become His own. There is nothing better than this unity. This is the Church. This is the Orthodox faith. This is Paradise. Let's read the High Priestly prayer from the Gospel of Saint John. Listen to the words: *...that they may be one as we are...that they may all be one, as you, Father, are in me and I am in you...that they may be one, even as we are*
John 17:11, *one...that they may be made perfect in one...that where I am they may*
21–4 *be with me also.*

You see? He says it over and over again. He emphasizes the unity. We need all to be one, one with Christ as our head! Just as Christ is one with the Father. This is where the profoundest depth of the mystery of the Church is concealed. No other religion says any such thing. No one else demands this refined sensibility which Christ demands: for us all to become one by the grace of Christ. This is where the fullness is to be found — in this unity, in this love in Christ. There is no room here for any separation or any fear. Neither death, nor devil, nor hell. Only love, joy, peace and worship of God. You can reach the point where you then say with Saint Paul: *It is no longer I who live; Christ lives in me.* Gal. 2:20

We can very easily reach this point. Good will is required, and God is ready to enter within us. He 'stands at the door and knocks', and Cf. Rev. 3:20 'makes all things new', as the Revelation of Saint John says. *Ibid.* 21:5 Our thinking is changed; it is ridded of evil and becomes better, more holy, more quick-witted. But if we don't open to Him who knocks, if we do not have the things He seeks for, if we are not worthy of Him, then He does not enter into our heart. But in order to become worthy of Him we need to die to our old self, so that we die no more. Then we will live incorporated in Christ along with the whole body of the Church. In this way divine grace will come. And when grace comes it will give us everything.

On the Holy Mountain I once saw something I liked very much. In a small boat out at sea there were monks who were carrying various sacred objects. Each of the monks came from a different place, but for all that they said, 'this is ours', and not 'this is mine'.

Let us scatter our love selflessly to all

Above everything is love. The thing that must concern you, my children, is love for the other person, for his soul. Whatever we do, whether it is prayer or offering advice or pointing out some error, let us do it with love. Without love prayer is of no benefit, advice is hurtful and pointing out errors is harmful and destructive to the other person who senses whether we love him or not and reacts accordingly. Love, love, love! Love for our brother prepares us to love Christ more. Isn't that perfect?

Let us scatter our love selflessly to all, without regard to the way they act towards us. When the grace of God enters us, we will not be concerned about whether they love us or not or whether they speak to us politely or not. We will feel the need to love all people. It's egotism on our part to wish for others to speak to us politely. If they don't we shouldn't be upset. Let them speak to us as they wish. We needn't become beggars for love. Our aim should be to love them and pray for them with all our soul. Then we will become aware that all people love us without our seeking it and without our begging for their love. They will love us freely and sincerely from the depths of their heart without our blackmailing them. When we love without seeking to be loved, people will gather around us like bees. This is true for everyone.

If your brother is annoying you and wearying you, you should think: 'Now I've got a pain in my arm or leg and I'll need to tend it with all my love.' But don't let's think that we will be rewarded for any possible good we might do or that we will be punished for any evil. You come to knowledge of truth when you love with the love of Christ. Then you no longer ask to be loved. That is bad. You love; you give your love. That is good. It
Cf. 1 Cor. depends on us to be saved. God wishes for our salvation. Scripture says,
12:21 God wishes for all men to be saved and to come to knowledge of truth.

We owe no one anything, except to love one another

When someone injures us in whatever way, whether with slanders or with insults, we should think of him as our brother who has been taken hold of by the enemy. He has fallen victim to the enemy. Accordingly we need to have compassion for him and entreat God to have mercy both on us and on him, and God will help both. If, however, we are filled with anger against him, then the enemy will jump from him to us and make a mockery of us both. A person who condemns others does not love Christ. Our egotism is at fault. This is where condemnation of others stems from. Let me give you a little example.

Let's suppose someone is all alone in the desert. Suddenly he hears a voice crying out in distress in the distance. He follows the sound and is confronted by a horrendous sight: a tiger has grabbed hold of a man and is savaging him with its claws. The man is desperately shouting for help. In a few minutes he will be torn to pieces. What can the person do to help? Can he run to his side? How? It's impossible. Can he shout for help? Who will hear him? There is no one within earshot. Should he perhaps pick up a stone and throw it at the man to finish him off? 'Certainly not,' we would say. But that's is exactly what can happen if we don't realize that the other person who is acting badly towards us has been taken hold of by a tiger, the devil. We fail to realize that when we react to such a person without love it is as if we are throwing stones at his wounds and accordingly we are doing him great harm and the 'tiger' leaps onto us and we do the same as him and worse. What kind of love do we have then for our neighbour and, even more importantly, for God?

We should feel the malice of the other person as an illness which is

tormenting him and which he is unable to shake off. And so we should regard our brethren with sympathy and behave with courtesy towards them, repeating in our hearts with simplicity the prayer 'Lord Jesus Christ', so that the grace of God may strengthen our soul and so that we don't pass judgment on anyone. We should regard all people as saints. We all carry within us the same 'old self'. Our neighbour, whoever he is, is 'flesh of our flesh'; he is our brother and, according to Saint Paul, *we
owe no one anything, except to love one another.* We can never pass judg- Rom. 13:8
ment on others, for *no one ever hated his own flesh.* Eph. 5:29

When someone has a vice we should try to bombard him with rays of love and compassion so that he may be cured and freed. These things are achieved only through the grace of God. Think that this person is suffering more than you. In a coenobitic monastery when someone is at fault, we should not tell him that he is to blame. We must adopt an attitude of care, respect and prayer. We must endeavour not to do anything harmful. When we endure insults from our brother, it counts as martyrdom. And it is something we should endure with joy.

A Christian is gracious. We should prefer to be wronged. If love enters us we forget the wrongs we have been done. This is where the secret lies. When the evil comes from afar, you cannot avoid it. The great art, however, is to show disdain for it. With the grace of God, even though you see it, it will not affect you, because you will be full of grace.

In the realm of the Spirit of God all things are different. Here one justifies all things in the behaviour of others. Everything! What have we
said? *Christ sends rain on the just and on the unjust.* I say that you are to Matt. 5:45
blame, even if you tell me that he or she is the one at fault. In the final analysis you are to blame in some respect and you will discover in what respect you are at fault when I tell you that you are to blame. You should acquire this sense of discrimination in your life. Inquire more deeply into everything and don't regard things superficially. If we don't go to Christ, if we don't endure patiently when we suffer unjustly, we will be tormented continually. The secret is to deal with situations in a spiritual way. Saint Symeon the New Theologian writes in a similar vein:

'We need to regard all of the faithful as one and think that each one of them is Christ. We need to have such love for each individual that we are ready to sacrifice our very life for him. Because we ought never to say or think that any person is evil, but rather to regard all as good. And if you see a brother troubled by passions, do not hate him. Hate rather the passions that are assailing him. And if you see that he is being tormented by desires and habits from former sins, have even greater compassion on him, lest

you also fall into temptation, since you are made of matter that easily turns from good to evil. Love for your brother prepares you to love God more. Accordingly, the secret of love for God is love for your brother. Because if you don't love your brother whom you see, how can you possibly love God whom you don't see? *He who does not love his brother whom he has seen,*
1 John 4:20 *how can he love God whom he has not seen?* *

Let us strive to radiate our good will

Let's have love, meekness and peace. In that way we help our brother when he is possessed by evil. Our example radiates mystically, and not only when the person is present, but also when he is not. Let us strive to radiate our good will. Even when we say something about a person whose way of life does not meet with our approval, the person is aware of it and we repel him. Whereas, if we are compassionate and forgive him then we influence him — just as evil influences him — even if he does not see us.

We shouldn't be enraged by people who blaspheme or who speak and act against God and the Church. Such rage is harmful. We may hate the words and the malice behind them, but we must not hate the person who spoke them nor become enraged against him. Rather we should pray for him. A Christian has love and graciousness and should behave accordingly.

Just as a hermit, who is seen by no one, benefits the world because the mystical waves of his prayers influence people and transmit the Holy Spirit into the world, so you, too, should scatter your love, without expecting anything in return — with love, patience and a smile...

Love needs to be sincere. And only the love of God is sincere love. To a person whom we find tiresome and troublesome, love needs to be offered in a subtle manner without the person being aware that we are striving to love him. It shouldn't be given much outward expression, because then the person will react. Silence saves us from all evils. Restraint of the tongue is a great thing. In a mystical way silence radiates out to our neighbour. Let me tell you a story.

A nun who was very concerned that life in her monastery should be

* This passage contains words of Saint Symeon interspersed with Saint Pophyrios's own words. Cf. Symeon the New Theologian, *One Hundred Theological and Practical Chapters*, ed. J. Darrouzès, Sources Chrétiennes 51, Paris 1957. Saint Porphyrios asked for this passage to written out in fine, legible characters, framed, and hung on the wall of his cell, and for photocopies to be made to be given to people for their benefit.

perfectly ordered came to her spiritual father in exasperation and said:

'Sister so-and-so is disrupting the whole monastery with her problems and her character. We simply can't endure her.'

Her elder replied:

'You are worse than she is.'

To begin with the nun was taken aback and protested, but after her elder explained things to her she understood what he meant and was very pleased. What her elder said was,'The evil spirit that takes hold of the other nun and causes her to behave badly takes hold of you too, even though you think you are in a better state, and it makes a mockery of you both. The other nun gets into the state she does without wishing to, but you, with your over-reaction and lack of love, do exactly the same. In that way you do no good to your sister and you yourself are harmed.'

With silence, tolerance and prayer we benefit others in a mystical way

When we see that the people around us have no love for God we are distressed. But with our distress we achieve nothing at all. Nor do we achieve anything by trying to persuade them to change their ways. That's not right either. There is a secret, however, and if we understand it, we will be able to help. The secret is our prayer and our devotion to God so that His grace may act. We, with our love, with our fervent desire for the love of God, will attract grace so that it washes over those around us and awakens them to divine love. Or rather God will send His love and will rouse them all. What we are unable to do, His grace will achieve. With our prayers we will make all worthy of God's love.

And you should be aware of something else. Souls that have known pain and suffering and that are tormented by their passions win most especially the love and grace of God. It is souls such as these that become saints, and very often we pass judgment on them. Remember what Saint Paul says, *Where sin abounded, grace flowed even more abundantly.* When Rom. 5:20
you remember this, you will feel that these people are more worthy than you and than me. We see them as weak, but when they open themselves to God they become all love and all divine *eros*. Whereas previously they had acquired different habits, they now give all the power of their soul to Christ and are set on fire by Christ's love. That is how God's miracle works in such souls, which we regard as 'lost'.

We shouldn't be discouraged, nor should we rush to conclusions, nor judge on the basis of superficial and external things. If, for example, you see a woman immodestly dressed, don't have regard only for her outward appearance, but look more deeply into her soul. She may be a very good soul with an existential restlessness, which she expresses through her shocking appearance. She has a dynamism within her, the power of self-projection; she wishes to attract the eyes of others. But through lack of awareness she has distorted things. Think what would happen if she were to come to know Christ. She would believe and she would turn all her passion towards Christ. She would do everything to attract the grace of God. She would become a saint.

It is a kind of self-projection of our own when we insist on other people becoming good. In reality, we wish to become good, but because we are unable to, we demand it of others and insist on this. And whereas all things are corrected through prayer, we often are distressed or become outraged and pass judgment on others.

Often through our anxieties and fears and our poor psychological state, without intending to and without being aware of it, we do harm to another person, even if we love him very much, as, for example, a mother loves her child. The mother transmits to the child all her anxiety about its life, about its health and about its progress, even if she doesn't speak to the child and even if she doesn't express what she has inside her. This love, this natural love, that is, can on occasion be harmful. This is not true, however, of the love of Christ that is combined with prayer and holiness of life. This love makes a person holy; it brings him peace, because God is love.

Let our love be only in Christ. In order to benefit others you must live in the love of God, otherwise you are unable to do good to your fellow man. You mustn't pressurize the other person. His time will come, as long as you pray for him. With silence, tolerance and above all by prayer we benefit others in a mystical way. The grace of God clears the horizon of his mind and assures him of His love. Here is the fine point. As soon as he accepts that God is love, then abundant light such as he has never seen will come upon him. Thus he will find salvation.

The best form of mission is through our good example, our love and our meekness

We should be zealots. A zealot is a person who loves Christ with all his soul and who serves his fellow men in Christ's name. Love for God and for our neighbour; they go together and cannot be divorced. Passion, yearning and tears along with contrition, not for a purpose, but all as an overflowing of the heart!

Fanaticism has nothing to do with Christ. Be a true Christian. Then you won't leap to conclusions about anybody, but your love will 'cover Cf. 1 Cor. all things'. Even to a person of another religion you will always act as a 13:7 Christian. That is to say, you will show respect for him in a gracious manner irrespective of his religion. You will care for a Muslim when he is in need, speak to him and keep company with him. There must be respect for the freedom of the other person. Just as Christ *stands at the door and knocks* and does not force an entry, but waits for the soul to accept Him Rev. 3:20 freely on its own, so we should stand in the same way in relation to every soul.

In our missionary endeavour we need to employ a very delicate manner so that people accept what we are offering, whether it be words, books or whatever, without reacting negatively. And something else: use few words. Words often provoke irritation. Prayer and living example find resonance. Living faith moves people, regenerates them and changes them, whereas words alone remain fruitless. The best form of mission is through our good example, our love and our meekness. Listen and I'll give you an example.

A priest once happened to attend a talk that was being given to an audience of intellectuals. A cousin of his had taken him along. The speaker spoke long and eloquently about some Marxist subject. The audience gave him an enthusiastic reception and clapped vigorously at the end. But while the speaker was still standing on the podium he caught sight of the priest and said:

'This evening we have a priest in our audience. Perhaps, if he could, he would say something to us about the subject from a religious and philosophical point of view.'

He said this ironically, believing that he would humiliate the priest and make the Church look foolish. The priest rose to his feet and said:

'What indeed could I tell you about the subject, my dear friend? I don't know. I have heard, however, that this wise thinker says this in this book and that philosopher says that in that work etc., etc. And Moses says this in this chapter and verse and Isaiah that, and David says such and such, and Christ refers to the matter in this way.'

He then continued, quoting the passage from Saint Paul:

Where is the wise man? Where is the scribe? Where is the disputer of this world? Has not God made foolish the wisdom of this world?... God has chosen the foolish things of the world to confound the wise...so that no 1 Cor. *flesh might boast before God.* 1:20, 27, 29

The 'wise' speaker was dumbfounded. What was most telling was the fact that the priest spoke in the mildest possible manner and without a hint of egotism. The priest in question was in fact a bishop belonging to the Ecumenical Patriarchate. He finished by saying:

'I confess I know nothing. It's up to you to judge what is right.'

With no little embarrassment the speaker said:

'The priest has indeed spoken to us very well! He has overturned everything I said.'

Mastery of a subject is a great thing when it is combined with meekness, graciousness and love. This is true in all fields. When you have the relevant mastery of the subject, then speak. Otherwise, speak through your example.

In debates, if you say a few words about religion you will prevail. Let the person who has a different opinion give free rein to his thoughts and speak as much as he likes... Let him sense that he is addressing himself to a calm and uncontentious person. Influence him through your graciousness and prayer and then speak briefly. You achieve nothing if you speak heatedly and tell him, for example, 'What you're saying is untrue,
Matt. 10:16 a downright lie!' What will you achieve? Be *as sheep among wolves*. What
should you do? Show indifference outwardly, but be praying inwardly. Be prepared, know what you are talking about and speak boldly and to the point, but with saintliness, meekness and prayer. But in order to be able to do this you must become saints.

Love is above everything

Love towards Christ is without limits, and the same is true of love towards our neighbour. It should radiate everywhere, to the ends of the earth, to every single person. I wanted to go and live with the hippies at Matala* in order to show them the love of Christ and how great it is and how it could change and transfigure them. Love is above everything. I'll give you an example:

There was a hermit with two monks in obedience. He did his utmost to foster their spiritual development and to make them good. He was unsure, however, whether they were really making any progress in the spiritual life and whether they were ready for the Kingdom of God. He looked for some sign from God about this, but he received no answer. One day there was going to be vigil service in the church of another hermitage that was many hours walk away from his own. They would have

* A resort in Eastern Crete.

to cross the desert. He sent off his two monks early in the morning so that they could help prepare the church and he planned to follow later in the afternoon. The monks had covered some considerable distance when suddenly they heard a groaning noise. A man was lying badly injured and was crying out for assistance.

'Take me with you, please,' he implored. 'Here in the desert no one else is going to pass by and who will help me? There are two of you. Lift me up and take me to the nearest village.'

'There's no way we can do that,' they replied. 'We're in a hurry to go to a vigil and we've got instructions to prepare everything.'

'Please take me with you! If you leave me, I'll die. I'll be eaten by the wild beasts.'

'We can't do it. We've got to do what we've been told to.'

And they walked on.

In the afternoon the elder set out along the same road to go to the vigil. He came to the spot where the injured man was lying. He saw him and went up to him and said, 'What's happened to you, good man of God? How long have you been lying here? Did no one see you?'

'Two monks passed by in the morning and I asked them to help me, but they were in a hurry to go to the vigil.'

'Don't worry. I'll carry you along,' said the elder.

'You won't be able to,' said the injured man. You're an old man and there is no way that you'll be able to lift me up.'

'Not at all, you'll see I'll manage. I can't leave you here. I'll bend down and you will grab hold of me and I'll carry you along until we get to the nearest village. A little today and a little tomorrow, but I'll get you there.'

With great difficulty he hoisted the man onto his back and set off. Walking in the sand with such a great weight was nearly impossible. Sweat was pouring from him in rivers. He thought to himself, 'It will take three days, but I'll get there.' As he continued on his way, however, he felt his burden getting lighter and lighter until he felt that he was carrying nothing at all. He turned round to see what was happening and was astonished to see an angel on his back. The angel said to him, 'God sent me to inform you that your two monks are not worthy of the Kingdom of God because they don't have love.'

ON DIVINE PROVIDENCE

God is love; He is not a simple spectator in our life.
He provides and cares for us as our Father,
but he respects our freedom

God has foreknowledge, but He does not pre-ordain

God's knowledge is beyond comprehension for our own mind. It is infinite and encompasses all beings, visible and invisible, from the beginning of time until the end of time. God knows all things with minute precision in all their depth and breadth. The Lord knows us before we know ourselves. He knows our predispositions and our slightest thought, the temptations we play with and our decisions — before we even take them. But even before our conception and before the creation of the world he knew us well. This is why David cries out in wonderment: *Lord, You tried me and knew me... You understood my thoughts from afar off... You traced out my path and You foreknew all my ways... You*
Ps. 138:1–5 *knew all things, the last things and the first things; You formed me and*
[139:1–5] *set your hand upon me.*

The Holy Spirit permeates everywhere. And that is why the person who is borne on and infused with the Holy Spirit also possesses the knowledge of God. He knows the past, the present and the future. The Holy Spirit reveals these things to him. Nothing of our actions is unknown to God; all are recorded. They are recorded and yet they are not recorded. They are born, brought into being, and exist, and yet they are not born. What you know now, God knows before the creation of the world. Let me remind you what Saint Symeon the New Theologian says in the Prayer of Preparation for Holy Communion: 'Your eyes knew my yet unaccomplished work; and in Your book the things I have not yet done are for You already written.'*

Some people misunderstand and confuse these words. They say, 'Since God has everything written down, we are ruled by fate and destiny. It was, for example, predestined for you to commit a murder; God had preordained you to do this.' And they ask, 'If I am destined to murder you, am I responsible or not responsible? Moreover, since "the things I have not yet

* Prayer 7; cf. psalm 138:16 [139:16].

done are for You already written", why should we humans be regarded as responsible for our actions? And can you, who affirm that God is good, tell me why he ordained this and didn't avert me from doing it?'

Here is the secret: God in His omnipotence and omniscience knows everything, including the things that will happen in the future, but He is not the cause of evil. God has foreknowledge, but He does not pre-ordain. For God there is no past, present and future. All things are *naked and laid bare* before Him. This is what Saint Paul says, *All things are naked*
and laid bare before His eyes. In His omniscience He knows both good Heb. 4:13
and evil. He cooperates with good, being, as God, good by nature and alien to evil. But since He is alien to evil, how is it possible for Him to pre-
ordain us for evil? God created everything *exceedingly good* and gave to Gen. 1:31
everything a good and holy purpose.

Evil is a problem which our faith explains in a marvellous way which cannot be bettered. The explanation which our faith gives is as follows: Evil exists and comes from the devil. Within us we have both the evil spirit and the good spirit and they battle with each other. *Either he will hate the one and love the other; or else he will cling to the one and despise*
the other. You cannot serve God and mammon. That is, within us a strug- Matt. 6:24
gle between good and evil takes place. But in this struggle a person is free to decide and to choose. Consequently it is not God who pre-ordains and decides, but man's free will.

God in His omniscience knows in all precision not simply beforehand, but before the creation of the world, that this person, for example, will commit a murder when he is thirty years old. But the person in his freedom of will (a gift which God gave the person and which he perverted) acts of his own volition. God is not the cause, nor does he pre-ordain us for that end. His omniscience does not constrain us. He respects our freedom; He does not abolish it. He loves us; he does not make us slaves; He gives us worth. God does not intervene in our freedom; He respects it fully. Consequently, we are responsible, because we do what we want. God does not compel us. It is known to God in advance that you will kill this man, but it is not arranged by God for you to do it. How is it possible for God — who created us out of infinite love and who Himself is absolute love and who desires only love — to will to lead you to evil and to murder? Does He give you freedom only to take it from you? You act freely and you decide to do the thing that God knows in advance without compelling you, and that is why it is you who are responsible.

These things are very delicate matters and require divine illumination for a person to understand them. They are mysteries. What is good in nature is a mystery. Isn't a tiny flower that attracts you with its variegated colours and makes you love it beautiful? You approach it and it has such a delicate fragrance that it awakens your love even more. That is 'the good'. Of course it is, but isn't it also a mystery? How did these colours come about? How did that fragrance arise? The same can be said of the birds, the animals and sea creatures. All express the goodness of God.

Some people say, 'Why does God make me suffer? Why does he make me fall easily into sin? Why did He give me this character?' And so on. And again I repeat. God created us as good. God gave to man what is most beautiful and best. He intended him to become perfect. But He gave him freedom and so it is up to him to follow good or evil. On the one hand there is God's love and on the other there is man's freedom. Love and freedom are interwoven. Spirit is united with the Spirit. This is the mystical life. When our spirit is united with the Spirit of God, then we do good — we become saints.

For our passions and vices another is responsible — our will. God does not wish to circumscribe our will; He does not wish to pressure us and impose on us. It depends on us what we will do and how we will live. Either we will live with Christ and we will have divine life and blessedness or we will live in melancholy and sorrow. There is no intermediate state — either the one or the other. Nature takes revenge — it abhors a vacuum. Everything can be good, but it can also not be. A kiss, for example, can be holy or it can be seductive. But that is what is of value, namely, that a person acts freely. If, on the contrary, God had made us will-less, and we did only what God willed, there would be no freedom. God made man seek himself to become good, to desire this himself and for it to be, in a sense, his own achievement, although in point of fact it comes from the grace of God. He comes first to the point where he wishes, loves and desires the good and then divine grace comes and he achieves it.

God provides and cares for us as a Father, but He also respects our freedom

God is love; He is not a simple spectator in our life. He provides and cares for us as our Father, but He also respects our freedom. He does not pressure us. We should have our hope in God's providence and, since we believe that God is watching over us, we should take courage and throw ourselves into His love and then we will see Him constantly beside us. We will not be afraid that we will make a false step.

How perfect the human body is! A great factory! It drinks water and the water goes to the stomach and to the kidneys and purifies the blood.

Or take the heart, the lungs, the liver, the gallbladder, the pancreas, the brain, the nervous system, the senses, vision, hearing… And what can we say about the mental powers and how all these systems work together in perfect harmony under the protection and providence of God!

All things are under God's providence. How many pine needles has each pine tree? Can you count them? God, however, knows them and without His will not one falls to the ground. Just as with the hairs of our head; they are all numbered. He provides for the smallest details of our life; He loves us and protects us.

We live as if we were completely insensitive to the magnificence of God's providence. God is very withdrawn and mystical. We cannot comprehend His actions. Don't imagine that God created things in one way and then corrected them. God is infallible. He corrects nothing. Who God is in His essence we do not know. We cannot discover the thoughts of God. *For my thoughts are not your thoughts, nor are your ways my ways, says the Lord. For as the heavens are higher than the earth, so are my ways higher than your ways and my thoughts than your thoughts.* Isa. 55:8–9

When God bestows on us the gift of humility, then we see all things, we sense all things and we experience God very manifestly. When we do not have humility, we see nothing. On the contrary, when we are made worthy of holy humility, we see all things and rejoice in all things. We experience God and we experience Paradise within ourselves for Paradise is Christ himself.

Let me tell you a story — I don't know if you've read it yourselves in the tales of the Desert Fathers — which shows God's providence and the power of an elder's prayer.*

An elder once sent the monk who was in obedience to him — Paisios was his name — on an errand far distant from their hermitage. The monk walked for hours on end. It was mid-day and the sun was burning down. He saw a large rock that cast a welcome shadow and he went and lay down in the shade of the rock to rest and there he fell asleep. While he was sleeping — he was either sleeping or dozing — he saw his elder before him shouting and saying:

'Paisios, Paisios, get up at once and get away from where you are!'

And as he heard his elder shouting loudly, he jumped up and leapt away. He had barely taken half a dozen steps when he saw the rock toppling over. It would have caught him like a bird in a trap and crushed every bone in his body. The elder was miles away from Paisios and yet he saw him.

* Cf. Saint John of Sinai, *The Ladder*, 'The Life of Saint John of Sinai'.

This is God's providence. The Lord's words are borne out: *And these signs will accompany those who believe: in my name they will cast out demons; they will speak in new tongues; they will pick up snakes in their*
Mark *hands, and if they drink any deadly thing, it will not harm them; they will*
16:17–18 *lay their hands on the sick, and they will recover.*

We can think to ourselves and say:

'My God, You are present everywhere and You see everything, wherever I am. You follow my every step with Your tender care.'

We should repeat the words of David:

Where can I go from Your spirit? Or where can I flee from Your presence? If I ascend to heaven, You are there; if I descend into Hades, you are present; if I take the wings of the morning and dwell in the uttermost parts
Ps. 138:7–10 *of the sea, even there Your hand shall lead me, and Your right hand shall*
[139:7–10] *hold me fast.*

Of course, it's not enough simply to know this, but it is a great support and comfort when we believe it, when we experience it and when we take it to heart.

ON THE UPBRINGING OF CHILDREN

A large part of the responsibility for a person's spiritual state lies with the family

A child's upbringing commences at the moment of its conception

A child's upbringing commences at the moment of its conception. The embryo hears and feels in its mother's womb. Yes, it hears and it sees with its mother's eyes. It is aware of her movements and her emotions, even though its mind has not developed. If the mother's face darkens, it darkens too. If the mother is irritated, then it becomes irritated also. Whatever the mother experiences — sorrow, pain, fear, anxiety, etc. — is also experienced by the embryo.

If the mother doesn't want the child, if she doesn't love it, then the embryo senses this and traumas are created in its little soul that accompany it all its life. The opposite occurs through the mother's holy emotions. When she is filled with joy, peace and love for the embryo, she transmits these things to it mystically, just as happens to children that have been born.

For this reason a mother must pray a lot during her pregnancy and love the child growing within her, caressing her abdomen, reading psalms, singing hymns and living a holy life. This is also for her own benefit. But she makes sacrifices for the sake of the embryo so that the child will become more holy and will acquire from the very outset holy foundations.

Do you see how delicate a matter it is for a woman to go through a pregnancy? Such a responsibility and such an honour!

I'll tell you something about other animate and non-rational beings and you will understand what I mean. In America the following experiment was carried out: in two identical rooms which were kept at exactly the same temperature flowers were planted in identical soil and watered in exactly the same way. There was, however, one difference: in the one room gentle, soothing music was played. And the result? The flowers in that room displayed an enormous difference in relation to the flowers in the other room. They had a quite different vitality, their colours were more attractive and they grew incomparably better.

What saves and makes for good children is the life of the parents in the home. The parents need to devote themselves to the love of God. They need to become saints in their relation to their children through their mildness, patience and love. They need to make a new start every day, with a fresh outlook, renewed enthusiasm and love for their children. And the joy that will come to them, the holiness that will visit them, will shower grace on their children. Generally the parents are to blame for the bad behaviour of the children. And their behaviour is not improved by reprimands, disciplining, or strictness. If the parents do not pursue a life of holiness and if they don't engage in spiritual struggle, they make great mistakes and transmit the faults they have within them. If the parents do not live a holy life and do not display love towards each other, the devil torments the parents with the reactions of the children. Love, harmony and understanding between the parents are what are required for the children. This provides a great sense of security and certainty.

The behaviour of the children is directly related to the state of the parents. When the children are hurt by the bad behaviour of the parents towards each other, they lose the strength and desire to progress in their lives. Their lives are constructed shoddily and the edifice of their soul is in constant danger of collapsing. Let me give you two examples.

Two sisters came to see me. One of them had gone through some very distressing experiences and they asked me what was the cause of these. I answered them:

'It's because of your home; it stems from your parents.'

And as I looked at the girl I said:

'These are things you've inherited from your mother.'

'But,' she said, 'my parents are such perfect people. They're Christians, they go to confession, they receive Communion and we had a religious upbringing. Unless it is religion that is to blame...'

I said to them:

'I don't believe a word of all that you're telling me. I see one thing only, and that is that your parents don't live with the joy of Christ.'

On hearing this, the other girl said:

'Listen, Maria, the Father's quite right. Our parents go to confession and receive Holy Communion, but did we ever have any peace at home? Our father was constantly complaining about our mother. And every day either the one refused to sit at the table or the other refused to go out somewhere together. So you see what the Father is saying is true.'

'What's your father's name?' I asked her.

She told me.

'What's your mother's name?'

She told me.

'Well,' I said, 'the feelings you've got inside you towards your mother are not at all good.'

You see, the moment she told me her father's name I saw his soul, and the moment she told me her mother's name, I saw her mother and I saw the way her daughter looked at her.

Another day a mother came to visit me with one of her daughters. She was very distressed and broke down in tears.

'What's the matter?' I asked.

'I'm in total despair over my older daughter. She threw her husband out the house and deceived us all with a pack of lies.'

'What kind of lies?' I inquired.

'She threw her husband out the house ages ago and she didn't tell us anything. We would ask on the phone, "How's Stelios doing?", and she would reply, "Oh, he's fine. He's just gone out to buy a newspaper." Each time she would think up some new excuse so that we wouldn't suspect anything. And this went on for two whole years. A few days ago we learned the truth from Stelios himself when we bumped into him by chance.'

So I said to her:

'The fault's your own. It's you that's to blame, you and your husband, but you most of all.'

'What do you mean!' she said indignantly. 'I loved my children to the point that I was never out of the kitchen. I had no life of my own at all. I took them to the church and I was always telling them the right thing to do. How can you say that I'm to blame?'

I turned to her other daughter who was with her and asked:

'What do you think about the matter?'

'The Father's right, Mum,' she said. 'We never ever enjoyed a single day when you weren't quarrelling with Dad.'

'Do you see then, how I'm right? It is you that are to blame. You traumatized the children. They are not to blame, but they are suffering the consequences.'

A psychological state is created in a child as a result of its parents that accompanies it throughout its life. Its later behaviour and its relationships with others are directly connected with the experiences that it carries with it from its childhood years. The child grows up and develops, but at bottom it does not change. This is manifested even in the smallest expressions of life. For example, you get a craving for food and want to eat. You take something and eat it, then you see something else and you want that. You feel hungry and think that if you don't eat you'll feel faint and you'll start to tremble. You're afraid you'll lose weight. This is a psychological state that has its explanation. Perhaps you never knew your father or your mother, and you feel deprived and hungry, poor and weak. And this psychological reality is expressed by way of reflex as a weakness of the body.

A large part of the responsibility for a person's spiritual state lies with the family. For children to be released from their various inner problems it is not enough for them to receive good advice, or to be compelled by force; nor do logical arguments or threats do any good. These things rather make matters worse. The solution is to be found through the sanctification of the parents. Become saints and you will have no problems with your children. The sanctity of their parents releases the children from their problems. Children want to have saintly people at their side, people with lots of love who will neither intimidate them nor lecture them, but who will provide a saintly example and pray for them. You parents should pray silently to Christ with upraised arms and embrace your children mystically. When they misbehave you will take some disciplinary measures, but you will not coerce them. Above all you need to pray.

Parents, especially the mother, often cause hurt to a child for some act of misbehaviour by scolding it excessively. The child is then wounded. Even if you don't scold the child outwardly but bristle with anger inwardly or look fiercely at the child, the child understands. The child believes that its mother doesn't love it and asks, 'Do you love me, Mummy?' The mother answers, 'Yes, dear,' but the child is not convinced. It has been wounded. The mother loves it, she'll caress it later, but the child will pull its head away. It refuses to be caressed, regarding this as hypocrisy because it has been wounded.

Over-protectiveness leaves children immature

Another thing that harms children is over-protectiveness, that is, excessive care or excessive anxiety and worry on the part of the parents.

A mother used to complain to me that her five-year-old child was disobedient. 'It's your fault,' I told her, but she didn't understand. Once I went for a walk by the seaside with this mother along with the child. The little boy let go of his mother's hand and ran towards the sea. There was a sand dune there and the sea came in directly behind it. The mother immediately reacted with anxiety and was about to shout out and run towards the boy who was standing on top of the dune with outstretched arms trying to keep his balance. I calmed her down and told to her to turn her back on the boy while I kept an eye on him askance. When the boy despaired of provoking his mother's attention and causing her to panic and scream as usual, he calmly climbed down and walked towards us. That was the end of it. Then the mother understood what I meant.

Another mother used to complain that her little boy wouldn't eat all his food, especially his yoghurt. The little one was about three years old and tormented his mother every day. I said to her:

'What you should do is this. Empty the refrigerator completely and then fill it with some yoghurt. When lunchtime comes you'll give Peter his yoghurt. He'll refuse to eat it. In the evening you'll give him it again and the same the next day. In the end he'll get hungry and will try some. He'll throw a tantrum, but you'll just put up with it. Thereafter he'll eat it quite happily.'

That's just what happened and yoghurt became Peter's favourite food.

These things aren't difficult, but many mothers are unable to do them and the result is that they give their children a very bad upbringing. Mothers who are always standing over their children and pressurizing them, that is, over-protecting them, have failed in their task. You need to leave the child alone to take an interest in its own progress. Then you will succeed. When you are always standing over them, the children react. They become lethargic and weak-willed and generally are unsuccessful in life. This is a kind of over-protectiveness that leaves the children immature.

A few days ago a mother came here in a state of despair because of her son's repeated failures in the university entrance exams. He had been an excellent pupil in elementary school and all the way through high school. But in the end he failed repeatedly and showed indifference and had strange reactions.

'It's your fault,' I said to the mother, 'educated woman though you are! How else did you expect the boy to react? Pressure, pressure, pressure all these years, "Make sure you're top of the class, don't let us down, get yourself an important position in society..." Now he's thrown in the towel; he doesn't want anything. Stop this pressure and over-protection and you'll see that the boy will regain his equilibrium. He'll make progress once you let him be.'

A child needs to be surrounded by people who pray and pray ardently

A child needs to be surrounded by people who pray and pray ardently. A mother should not be satisfied by giving her child a physical caress, but should also coddle it with the caress of prayer. In the depths of its soul the child senses the spiritual caress that its mother conveys to it and is drawn to her. It feels security and certainty when its mother mystically embraces it with constant, intense and fervent prayer and releases it from whatever is oppressing it.

Mothers know how to express anxiety, offer advice and talk incessantly, but they haven't learned to pray. Most advice and criticism does a great deal of harm. You don't need to say a lot to children. Words hammer at the ears, but prayer goes to the heart. Prayer is required, with faith and without anxiety, along with a good example.

One day a mother came here distraught about her son, George. He was very mixed-up. He stayed out late at night and the company he kept was far from good. Every day things were getting worse. The mother was overcome by anxiety and distress.

I said to her:

'Don't say a word. Just pray.'

We agreed that between ten and ten fifteen every evening we would both pray. I told her to say not a word and to leave her son to stay out till whatever time he wanted, without asking him, 'What sort of time is this to come home? Where were you?', or any such thing. Instead she would say to him as lovingly as possible, 'Come and eat, George, there's food in the fridge.' Beyond this she was to say nothing. She would behave towards him with love and not stop praying.

The mother began to apply this tactic, and after about twenty days had passed the boy asked her:

'Mother, why don't you speak to me?'

'What do you mean, George, that I don't speak to you?'

'You've got something against me, Mother, and you're not speaking to me.'

'What strange idea is this that you've got into your head, George? Of course I speak to you. Am I not speaking to you now? What do you want me to say to you?'

George made no reply.

The mother then came to the monastery and asked me:

'Elder, what was the meaning of this that the boy said to me?'

'Our tactic has worked!'

'What tactic?'

'The tactic I told you — of not speaking and simply praying secretly and that the boy would come to his senses.'

'Do you think that that is it?'

'That is it,' I told her. 'He wants you to ask him "Where were you? What were you doing?" so that he can shout and react and come home even later the next night.'

'Is that so?' she said. 'What strange mysteries are hidden!'

'Do you understand now? He was tormenting you because he wanted you to react to his behaviour so that he could stage his little act. Now that you're not shouting at him he is upset. Instead of you being upset when he does what he wants, now he is upset because you don't appear distressed and you display indifference.'

One day George announced that he was giving up his job and going to Canada. He had told his boss to find a replacement because he was leaving. In the meantime I said to his parents:

'We'll pray.'

'But he's ready to leave… I'll grab him by the scruff of the neck!' said his father.

'No,' I told him, 'don't do anything.'

'But the boy's leaving, Elder!'

I said: 'Let him leave. You just devote yourselves to prayer and I'll be with you.'

Two or three days later early one Sunday morning George announced to his parents:

'I'm going off today with my friends.'

'Fine,' they replied, 'do as you want.'

He left, and along with his friends, two girls and two boys, he hired a car and set off for Chalkida. They drove around aimlessly here and there. Then they went past the church of Saint John the Russian and from there to Mantoudi, Aghia Anna and beyond to Vasilika. They had a swim in the Aegean Sea, they ate, drank and had a fine time. At the end of it all they set off on the road home. It was already dark. George was driving. As they were passing through Aghia Anna the car hit the corner of a house and was badly damaged. What could they do now? They managed to bring the car back to Athens at a crawling pace.

George arrived back home in the early hours of the morning. His parents said nothing to him and he went off to sleep. When he woke up he came and said to his father:

'Do you know what happened?… Now we'll have to repair the car and it will cost a lot of money.'

His father said:

'Well, George, you'll have to find a solution to this yourself. You know I've got debts to pay and your sisters to look after…'

'What can I do, father?'

'Do whatever you like. You're grown-up and you've got a brain of your own. Go off to Canada and make some money…'

'I can't do that. We have to repair the car now.'

'I've no idea what you should do,' said his father. 'Sort it out yourself.'

So, seeing that further dialogue with his father was pointless, he said no more and left. He went to his boss and said:

'I had an accident with a car. I don't want to leave now, so don't hire anyone else.'

His boss said:

'That's all right by me, lad.'

'Yes, but I would like you to give me some money in advance.'

'That's fine, but you were wanting to leave. If you want money, your father will have to sign for it.'

'I'll sign for it myself. My father doesn't want to get involved. He told me so. I'll work and I'll repay it.'

Now isn't that a miracle?

When the boy's mother came again to see me I said to her:

'The method we employed worked and God heard our prayer. The accident was from God and now the boy will stay at home and will come to his senses.'

That's what happened through our prayer. It was a miracle. The parents fasted, prayed and kept silent and they were successful. Some time later the boy himself came and found me — without any of his family having said anything to him about me. George became a very fine man and now works in the air force and is married with a lovely family.

With children what is required is a lot of prayer and few words

All things are achieved through prayer, silence and love. Have you understood the effects of prayer? Love in prayer, love in Christ. That is what is truly beneficial. As long as you love your children with human love — which is often pathological — the more they will be mixed-up, and the more their behaviour will be negative. But when the love between you and towards your children is holy and Christian love, then you will have no problem. The sanctity of the parents saves the children. For this to come about, divine grace must act on the souls of the parents. No one can be sanctified on his own. The same divine grace will then illuminate, warm and animate the souls of the children.

People often telephone me from abroad and ask me about their children and about other matters. Today a mother phoned me from Milan and asked me how she should behave towards her children. What I said to her was this:

'Pray, and when you have to, speak to your children with love. Lots of prayer and few words. Lots of prayer and few words for everyone. We mustn't become an annoyance, but rather pray secretly and then speak, and God will let us know in our hearts whether the others have accepted what we have said. If not, we won't speak. We will simply pray mystically. Because if we speak we become an annoyance and make others react or even infuriate them. That is why it is better to speak mystically to the heart of others through secret prayer rather than to their ears.

'Pray and then speak. That's what to do with your children. If you are constantly lecturing them, you'll become tiresome and when they grow up they'll feel a kind of oppression. Prefer prayer and speak to them through prayer. Speak to God and God will speak to their hearts. That is, you shouldn't give guidance to your children with a voice that they hear with their ears. You may do this too, but above all you should speak to God about your children. Say, "Lord Jesus Christ, give Your light to my children. I entrust them to You. You gave them to me, but I am weak and unable to guide them, so, please, illuminate them." And God will speak to them and they will say to themselves, "Oh dear, I shouldn't have upset Mummy by doing that!" And with the grace of God this will come from their heart.'

This is the most perfect way — for the mother to speak to God and for God to speak to the children. If you do not communicate in this way, constant lecturing becomes a kind of intimidation. And when the child grows up it begins to rebel, that is, to take revenge, so to speak, on its father and mother who coerced it. One way is the perfect way — for the mother's and father's holiness and love in Christ to speak. The radiance of sanctity and not human effort makes for good children.

When the children are traumatized and hurt on account of some serious situation, don't let it affect you when they react negatively and speak rudely. In reality they don't want to, but can't help themselves at difficult times. They are remorseful afterwards. But if you become irritated and enraged, you become one with the evil spirit and it makes a mockery of you all.

The sanctity of the parents is the best way of bringing up children in the Lord

We must see God in the faces of our children and give God's love to our children. The children should learn to pray. And in order for children

to pray they must have in them the blood of praying parents. This is where some people make the mistake of saying, 'Since the parents are devout and pray, meditate on Holy Scripture and bring up their chil-
Eph. 6:4 dren *in the nurture and admonition of the Lord*, it is natural that they will become good children.' But nevertheless we see the very opposite result on account of coercion.

It is not sufficient for the parents to be devout. They mustn't oppress the children to make them good by force. We may repel our children from Christ when we pursue the things of our religion with egotism. Children cannot endure coercion. Don't compel them to come with you to church. You can say, 'Whoever wants can come with me now or come later.' Leave God to speak to their souls. The reason why the children of some devout parents become rebellious when they grow up and reject the Church and everything connected with it and go off to seek satisfaction elsewhere is because of this pressure which they feel from their 'good' parents. The so-called 'devout' parents, who were anxious to make 'good Christians' of their children with their human love, pressurized their children and produced the opposite result. The children are pressurized when they are young, and when they reach the age of sixteen, seventeen or eighteen years old, they end up the opposite of what was intended. By way of reaction they start to mix with bad company and to use bad language.

When children grow up in an atmosphere of freedom and at the same time are surrounded by the good example of grown-ups, they are a joy to see. The secret is to be good and saintly and to inspire and radiate. The life of the children seems to be affected by the radiation of their parents. If the parents insist, 'Come on now, go and make confession, go and receive Communion', and so on, nothing is achieved. But what does your child see in you? How do you live and what do you radiate? Does Christ radiate in you? That is what is transmitted to your child. This is where the secret lies. And if this is done when the child is young, it will not be necessary for it to undergo '*great travail*' when it grows up. Solomon the Wise uses a beautiful image about exactly this subject, underlining the importance of a good start and good foundations: *He who seeks her* [Wisdom]
Wisd. 6:14 *early shall have no great travail; for he shall find her sitting at his doors.* The
[DC] person who '*seeks her early*' is the person who occupies himself with Wisdom from an early age. Wisdom is Christ.

When the parents are saintly and transmit this to the child and give the child an upbringing 'in the Lord', then the child, whatever the bad influences around it, will not be affected because by the door of its heart will be Wisdom — Christ Himself. The child will not undergo great travail to acquire Wisdom. It seems very difficult to become good, but in reality it is very easy when from an early age you start with good experiences. As you grow up effort is not required; you have goodness within you and you experience it. You don't weary yourself; it is yours, a possession which you preserve, if you are careful, throughout your life.

With prayer and sanctity you can also help children at school

What is true for parents is also true for teachers. With prayer and sanctity you can also help children at school. The grace of God can overshadow them and make them good. Don't attempt with human methods to correct bad situations. No good will come of this. Only with prayer will you produce results. Invoke the grace of God on all the children — for divine grace to enter their souls and transform them. That is what it means to be a Christian.

You teachers transmit your anxiety to the children, without realizing it, and this affects them. With faith anxiety dissolves. What is it that we say? 'We commit our whole life to Christ our God.'*

Respond to the love of the children with discernment. And once they love you, you will be able to lead them to Christ. You will become the means. Let your love be genuine. Don't love them in a human way, as parents usually do. This does not help them. Love in prayer, love in Christ. This is truly beneficial. Pray for each child you see, and God will send His grace and will unite the child to Him. Before you enter the classroom, especially difficult classes, repeat the prayer, 'Lord Jesus Christ…'. And as you enter, embrace all the children with your gaze, pray and then start your lesson, offering your whole self. By making this offering in Christ, you will be filled with joy. And in this way both you and the children will be sanctified. You will live in the love of Christ and of His Church, because you will become good during your work.

If a pupil causes a problem, make a general observation first, such as:

'Children, we're all here for a lesson, for a serious business. I'm here to help you. You are working hard to succeed in life, and I, who love you all very much, am also working hard. So please be quiet so that we can achieve our aim.'

And while you're saying this don't look at the pupil who's misbehaving. If he continues, address yourself to him, not with anger, but with seriousness and resolution. You need to be watchful and to keep control

* Words repeated again and again throughout the Divine Liturgy.

of the class to be able to influence their souls. The children are not at fault if they cause problems. It is the grown-ups who are to blame.

Don't speak much about Christ and God to the children, but pray to God for the children. Words enter the ears, but prayer enters the heart. Listen to a secret. The first day you enter a class, don't have a lesson. Speak to the children warmly and clearly and behave with love towards them. To begin with don't speak to them at all about God or about the soul. This comes later. But on the day when you decide to speak to them about God, prepare yourself well and say:

'There is a subject about which many people have great doubts. It is the subject 'God'. What's your opinion about this?'

And then you will have a discussion. On another day you will broach the subject of the 'soul'.

'Is there such a thing as the "soul"?'

Then you can talk about evil from a philosophical point of view. Tell them that we have two selves, a good and a bad. We must cultivate the good self. It is the good self that desires progress, kindness and love. We need to wake up this good self in order to become right-minded people in society. Remember that hymn: 'O soul, my soul, arise, why are you sleeping?' * Don't tell them it like this, but with other words, for example: 'Be bright and awake for good things — for education, for love. Only love makes all things beautiful and fills our life and gives it meaning. Our wicked self desires laziness and indifference. But that takes all flavour from life and takes away all meaning and beauty.'

All these things, however, require preparation. Love demands sacrifices and very often sacrifice of time. Make sure you have mastery of your subject and are ready to give to the children. Be prepared and say everything with love and above all with joy. Show them all your love and know what you want and what you are saying. But how to behave towards children is an art. I heard a lovely story about this. Listen.

There was a teacher who was being tormented by the behaviour of one of the boys and wanted to expel him from the school. In the meantime, however, a new teacher arrived and took over the class. The new teacher was told in advance about the problem pupil. He also heard that the boy in question was mad about bicycles. So, on the second day, when he entered the classroom he said:

'Children, I've got a problem. I live far from the school and I want to get a bicycle so that I don't tire my feet out every day walking here, but

* The *Kontakion* from the Great Canon by Saint Andrew of Crete.

I don't know how to ride one. Could any one of you teach me how to ride a bike?'

The mischievous boy jumped up at once and said, 'I'll teach you, Sir.'

'Do you know how to ride a bike?'

'Yes, Sir.'

From that moment on they became best friends, to the point that the old teacher got upset when he saw them. He felt a sense of inadequacy that he had been unable to evoke respect from the boy.

There are often orphan children at a school. It's a hard thing to be an orphan. A child who's deprived of its parents, especially at an early age, becomes unhappy in life. But if it acquires spiritual parents in Christ and our Holy Lady, it becomes a saint. Treat orphan children with love and understanding, but above all bring them into contact with Christ and the Church.

Teach the children to seek God's help

The medicine and great secret for children's progress is humility. Trust in God gives perfect security. God is everything. No one can say that I am everything. That cultivates egotism. God desires us to lead children to humility. Without humility neither we nor children will achieve anything. You need to be careful when you encourage children. You shouldn't say to a child, 'You'll succeed, you're great, you're young, you're fearless, you're perfect!' This is not good for the child. You can tell the child to pray, and say, 'The talents you have, have been given to you by God. Pray and God will give you strength to cultivate them and in that way you will succeed. God will give you His grace.' That is the best way. Children should learn to seek God's help in everything.

Praise is harmful to children. What does Scripture say? *O my people, those who call you blessed lead you astray, and pervert the path of your feet.* The person who praises us leads us astray and perverts the paths of Isa. 3:12
our life. How wise God's words are! Praise does not prepare children for any difficulties in life and they grow up badly adjusted; they lose their way and in the end they become failures. Now the world has gone haywire. Little children are constantly being praised. We are told not to scold children, not to go against their will and not to impose on them. The child learns to expect this, however, and is unable to deal maturely with even the slightest difficulty. As soon as it encounters opposition, it is defeated and drained of all strength.

Prime responsibility for the failure of children in life lies with their parents and thereafter with their teachers. They praise them constantly. They fill them with egotistical words. They do not lead them to the spirit of God and they alienate them from the Church. When the children grow up a little and go to school with this egotism they abandon and disdain religion and they lose their respect for God, for their parents and for everyone. They become stubborn, hard and unfeeling, with no respect for religion or for God. We have produced a generation of egotists and not of Christians.

Children are not edified by constant praise

Children are not edified by constant praise. They become self-centred and vain. All their lives they will want everyone to be praising them constantly, even if they are being told lies. Unfortunately, nowadays all people have learned to tell lies and the conceited accept those lies as their daily sustenance. 'Say it, even if it's not true, even if it's ironical,' they say. God does not want this. God wants truth. Unfortunately, not all people understand this and they do the very opposite.

When you praise children constantly and indiscriminately, they fall prey to the temptations of the evil one. He sets the mill of egotism in motion, and accustomed as they are to praise from their parents and teachers, they make progress at school perhaps, but what is the gain? In life they will be egotists and not Christians. Egotists can never be Christians. Egotists desire to be praised constantly by everyone, for everyone to love them and for everyone to speak well of them, and this is something that our God, our Church and our Christ do not want.

Our religion does not wish for this kind of upbringing. On the contrary, it wants children to learn the truth from an early age. The truth of Christ emphasizes that if you praise a person you make him an egotist. An egotist is mixed-up and is led by the devil and the evil spirit. And so, growing up in the spirit of egotism, his first task is to deny God and to be a badly adjusted egotist in society.

You must tell the truth for a person to learn it. Otherwise you sustain him in his ignorance. When you tell someone the truth, he finds his bearings, he takes care, he listens to other people and he restrains himself. And so to a child also you must tell the truth and scold it so that it knows that what it is doing is not good. What does Solomon say? *He that spares*
Prov. 13:24 *the rod hates his son, but he that loves him chastens him diligently.* I don't mean, of course, for you to beat the child with a stick. Then we overstep the bounds and produce the opposite result.

By praising our children from an early age we lead them to egotism. And you can hoodwink an egotist, provided you tell him how good he is and inflate his ego. And so he tells you, 'This person who praises me is good.' These things are not right. Because such a person grows up with egotism, confusions arise within him, he suffers and he doesn't know what he is doing. The cause of psychological instability and disorder is egotism. This is something that psychiatrists themselves, if they explore the matter, will discover, namely, that the egotist is sick.

We should never praise and flatter our fellow men, but rather lead them to humility and love of God. Nor should we seek to be loved by flattering others. Let us learn to love and not seek to be loved. Let us love everyone and make sacrifices, as great as we are able, for all our brothers and sisters in Christ, without expecting praise and love from them in return. They will do for us whatever God inspires them to. If they are Christians, they will give glory to God that we helped them or spoke a good word to them.

This is also the way you should guide the children at school. This is the truth. Otherwise they grow up maladjusted. They don't know what they are doing and where they are going, and we are the cause of it, on account of the way we have brought them up. We have not led them to truth, to humility and to the love of God. We have turned them into egotists and look at the result!

There are also, however, children who come from humble parents who spoke to them from an early age about God and about holy humility. These children do not create problems to their fellow men. They do not get angry when you point out their error, but try to correct it and pray that God may help them not to become egotists.

When I went to the Holy Mountain I lived with exceedingly saintly elders. They never said to me, 'Well done.' They always counselled me how to love God and how to be always humble, to invoke God to fortify my soul and to love Him greatly. I didn't know what 'well done' was, nor did I ever desire it. On the contrary, I was distressed if my elders didn't scold me. I said to myself, 'Heavens above, I haven't found myself good elders!' I wanted them to correct me, to censure me and behave strictly towards me. If a Christian were to hear what I'm saying now, what would he say? He would be taken aback and reject it. But nevertheless that is what is right, humble and sincere.

My parents never said 'well done' to me either. For that reason, whatever I did, I did selflessly. Now that I hear people singing my praises, I feel very bad. There's something that kicks in protest inside me when other people say to me, 'well done'. The fact that I learned humility did me no harm. And why do I not want to be applauded now? Because I know that praise makes a person empty and expels the grace of God. The grace of God comes only with holy humility. A humble man is a perfect man. Is that not a fine thing? Is that not true?

If you tell this to anyone they will immediately say, 'What a piece of nonsense! If you don't praise your child he won't be able to do his schoolwork or anything…' But that happens because that's what we're like, and we have made our children the same. In other words, we have strayed from the truth. Egotism evicted man from Paradise; it is a great evil. Adam and Eve were simple and humble; that's why they lived in Paradise. They didn't have egotism. They did, however, have the 'primal nature', as we call it in theological language. When we say 'primal nature' we mean the gifts of grace that God bestowed on man in the beginning when He created him, namely, life, immortality, consciousness, freedom of will, love, humility, etc. Through flattery, however, the devil managed to delude them. They became filled with egotism. The natural state of man as created by God, however, is humility. Egotism, on the contrary, is something unnatural, an illness and contrary to nature.

When we, with our laudations, create this 'superego' in the child, we inflate its egotism and we do it great harm. We make the child more susceptible to demonic influence. And so, as we bring it up, we steadily distance it from the values of life. Don't you believe that this is the reason why children go astray and people rebel? It is the egotism that their parents have implanted in them from an early age. The devil is the great egotist, the great Lucifer. In other words, we live with Lucifer inside us, with the devil. We don't live with humility. Humility is from God; it is something essential for the human soul. It is something organic. And if it is missing, it is as if the heart were missing from the human organism. The heart gives life to the body and humility gives life to the soul. With egotism a person is given over to the part of the evil spirit, that is, he develops with the evil spirit and not with the good spirit.

This is what the devil has succeeded in achieving. He has turned the earth into a labyrinth so that we are unable to come to an understanding with one another. What has happened to us without our realizing it? Do you see how we have been led astray? We have turned our world and our age into one large psychiatric hospital! And we don't understand what's gone wrong. We all ask, 'What's become of us, where are we going, why have our children taken off, why have they left their homes, why have they resigned from life, why have they given up their studies?

Why is all this happening?' The devil has succeeded in concealing himself and in making people use other names. Doctors and psychologists often say when someone is tormented, 'Ah, this person has a neurosis or is suffering from anxiety.' They don't accept that the devil is inciting and arousing egotism in the person. But yet the devil exists and is the spirit of evil. If we say he doesn't exist, it is as if we are rejecting the Gospel that speaks of him. He is our enemy, our adversary in life, the contrary of Christ, which is why he is called the Anti-Christ. Christ came to earth to release us from the devil and to grant us salvation.

The conclusion is that we need to teach our children to live humbly and simply and not continually to seek praise and applause. We need to teach them that there is humility and that this is the healthy state of life.

The mind-set of our contemporary society does harm to children. It is based on another psychology and another theory of education that is addressed to the children of atheists. This frame of mind leads to complete disregard for the consequences of one's actions. And you see the results in our children and young people. Young people nowadays say, 'You need to understand us!' But we mustn't go to them. On the contrary, we need to pray for them, to say what is right, to live by what is right, and proclaim what is right, and not conform ourselves to their way of thinking. We mustn't compromise the magnificence of our faith. We cannot, in order to help them, adopt their own frame of mind. We need to remain the people that we are and proclaim the truth and the light.

The children will learn from the Holy Fathers. The teaching of the Fathers will instruct our children about confession, about the passions, about evils and about how the saints conquered their evil selves. And we will pray that God will enter into them.

ON DISPOSITIONS OF THE HEART

We need always to have thoughts of love for our brothers and sisters

We need to have goodness and love in our soul

Man has such powers that he can transmit good or evil to his environment. These matters are very delicate. Great care is needed. We need to see everything in a positive frame of mind. We mustn't think anything evil about others. Even a simple glance or a sigh influences those around us. And even the slightest anger or indignation does harm. We need to have goodness and love in our soul and to transmit these things.

We need to be careful not to harbour any resentment against those who harm us, but rather to pray for them with love. Whatever any of our fellow men does, we should never think evil of him. We need always to have thoughts of love and always to think good of others. Look at Saint Stephen the first martyr. He prayed, *Lord, do not hold this sin against*
Acts 7:60 *them.* We need to do the same.

We should never think about someone that God will send him some evil or that God will punish him for his sin. This thought brings about very great evil, without our being aware of it. We often feel indignation and say to someone: 'Have you no fear of God's justice, are you not afraid of God's punishment?' Or else we say, 'God will punish you for what you've done,' or, 'O God, do not bring evil on that person for what he did to me,' or, 'May that person not suffer the same thing.'

In all these cases, we have a deep desire within us for the other person to be punished. Instead of confessing our anger over his error, we present our indignation in a different way, and we allegedly pray to God for him. In reality, however, in this way we are cursing our brother.

And if, instead of praying, we say, 'May God repay you for the evil you have done to me,' then once again we are wishing for God to punish him. Even when we say, 'All very well, God is witness,' the disposition of our soul works in a mysterious way and influences the soul of our fellow man so that he suffers evil.

When we speak evil about someone, an evil power proceeds from within us and is transmitted to the other person, just as the voice is transmitted on sound waves, and in point of fact the other person suffers evil.

It is something like the bewitchment of the evil eye, when someone has evil thoughts about others. This occurs through our own indignation. We transmit our evil in a mystical way. It is not God who provokes evil, but rather people's wickedness. God does not punish, but our own evil disposition is transmitted to the soul of the other in a mysterious way and does evil. Christ never wishes evil. On the contrary, He commands, *Bless those who curse you...* Matt. 5:44

The evil eye is a very bad thing. It is the evil influence that occurs when someone is jealous of, or desires something or someone. It needs great care. Jealously does great harm to the other person. The person who exercises the evil eye doesn't think for a moment that he is doing harm. Remember what the Old Testament says: *For the bewitching eye of wickedness obscures what is good.* Wisd. 4:12 [DC]

When the other person, however, is a man of God and makes confession and receives Holy Communion and wears a cross, nothing does him any harm. Even if all the demons were to fall on him, they would achieve nothing.

'The noise of murmurings shall not be hidden'

Within us there is a part of the soul called the 'moralist'. This 'moralist', when it sees someone going astray, is roused to indignation, even though very often the person who judges has strayed in the same way. He does not, however, take this as an occasion to condemn himself, but the other person. This is not what God wants. Christ says in the Gospel: *You, then, that teach others, will you not teach yourself? While you preach against stealing, do you steal?* It may be that we do not steal, but we commit murder; we reproach the other person and not ourselves. Rom. 2:21 We say, for example: 'You should have done that and you didn't do it. So see now what's happened to you!' When we think of evil, then it can actually happen. In a mysterious and hidden manner we diminish the power of the other person to move towards what is good, and we do him harm. We can become the occasion for him to fall ill, to lose his job or his property. In this way we do harm, not only to our neighbour, but also to ourselves, because we distance ourselves from the grace of God. And then we pray and our prayers are not heard. We 'ask and do not receive'. Cf. Jas. 4:3 Why? Have we ever thought of this? 'Because we ask wrongly.' *Ibid.* We need to find a way to heal the tendency within us to feel and think evil about others.

It's possible for someone to say, 'The way that person is behaving, he will be punished by God,' and to believe that he is saying this without evil intent. It is not a simple thing, however, to discern whether he has or does not have evil intent. It does not appear clearly. What is hidden in our soul and how that can exercise influence on people and things is a very secret matter.

The same is not true if we say with a sense of awe that another person is not living well and that we should pray for God to help him and grant him repentance; that is, neither do we say, nor deep down do we desire that God will punish him for what he does. In this case not only do we not do harm to our neighbour, but we do him good. When someone prays for his neighbour, a good force proceeds from him and heals, strengthens and revives him. It is a mystery how this force leaves us. But, in truth, the person who has good within him radiates this good power to others, mystically and gently. He sends light to his neighbour and this creates a shield around him and protects him from evil. When we possess a good disposition towards others and pray, then we heal our fellows and we help them progress towards God.

There is an invisible life, the life of the soul. This is very powerful and can have effect on the other, even if we are miles apart. This also happens with the curse, which is a power that works evil. But if, conversely, we pray with love for someone, whatever the distance that separates us, the good is transmitted. So distances do not affect the power of good and evil. We
Cf. Wisd. can transmit these across boundless distances. Solomon the Wise says this
1:10 [DC] very thing: 'The noise of murmurings shall not be hidden.' The noise of our soul is transmitted mysteriously and affects the other, even if we don't say a word. Even without speaking we can transmit good or evil, irrespective of the distance which separates us from our neighbour. What is not expressed generally has greater power than words.

'My Holy Lady, make him glorify your name!'

Listen, and I'll tell you one of my own experiences. Once I was on my way to my village via Chalkida. Near the railway station at Chalkida I saw a boy on a cart who was trying to cross the railway line. His horse was refusing to obey him and he started to curse our Lady. I was distraught at his behaviour and instinctively I said, 'My Holy Lady, make him glorify your name!' Five minutes later the boy's cart overturned and trapped him underneath. The barrel that was in the back of the cart broke open and the grape must that was in it poured all over him. The boy, holding his head and trembling in shock, started to shout: 'My Holy Lady, my Holy Lady, my Holy Lady!!!' When I saw him from the vantage point where I was standing, I wept in remorse and said to our Lady: 'My Holy Lady, why did you do it like this? I asked for him to glorify your name, but not in that way.' I was distraught about the boy. I repented that I had become the cause of him suffering what he suffered. I believed that I had made that prayer to our Lady with goodness of heart when I heard him cursing her name, but perhaps in my soul some hidden indignation had been created.

I'll tell you about another incident and you will be amazed. It's not a figment of my imagination. What I'm going to tell you is true. Listen.

One afternoon a lady went to visit one of her friends. In the sitting room she saw a beautiful Japanese vase of great value filled with flowers.

'What a beautiful vase!' she exclaimed. 'When did you buy it?'

'My husband brought it to me,' answered her friend.

The next morning at eight o'clock the lady who had visited her friend was sitting with her husband drinking coffee and she remembered the vase. It had made a great impression on her. So she said to her husband in a tone of admiration:

'You should see what my friend's acquired. Her husband brought her a most beautiful Japanese vase, brightly coloured and painted with idyllic scenes; her whole living room has been transformed.'

Later the same day she called on her friend once again to discuss something. She looked and saw that the vase was missing. She asked:

'What did you do with your vase?'

'What can I say?' she answered. 'Early this morning at eight o'clock while I was sitting quietly in the room I heard a loud 'crack!' and the vase shattered into pieces — on its own, without anyone touching it, without the wind blowing, without anyone moving a finger!'

To begin with the lady said nothing. Then she confessed:

'Well, you know… At eight o'clock this morning I was drinking coffee with my husband and I was describing your vase to him with admiration. I described it to him really vividly and passionately. What do you think? Could I have released some evil power? But that would have happened only if I didn't love you.'

And yet that was exactly what had happened. She didn't realize that she had jealousy within her. That was envy, jealousy, evil bewitchment. The evil power can be transmitted, however far apart we are. This is a mystery. Distance is irrelevant. That's why the vase broke. I remember something else that also happened out of jealousy.

There was a mother-in-law who was very jealous of her daughter-in-law; she didn't want to believe that there was any good in her at all. One day the girl bought some lovely printed fabric to make a dress. The mother-in-law saw it and was filled with envy. Her daughter-in-law locked the material in the bottom of a chest beneath all the other clothes until the dress-maker would come to make it up. The day came when the dress-maker arrived. The girl went to take out the material, and what did she see! The whole of the fabric was cut into tiny shreds and useless. And yet it had been locked in the chest.

The evil power knows no barriers; it is impeded neither by locks nor by distances. The evil power can cause a car to crash without there being any mechanical fault.

With the Spirit of God we become incapable of every sin

You see, then, how our evil thoughts, our evil disposition affect others. That's why we need to find the way of purifying the depths of our soul from every evil. When our soul is sanctified, it radiates goodness. We then silently emit our love without words.

Certainly, to begin with this is somewhat difficult. Remember Saint Paul. That's what it was like for him too in the beginning. He said in distress: *For I do not do the good I want, but the evil I do not want, that I do.* And he continues, *I see in my members another law at war with the law of my mind, making me captive to the law of sin that dwells in my mem-*
Rom. 7:19 *bers. Wretched man that I am! Who will rescue me from this body of death?* He was very weak then and couldn't do what was good, even though he desired it and longed for it.

That is what he said at the beginning. But when in this way Paul devoted himself ever more fully to the love and worship of God, God, seeing the disposition of heart, entered into him and divine grace came to dwell in him. In this way he succeeded in living in Christ. Christ Himself entered into him, and the man who had said 'I cannot do what is good, even though I desire it', succeeded by the grace of God in becoming incapable of evil. At first he was incapable of doing what was good, but after Christ entered within him he became incapable of doing what was
Gal. 2:20 evil. Indeed he proclaimed: *It is no longer I who live; Christ lives in me.* He proclaimed boasting that 'I have Christ in me', whereas he had previously said: 'I wanted to do what was good, but I couldn't.' Where did that '*wretched man that I am*' go? It disappeared. The grace of God within him completed its work. From being wretched he became filled with grace. Grace permeated him, after he had first been humbled.

Do you see what happens? With the Spirit of God we all become incapable of every sin. We are made incapable because Christ dwells within us. We are henceforth capable only of good. Thus we will acquire the grace of God and become possessed by God. If we abandon ourselves to the love of Christ, then all will be overturned, all will be transfigured, all will be transformed, all will be transubstantiated. Anger, resentment, jealousy, indignation, censure, ingratitude, melancholy and depression will all become love, joy, longing, divine *eros*. Paradise!

ON CREATION

All things around us are droplets of the love of God

The beauties of nature are the little loves
that lead us to the great Love that is Christ

Take delight in all things that surround us. All things teach us and lead us to God. All things around us are droplets of the love of God — both things animate and inanimate, the plants and the animals, the birds and the mountains, the sea and the sunset and the starry sky. They are little loves through which we attain to the great Love that is Christ. Flowers, for example, have their own grace: they teach us with their fragrance and with their magnificence. They speak to us of the love of God. They scatter their fragrance and their beauty on sinners and on the righteous.

For a person to become a Christian he must have a poetic soul. He must become a poet. Christ does not wish insensitive souls in His company. A Christian, albeit only when he loves, is a poet and lives amid poetry. Poetic hearts embrace love and sense it deeply.

Make the most of beautiful moments. Beautiful moments predispose the soul to prayer; they make it refined, noble and poetic. Wake up in the morning to see the sun rising from out of the sea as a king robed in regal purple. When a lovely landscape, a picturesque chapel, or something beautiful inspires you, don't leave things at that, but go beyond
Ps. 44:2 this to give glory for all beautiful things so that you experience Him who
[45:2] alone is *comely in beauty*. All things are holy — the sea, swimming and eating. Take delight in them all. All things enrich us, all lead us to the great Love, all lead us to Christ.

Observe all the things made by man — houses, buildings large or small, towns, villages, peoples and their civilizations. Ask questions to enrich your knowledge about each and everything; don't be indifferent. This helps you meditate more deeply on the wonders of God. All things become opportunities for us to be joined more closely with everything and everyone. They become occasions for thanksgiving and prayer to the Lord of All. Live in the midst of everything, nature and the universe. Nature is the secret Gospel. But when one does not possess inner grace, nature is of no benefit. Nature awakens us, but it cannot bring us into Paradise.

The spiritual man, the man who has the Spirit of God, is attentive wherever he passes by; he is all eyes, all sense of smell. All his senses are alert, but they are alert in the Spirit of God. He is different. He sees everything and hears everything: he sees the birds, the stone, the butterfly… When he walks by somewhere, he senses each thing, a fragrance, for example. He lives amid everything — the butterflies, the bees and so on. Grace makes him attentive. He wishes to be together with all things.

Ah, what can I say! I experienced this when divine grace visited me on the Holy Mountain. I remember the nightingale bursting its throat in song among the trees with its wings stretched back to give its voice more power. So wonderful! If only I had a glass of water to give it to drink every so often, to quench its thirst… Why does the nightingale sing madly, why? But it too takes delight in its song. It senses what it is doing, and that's why it sings so passionately.

The birds in the forest inspired me greatly. Go to Kallisia one day and listen to the nightingales. Even if you have a heart of stone, you will be moved. How can you fail to sense that you are together with all things? Reflect deeply on their purpose. Their purpose is defined by their Maker. The teleology of creation displays the greatness of God and His providence. God's purposefulness is expressed differently in us, in mankind. We have freedom and reason.

One day I made a plan for this place here. I thought of placing a cistern in among the pine trees with a water tank holding two cubic metres of water which would release water automatically. Then the nightingales would come because they need water a lot and midges and flies…

Once when I was living in Kallisia I returned to the monastery after a period of illness and Maria the herdswoman came to take me by donkey. On the way I asked her:

'How are all the beauties doing — the meadows, the colours, the butterflies, the fragrances and the nightingales?'

'There's nothing doing at all,' she replied.

'Really?' I said. 'Even though it's the month of May, yet there's nothing at all?'

'Not a thing!' she retorted.

As we progressed along the path we encountered all these things: flowers, fragrances and butterflies.

'What have you to say now, Maria?' I asked.

'I hadn't noticed!' she said.

We arrived at the plane trees and the nightingales were singing their heads off.

'You've been telling me lies, Maria!' I said.

'No, not at all,' she replied. 'It's just that I hadn't noticed at all.'

To begin with I was also insensitive and didn't notice. Then God gave me His grace and everything changed. This occurred after I had begun my obedience.

I remember the fossilized trees, the trunks, which we saw in Mytilene. They've been there for fifteen million years. They made a great impression on me! And that is prayer — to see the fossils and to glorify the greatness of God.

Prayer is to approach everything made by God with love

Prayer is to approach everything made by God with love and to live in harmony with everything, even with wild nature. That is what I desire and attempt to do. Listen and I'll tell you something related to all this.

Some time ago someone gave me a parrot. For the first few days it was very unmanageable and wild. You couldn't go near it. It was ready with its beak to peck your hand off. I wanted to tame it with the grace of God and with the Prayer. I repeated the words 'Lord, Jesus Christ, have mercy on me' silently or out loud and gently touched its back with a stick while the parrot was in its cage. I did this carefully three times. Then in the evening of the same day I repeated the same thing. And the next day I did this again. After a few days I placed the stick gently on the bird's head, once again while repeating, 'Lord, Jesus Christ, have mercy on me'. I was always very careful to avoid making the bird aggressive. I didn't do this for very long at any one time. After a few more days I placed the stick on the bird's head and slowly moved it down its back and tail. When I didn't see any reaction, I started to place the stick under its neck and to stroke its chest very gently so as not to excite it, all the time repeating the prayer. After a while I took courage and set the stick aside and took a pencil and made the same motions. Finally, I laid aside the pencil and started to use my hand. The bird had now acquired familiarity with me and so I took it out of the cage and placed it on my shoulder. We went for a walk together up and down the corridor. And when I would sit down to eat, the bird would come and we would eat together. I would give it a little apple and it would come next to me and eat. Unfortunately, however, we lost it. A priest with lots of children came one day and the children opened the cage and the parrot flew away.

After some time I was given another parrot — the one we've got now. It was also wild to begin with, just like the first one. In the same way, with prayer and gentleness, I tamed this one. It started gradually to say various words, to squawk out names, to come out of its cage, to sit on my shoulder and to eat with me. Its cage has a latch. When it comes out, I close the latch and the bird sits on top of the cage. When I want it to go back in, I make a sign for it to come down and go back in. Then it comes down, opens the latch and goes into the cage. It is a great egotist, however, and is always wanting attention. It wants you to talk sweetly to it and not ignore it. It's particularly jealous and doesn't want you to speak to anyone else, or love anyone else. Otherwise it gets very enraged. Now that we've become very good friends, it's learned not only words and names, but it says the prayer: 'Lord. Jesus Christ, have mercy on me.' It also says: 'O Virgin who brought forth God, Hail Mary full of grace, the Lord is with You', 'God is good', and it knows how to sing 'Lord have mercy' and other things.

What I want to do now is to tame an eagle. I've found him in the north of Evia. A short distance from the place where I go to rest, I found a spot which I've named 'the eyrie'. I didn't call it that without reason. It's very difficult to get up there. It's very rocky, and down below you see the Aegean Sea. When the atmosphere is right you can even make out Kavsokalyvia on the Holy Mountain from there.

One day we saw an eagle there with a wingspan of two and a half metres. A great beast! It was encircling above us calmly without moving its wings at all. I made up a plan: just as I tamed the parrot, so I would tame the eagle. And I believe that with the help of God I'll become friends with the eagle. We'll do it in a holy way. Birds also like God's ways and to pray. They like it when you read. The eagle also likes meat.

My plan is to go up there with two companions very early in the morning. To begin with we will pray and then we will read out loud some of the psalms from Matins. Then we'll sing some hymns — the lauds and others. And at the same time we will burn a little incense. The singing of the psalms and the aroma of the incense will play an important role. Incense has a fragrance which is soothing. I'll also take a long piece of dry wood, a metre and a half long, and I'll strike it rhythmically with another piece of wood, just as they strike the *simantron* in monasteries as a call to prayer. And every so often I'll shout, 'Jooohn!! Jooohn!!' That's the name I'm going to give him. We'll also have some roast meat with us. We'll leave it on the rock little bit by little bit and we'll back off about two hundred metres. From that distance I'll see it and say the prayer, 'Lord, Jesus Christ, have mercy on me'. And in a short time the eagle will very certainly come down to eat the meat.

The next day we'll do the same thing. The eagle will encircle above us, and as soon as we've finished our programme, he'll come down to eat the meat. After two or three times the eagle will be ours. Whenever we strike the *simantron*, he'll come to eat the meat. Then I'll bring him down whenever I want. I'll gradually tame him and then I'll be able to go and catch him. He may, of course, make mincemeat of me. He is a great monster of a beast with huge legs. If he were to sit on your shoulder, he would rip you up with his talons, even if he had no evil intent. But there is a way. I'll take along Saint Gerasimos's walking stick and I'll touch him gently on the back with it twice and say at the same time: 'Joohn!! Joohn!!' I've given him a fine name. The eagle is the symbol of Saint John the Theologian. The next day when he comes, as soon as he's eaten the meat, I'll stroke him on the back with the stick three times. The next day four. The day after, five. Then I'll proceed to his throat. Then I'll stroke him from head to tail. The next day from the beak to the chest. And so I'll proceed until we've become friends. Then I'll stroke his head, wings and back with my hand and do what I previously did with the stick. But great care is needed because he's highly dangerous. If he were to grab you, he would tear you to pieces with his talons. His talons are like iron. Even if you simply smell of meat he might make a grab at you. But the eagle is a very clever and active bird, a real king. If we do this, then we'll really see the grace and visitation of God.

Let me tell you something else.

A woman once came to me up there in north Evia with her goats and asked me if I could make a prayer for her herd because they weren't doing well. I stood up and the goats approached me on their own; she didn't bring them to me. I stretched out my arms and read a prayer. They were all close to me and lifted up their heads to look at me. A billy goat approached more closely, bowed, and kissed my hand. He wanted me to stroke him. I stroked him and he was pleased. They all pressed around me and looked up at me. They looked me in the face. I blessed them. I spoke and made a prayer.

We once had a dog. Whenever it saw me outside, it would come and kiss my hand. It covered me in saliva and then ran off in case I scolded it.

The person who has divine wisdom sees all things with love

All these things connected with nature help us greatly in our spiritual life when they are conjoined with the grace of God. When I sense the harmony of nature, I am brought to tears. Why should we be bored with life? Let us live life with the Spirit of God, the Spirit of Truth. The person who has the Spirit of God, who has Divine Wisdom, sees all things with love of God and notices all things. The wisdom of God makes him grasp all things and delight in all things.

Listen and I'll recite my poem to you. It's by Lambros Porphyras. This captures my present state; I've got it constantly before me. It fits with my life.

If only the pine trees that cover the hillside
would give me a pile of their numberless branches,
then finding a spot in a hollow beside them,
I'd build there my dwelling, a hut low and lonely.

If only 't were summer-time, then they could give me
a couch of their dry leaves, pine needles, to lie on,
and then I would join in the song of the pine trees,
their chorus at dawn-break of whispers and rustlings.

And nothing beyond this would I wish thereafter.
And when full of joy from this life I'd be parted,
again they would lend me a few of their branches
*and make me a bower, a bed everlasting.**

* 'Pine Trees' in: Lambros Porphyras, *Τὰ Ποιήματα*, Athens 1993, p. 248.

ON ILLNESS

I feel illness as the love of Christ

'My Christ, Your love knows no limits!'

I thank God for granting me many illnesses.* I often say to Him: 'My Christ, Your love knows no limits!' How I am alive is a miracle. Among all my other illnesses I also have cancer of the pituitary gland. A tumour appeared there which has grown and presses against the optic nerve. That's why I don't see any more. I am in dreadful pain. But I pray, taking up the cross of Christ with patience. Have you seen what my tongue is like? It has grown; it's not as it used to be. That's also a result of the cancer I've got in my head. And as time goes on, things will get worse. It will grow even more and I'll have difficulty in speaking. I'm in great pain, but my illness is something very beautiful. I feel it as the love of Christ. I am given compunction and I give thanks to God. It is on account of my sins. I am sinful and God is trying to purify me.

When I was sixteen years old I asked God to give me a serious illness, a cancer, so that I would suffer for His love and glorify Him through my pain. I made this prayer for a long time. But my elder told me that this was egotism and that I was coercing God. God knows what He is doing. So I didn't continue with this prayer. But, you see, God did not forget my request and He gave me this benefaction after so many years!

Now I do not pray for God to take away from me the thing I asked Him for. I am glad that I have it so that I can participate in His sufferings through my great love. I have the chastisement of God: *For the Lord chas-*
Heb. 12:6 *tises the one he loves.* My illness is a special favour from God, who is inviting me to enter into the mystery of His love and to try to respond with His own grace. But I am not worthy. You'll say to me, 'Don't all these things that God reveals to you make you worthy?' These rather condemn me. Because these are things that belong to the grace of God. There

* Saint Porphyrios suffered from the following illnesses: myocardial infarction (anterior diaphragm with lateral ischaemia), chronic kidney disease, duodenal ulcer (with repeated perforations), operated cataract (loss of lens and blindness), herpes zoster (shingles) on the face, staphylococcus dermatitis on the hand, inguinal hernia (frequently strangulated), chronic bronchitis and cancer of the pituitary gland. Cf. Dr Georgios Papazachou in an article in the periodical *Synaxis*, 41 (Jan–Mar) 1992, p. 93.

is nothing of my own. God gave me many gifts, but I did not respond; I proved myself unworthy. But I have not abandoned my efforts, not even for a moment. Perhaps God will give me His help so that I can give myself to His love.

That's why I do not pray for God to make me well. I pray for Him to make me good. I'm certain that God knows that I am in pain. But I pray for my soul, for God to forgive my transgressions. I am not taking medicines, nor did I go for surgery, not even for tests, and nor will I accept surgery. I will leave God to sort things out. The only thing I do is to try to become good. This is what I ask you to pray for me. The grace of God sustains me. I try to give myself to Christ, to approach Christ and to be one with Christ. This is what I desire, but I haven't succeeded — and I don't say this out of humility. But I don't lose my courage. I persevere. I pray for God to forgive my sins. I've heard many people saying, 'I'm unable to pray.' I haven't suffered this. Only on the day that I was disobedient on the Holy Mountain did I suffer that.

It doesn't concern me how long I will live or whether I will live. That is something I have left to God's love. It often happens that you don't want to remember death. It's because you desire life. That, from one point of view, is a proof of the immortality of the soul. But *whether we live, or whether we die, we are the Lord's.* Death is a bridge which will Rom. 14:8
lead us to Christ. As soon as we close our eyes, we will open them on eternity. We will appear before Christ. In the next life we will experience the grace of God more intensely.

I felt great joy at the thought that I would meet the Lord

Once I came to the point of death. I had suffered severe perforation of the stomach as a result of the steroids I was given in hospital when I went for an operation on my eye — which I lost in the end. At that time I was living in a little hut; the monastery had not yet been built. I was so exhausted that I didn't know whether it was day or night. I came to the point of death and yet I survived. I lost a lot of weight and had no appetite. For three months I survived with three spoons of milk a day. I was saved by a goat!

I lived with the thought of leaving this world. I felt great joy at the thought that I would meet the Lord. I had a very deep sense of the presence of God. And God desired at that time to strengthen and comfort me with something very blessed. Every so often I would feel that my soul was about to depart. I saw in the sky a star which twinkled and emitted sweet rays of light. It was bright and very sweet. It was so beautiful! Its light possessed a great sweetness. Its colour was a light sky blue, like a diamond, like a precious stone. Whenever I saw it I was filled with comfort and joy because I felt that the whole Church — the Triune Godhead, our Lady, the angels and the saints — was contained in that star. I had the sense that in it were contained all the souls of all my loved ones, of my elders. I believed that when I would leave this life I, too, would go to that star through the love of God, not through my virtues. I wanted to believe that God, who loves me, revealed it to me in order to tell me, 'I'm waiting for you!'

I didn't want to think about hell and about tollgates.* I didn't remember my sins, although I had many. I set them aside. I remembered only the love of God and was glad. And I made entreaty, 'O my God, for the sake of your love, may I also be there. But if on account of my sins I must go to hell, may your love place me wherever it wishes. It is sufficient for me to be with You.' For so many years I lived in the desert with love for Christ. I said to myself: 'If you go to heaven and God says to you,
Matt. 22:12 "*Friend, how did you get in here without a wedding robe?* What do you want here?" I'll reply, "Whatever You want, my Lord, whatever Your love desires; place me wherever Your love wishes. I abandon myself to Your love. If You want to place me in hell, then do so, only don't let me lose Your love."'

I had an acute sense of my sinfulness, and that's why I constantly repeated to myself the prayer of Saint Symeon the New Theologian:

I know, Saviour, that none other
has, as I have, sinned against You,
nor done the deeds that I have done.
But this again I surely know:
neither magnitude of errors,
nor multitude of transgressions,
can surpass my God's great patience
and His love for man unbounded.†

What the prayer says are not our own words. We are unable to conceive and express such words. They were written by saints. But our soul needs to embrace these words written by the saints and to sense and experience them. I also like the other words of the prayer:

* A theory that a soul after death has to pass through a series of 'tollgates' where it is interrogated about a variety of sins.

† Prayers of Preparation for Holy Communion, Prayer 7.

Neither tears shed in my weeping
nor the slightest falling tearlet,
O my God, escapes Your notice,
O my Maker, my Redeemer.

And my work yet unaccomplished
is to Your eyes already known
and all the things I've not yet done
are for You already written,
in Your book already entered.

Look down on my humbled being,
look on my so great contrition
and forgive me my transgressions,
all my sins, O God of all things...

I repeated this prayer continually and intensely to escape from these thoughts. The more I repeated it, the more, up in the infinity of space, appeared the star, my comfort. It came all these days that I was suffering. And when it appeared, my soul took wings and I said to myself: 'My star has come!' It felt as if it were drawing me up from the earth towards it. I felt great joy when I saw it. I didn't want to think of my sins, as I've said, because these would exclude me from this mystery. Only once, once only, did I sense that the star was empty, it wasn't twinkling, it wasn't full. I realized what it was. It was from the 'contrary one'. I ignored him, and turned my mind elsewhere. I spoke to my sister about some jobs that were to be done. After a while I saw it shining brightly again. Joy came again even more intensely within me.

All that time I had fearful pains throughout my body. Other people saw that I was dying. I had given myself over to the love of God. I did not pray to be released from the pains. My desire was for God to have mercy on me. I had leant on Him, and I waited for His grace to work. I was not afraid of death. For I would go to Christ. As I've told you, I repeated constantly the prayer of Saint Symeon the New Theologian, but not in a selfish spirit, and not for my health to be restored. I sensed every single word of the prayer.

The secret in illness is to struggle to acquire the grace of God

We benefit greatly from our illnesses, as long as we endure them without complaint and glorify God, asking for His mercy. When we become ill, the important thing is not that we don't take medicines or that we go and pray to Saint Nektarios. We need also to know the other secret, namely, to struggle to acquire the grace of God. This is the secret. Grace will teach us all the other things, namely, how to abandon ourselves to Christ. That is, we ignore the illness, we do not think about it, we think about Christ, simply, imperceptibly and selflessly and God works His miracle for the good of our soul. Just as we say in the Divine Liturgy, 'we commend all our life to Christ our God.'

But we need to wish to ignore the illness. If we don't wish to, it's difficult. We can't simply say, 'I ignore it'. And so although we think that we are ignoring it and giving no thought to it, in point of fact we have it in our mind continually and we cannot find peace within ourselves. Let me prove this to you. We say: 'I believe that God will cure me. I won't take any medicine. I'll stay awake all night and I'll pray to God about it and He will hear me.' We pray all night long, we make entreaty, we call on and coerce God and all the saints to make us well. We go to one place and another. With all these things don't we show that we are far from ignoring the illness? The more we insist and blackmail the saints and God to make us well, the more acutely we feel our illness. The more we strive to get rid of it, the more we feel it. And so we achieve nothing. And we have the impression that a miracle will happen, and yet, in reality, we don't believe it, and so we do not become better.

We pray and we don't take medicine, but we don't find any peace and no miracle happens. But you will say: 'What do you mean that I don't believe? Don't you see I haven't taken any medicine?' And yet, at bottom, we have doubt and fear within us and we think to ourselves, 'Will it really happen?' Here the words of Scripture hold good: *If you have faith and do not doubt, not only will you do what has been done to the fig tree, but even if you say to this mountain, 'be lifted up and thrown into the sea',*
Matt. 21:21 *it will be done.* When faith is real, whether you take medicine or not, the grace of God will act. And God acts through doctors and medicines. The Wisdom of Sirach says: *Honour the physician with the honours due to him, according to your need of him, for the Lord created him. The Lord created medicines from the earth, and a man of sense will not despise them.*
Sir. 38:1, 4, *And give the physician his place, for the Lord created him; let him not*
12 [DC] *leave you, for there is need of him.*

Wisd. 1:1 The whole secret is faith — without doubts, gentle, simple and art-
[DC] less: *in simplicity and artlessness of heart.* It is not a question of 'will power' or 'mind over matter'. A fakir can display this kind of 'will power'. It is a question of having faith that God loves us with infinite love and

wants us to become His own. That is why He allows illnesses, until we surrender ourselves in trust to Him.

If we love Christ, all things will change in our lives. We do not love Him in order to receive some reward such as health. Rather we love Him out of gratitude, without thinking of anything, only of the love of God. Nor should we pray with any ulterior motive and say to God: 'Make such-and-such a person well, so that he may come close to You.' It is not right to point out ways and means to God. How can we presume to say to God, 'make me well'? What can we tell to Him who knows everything? We will pray, but God may not wish to listen to us.

A person asked me a little while ago, 'When will I get well?'

'Ah,' I told him, 'if you say, "When will I get well?" then you never will get well. It's not right to entreat God about such things. You entreat anxiously for God to take the illness from you, but then the illness lays even tighter hold on you. We mustn't ask for this. Nor should you pray about this.'

He was taken aback and said, 'Do you mean I shouldn't pray?'

'Not at all,' I answered. 'On the contrary, pray a great deal, but for God to forgive your sins and to give you strength to love Him and to give yourself to Him. Because the more you pray for the illness to leave you, the more it adheres to you, winds its tentacles around you and squeezes you, and becomes inseparable from you. If, of course, you feel an inner human weakness, then you may humbly entreat the Lord to take the illness from you.'

Let us abandon ourselves in trust to the love of God

When we surrender ourselves to Christ, our spiritual organism finds peace, with the result that all our bodily organs and glands function normally. All these are affected. We become well and cease to suffer. Even if we have cancer, if we leave everything to God and our soul finds serenity, then divine grace may work through this serenity and cause the cancer and everything else to leave.

Stomach ulcers, you know, are caused by stress. The sympathetic system, when it is subjected to pressure, is constricted and suffers harm and so the ulcer is created. With stress, pressure, distress, anxiety, an ulcer or cancer comes about. When there are confusions in our soul, these have influence on our body and our health suffers.

The most perfect way is not to pray for our health — not to pray to become well, but to become good. That is what I pray for myself. Do you hear? I don't mean to be good in the sense of virtuous, but in the sense of acquiring divine zeal, of abandoning ourselves in trust to God's love, and of praying rather for our soul. And we mean our soul as it is incorporated in the Church, whose head is Christ, along with all our fellow men and our brothers and sisters in Christ.

And I open my arms and pray for all people. When I am about to receive Holy Communion, as I am standing before the Holy Chalice, I open my soul to receive the Lord, and I bow my head and I pray for you, for this person and that, and for the whole Church. You should do the same. Do you understand? Don't pray for your health. Don't say, 'O Lord, make me well.' No! Rather say, 'Lord, Jesus Christ, have mercy on me', with selflessness, with love and without expecting anything. 'Lord, whatever Your love desires…' Only in this way will you act from now on, loving Christ and our brothers and sisters. Love Christ. Become saints. Throw yourselves into becoming friends with Christ, into His love alone, into divine *eros*.

Isn't perhaps this what is happening to me, since I feel this zeal and adoration? Even though I feel that my body has rotted away, I don't succumb to my illness, not even to my cancer. I shouldn't speak, but my love for you and for the whole world doesn't allow me to remain silent. When I speak, my lungs remain without oxygen and that's very bad because the heart is harmed. I have suffered something much worse than a heart attack. And yet I live. Isn't that an intervention of God? Yes, and I am obedient to God's will, to my illness. I suffer without complaint and…with annoyance at myself because no one is devoid of unclean-
Cf. Job 14:4 ness. I'm in a bad state. My spirit is also sick.

I say to a hermit with whom I am in contact, 'Pray for me. I love you. Love me too and pity me and pray for me and God will have mercy on me.'

'You're the one who should pray,' he says to me.

'I'm beginning now to be unable to do all that I did for so many years,' I tell him. What does the hymn say?

> *My mind is sorely wounded, my body has grown enfeebled,*
> *my spirit is sick, my speech has lost its power,*
> *my life is brought to death; the end is at the door.*
> *And so, O wretched soul of mine, what will you do*
> *when the Judge appears before you to investigate your deeds?**

This hymn reflects my present state. I think that if I hadn't done this or that I wouldn't be in pain now, I would be close to Christ. I say this about myself because I'm thoughtless…

* Great Canon by Saint Andrew of Crete (1st *troparion* of the 9th Ode).

If you want to enjoy good health and live for many years, then listen to what Solomon the Wise has to say: *Fear of the Lord is the beginning of wisdom and the counsel of saints is understanding; for to know the law is the mark of a sound mind, for in this way you will live long and years of* Prov.
your life will be added to you. This is the secret: for us to acquire this wis- 9:10–11
dom, this knowledge, and then everything functions smoothly, all things are put in order and we will live with joy and health.

ON THE GIFT OF CLEAR SIGHT

Only a person who has humility receives gifts from God;
he attributes them to God
and uses them for His glory

The mysteries of God are revealed to the person who possesses a healthy soul

The person who is worthy of God is filled with the Holy Spirit. He has divine grace. God, in the mystery of Christ, gives him joy, peace, meekness, and love. He gives him those characteristics enumerated
by Saint Paul: *The fruit of the Spirit is love, joy, peace, long-suffering,*
Gal. 5:22–3 *gentleness, goodness, faith, meekness, continence...* God knows no
past, present or future. *Neither is there any creature that is not man-*
Heb. 4:13 *ifest in His sight, but all things are naked and opened to His eyes...*
Thus also the mysteries of God are revealed to the person who possesses a healthy soul, and His counsels are made known to him to the degree that God permits.

There are, however, preconditions for divine grace to come and dwell in a person. Only a person who has humility receives these gifts from God; he attributes them to God and he uses them for His glory. The good, humble, devout man who loves God, the man who possesses virtue, is not, by the grace of God, deluded or led astray. He feels in his heart that he is truly unworthy, and that all those things are given to him so that he may become good, and for that reason he makes his ascetic struggle.

On the contrary, the grace of God does not go to egotists, to people who have no awareness of what is happening to them. The person who has Luciferic egotism believes that he is filled with divine grace, but he is deluded; he is a man of the devil.

Delusion is a psychological state, erroneous discernment; at bottom the delusion proceeds from egotism. Fantasies provoked by demonic temptation are produced in the person who is deluded and he is tormented. Such delusion is very difficult to overcome. It is overcome only through divine grace. Someone else may pray, and God may have mercy on the person who is deluded. If he, too, makes an effort and goes to look in the 'mirror' of a good spiritual guide, and makes honest, heartfelt confession, the grace of God will heal him.

We frequently see saintly people nowadays, but we also see deluded people who have gone astray. You can go to a hermit or an ascetic, and as soon as he sees you he will greet you by name and say, 'Why weren't you more careful? Now you've got yourself involved in such-and-such a situation.' Without knowing you, he calls you by your name and tells you about a situation which is known only to you. And you exclaim, 'The man's a saint! He knows my name and my secrets!' Then you go to a medium — and mediums and charlatans making pots of money have sprung up all over the place — and he also tells you where you're from and where you're going. So you are bewildered and you ask yourself, 'What's going on here? Where is the truth? The saint told me the truth and so did this wizard. He also knew my name... Is he a saint too?' That's how we get mixed up.

Holy Scripture enlightens us and enables us to make discrimination of spirits. That's why we must know Scripture and listen to its words with acuity. The inebriation of the Apostles through the divine grace of the Holy Spirit is one thing, and the inebriation of the Corybants, in which, unmistakably, you see the spirit of Satan, is quite another. What happens with the medium is delusion, spiritual solecism. The contrary spirit appears as an *angel of light*. If you do not know his wiles, you are 2 Cor. 11:14
unable to say that this does not come from the Holy Spirit and you may be led astray, believing that this enthusiasm is good. Many people fall into this trap.

In these situations, two things exist — the good and the evil, the good angel and the evil angel, the demon, the evil spirit. Similarly within us there is the good and the evil, namely, the 'old man' and the man who is formed according to Christ. The 'old man' is the one who gives in to his old self. The evil spirit exerts a strong influence on him and he becomes evil. Everyone looks askance on him, he wishes ill on everyone and curses continually. He is like the old woman 'Frankoyiannou' in the story by Papadiamantis* who had undergone countless torments in her life and had been left with thousands of wounds in her soul.

Thus a person who is under the influence of the evil spirit, a medium, let us say, blasphemes continually. He may prophecy and tell the future, but all in the direction of evil. His orientation is downwards, and out of wickedness he does base things proceeding from his old self. He enters

* Cf. the novella by Alexandros Papadiamantis, *The Murderess.*

into a demonic state, not into a state of elevation. And there God is not to be found. Nevertheless, he claims to be inspired by Christ. And he may, in point of fact, to all appearances belong to the Church, he may be baptized, and may know the Gospel. But he is entangled in evil and his thought, imagination and soul are sick. Such a person may lead others astray. He says: 'I saw Christ, I saw our Lady. She told me that there would be a war, that a murder would take place or that such and such would happen.' And it does indeed happen. It happens because the devil plans evil and therefore he knows all about it. Do you understand? All these matters are highly confused. For all that he tells you that he saw our Lady, or the Holy Trinity, or Saint Seraphim and was told this or that, he may still, in point of fact, be a medium. Do you understand? And he falls down, loses his senses and foams at the mouth and weeps. Then it becomes apparent that this person is not of Christ. He may believe that he is inspired by Christ or by our Lady and the saints, but this is not the case.

If ever someone goes up to a person who is possessed by the evil spirit and tells him, 'you're a charlatan', and gives him a slap and speaks rudely to him, he will swear and curse even sacred things. He is in a demonic state which will gradually lead him to the madhouse. In other words, all these states, spiritualisms and such like, are states of sickness.

God makes great revelations to those who are worthy of Him in a simple and natural manner

I'll give you a few examples so that you will understand that God makes great revelations to those who are worthy of Him in a simple and natural manner. He reveals events from the past and the present and what will happen in the future. He reveals to them the depths of people's souls, their pains and their joys, their sins and their charismas, their illnesses of body and soul, the time and mode of their death. Listen.

High up on Mount Sinai there are many hermitages. There once was an elder who lived there with the monk in obedience to him. The elder was a hundred years old. He had received intimation that he would die. On a slope lower down there was some soil. So he said to his disciple:

'Go down and dig my grave because I am going to die. I'll call you in a little while.'

The disciple obeyed at once and dug the grave. The elder gave himself over to prayer. After a short time he called out:

'Paphnutius, my child, come up and take me by the arm and lead me to the grave, because when I die how will you manage to carry me down there on your own? Come on, take me by the arm.'

Gradually, with the help of his walking stick and his disciple, they went down the slope. When they arrived at the grave he said:

'Hold me now, hold me!'

And with his disciple's help — after they had first embraced each other and bidden each other farewell — he descended into the grave. He went into the grave, laid down, closed his eyes, and as he prayed he gave up his spirit.*

You see? These things seem incredible. And yet they happened.

Many saints were given the grace by God to transport themselves to other places as they desired and to go there, *whether in the body or out of the body*, and to be seen by others. 2 Cor. 12:2

Father George, the abbot of the Holy Monastery of Mount Sinai, was ill at one time. He had, however, a strong desire to go and receive Holy Communion from the Patriarch of Jerusalem. At that moment some of his disciples went to his cell in Sinai and asked him if he would be able to come to the Church.

'No,' he replied, 'I won't come.'

As soon as they had gone, the elder was left alone in body, but in spirit, with his mind, he went to the Holy Church of the Resurrection in Jerusalem and attended the Liturgy there. He saw the Patriarch entering the Sanctuary. And all the priests and deacons and bishops there saw the abbot during the Divine Liturgy and when it came to the time for Holy Communion they placed a priest's stole on him. He approached the Holy Table and received the Immaculate Mysteries from the hands of the Patriarch. When the Communion was over, all the priests went to the lavabo and washed their hands. Father George passed next to the Patriarch who said to him:

'At mid-day I'll expect you in the refectory.'

Father George didn't speak, but made a reverential bow.

In the meantime on Mount Sinai, after the Divine Liturgy there, the deacon, the priest and a monk holding a candle and censer entered Father George's cell and gave him Holy Communion.

In Jerusalem, when lunch-time arrived, the Patriarch waited for Father George to appear. The time passed until they couldn't wait any longer and they started their meal. The Patriarch was very upset and sent three monks from Jerusalem to Sinai to see why he had disobeyed him and had left, in spite of the fact that he was so well known for his

* Cf. Abba Michael in: *Γεροντικὸν τοῦ Σινᾶ*, ed D. Tsamis, Thessalonica 1991, p. 280.

obedience. The Patriarch's envoys arrived, and as soon as they entered the monastery they said:

'Your elder came down to Jerusalem and received Communion in the church of the Resurrection. We all saw him there and the Patriarch invited him to dine with him, but he left. The Patriarch was very upset and sent us to reprimand him for his disobedience.'

The monks in the monastery were taken aback.

'Whatever do you mean?' they asked. 'Our elder hasn't been out of the monastery for the last fifty years. You're obviously mistaken.'

'No,' they insisted, 'we all saw him.'

'Come then and we'll take you to the elder and we'll prove to you the truth of the matter.'

As soon as the envoys saw the elder, they communicated the Patriarch's displeasure. The elder didn't speak at first, but then he said:

'Tell His Beatitude to forgive me and give him a joyous message: God has revealed to me that in six months we will be together, so tell him to prepare himself.'

You see how the abbot of Sinai went to Jerusalem without knowing himself whether it was in the body of out of the body, but at all events people saw that he went.*

Many of our saints also communicate at a distance and pray together. All is done by the grace of God. With the grace of God distances are abolished. May God forgive me for saying this, but in the past I often communicated with a priest-monk from the Monastery of Saint Charalambos in Evia, Father Paul, at a distance. Let me give you a characteristic example.

When I went there after leaving the Holy Mountain I had a serious problem. As I've told you, I returned from the Holy Mountain very ill, and on account of my health I had to eat an egg or two and drink some milk. I couldn't eat beans, lentils and so on. The staple diet of the monks was beans and chick-peas. My health didn't allow me to share their diet nor did I wish to scandalize the others by eating special food. That's how I felt. I felt ashamed, however, to say so, and I thought of leaving the monastery. One day I was sitting under a large tree absorbed in these thoughts of leaving, when suddenly I saw Father Paul before me. He was holding a large book. It was the Holy Bible, the Old and New Testament. He had gone deep into the woods and was reading. Suddenly he got up and came over to me and said:

* Cf. 'George, The Abbot of Sinai', in: John Moschos, *The Meadow*, 127 (*PG* 87. 2988C – 2989C).

'How are you, Father Porphyrios? You know what I was thinking? I know you're ill and suffer with your stomach because you can't digest the food we eat at the monastery. So I was thinking that we should give you milk and eggs. It's quite justified to have a special diet when you're ill.'

I asked him, 'How did you come to think of that?'

'Well,' he said, 'as I was walking this way…'

You see, the grace of God does everything.

Often in the past, and even now, I 'fly' to the Holy Mountain above Mount Athos and pray with the fathers there. I have a strong sense of the grace of the hermits and the incense which gives off such a fragrance as it rises to heaven. The incense forms a cloud round Mount Athos! These places have been trodden by saints with great devotion and prayer. Even the rocks are impregnated with the grace of God which the saints attracted to themselves. These people there were angels of God sent to the earth. They lived an angelic life. They lived with fervent love towards God and devotion.

When I wake up here in the monastery during the night, I see that the Holy Mountain is flooded with grace on account of the nocturnal prayers of the fathers there. As soon as the *simantron* is sounded, they hasten to hear the words 'Having risen from sleep…'* and they begin their prayer with longing, love and joy. What can I say! The gates of Paradise are opened. That's how I sense it with the grace of God and I tell you so. Let me tell you. I want to tell you. I do it out of my love for you!

I'll tell you now another secret. During the night I communicate by telephone with a hermit on the Holy Mountain. He studies the writings of the Fathers deeply and explains a lot of things to me. We talk about spiritual matters. Utter madness, what can I say! This happened this morning at three o'clock. The bells started to ring as we were talking. For half an hour we spoke of wonderful things. Truly, I felt great joy, much greater than I can express. Glory to You, O God! While we were speaking about these spiritual things, he said to me:

'The bell is sounding for church. I'm going off now to be in time.'

I said to him, 'Don't leave me, Elder!'

'Very gladly,' he replied. 'Come on and we'll go to the church. We'll be together and see the greatness of God, the Divine Liturgy and the grace of Christ. Come now, there is no distance in our Lord Jesus Christ. No distance at all!'

And I 'went' with him to the church. We prayed together all the time.

* The first words in the daily cycle of prayer.

I saw all the sacred and holy icons, the candles, the sibilant oil-lamps. I saw the priests celebrating in transports of joy. The church was filled with ascetics, all possessed with deep heartfelt joy and singing the Christmas hymns, 'Come, O faithful, let us see where Christ was born… Your nativity, O Christ… Christ is born, give glory…' At the summons, 'With the fear of God', he went to receive Communion. I was at his side, by the grace of our Lord, deeply moved. Forgive me for telling you all this. I saw all the monks praying. I felt a great exaltation. What they saw, I saw too. This Liturgy was a true spiritual banquet with the holy ascetics, their joyful souls experiencing everything as they truly lived the Feast of the Nativity. They really lived it. How I wish you had been there too, and could have heard the words they were singing!

My joy becomes very great when someone else confirms that what I see is really so, because I realize that this knowledge comes only from God. Let me tell you what I mean. I often ask you to read for me a paragraph from one of the Fathers, for example, and I say to you: 'Look on page ten at the second paragraph in the middle of the page and you'll find the passage I've just quoted you.' You open the book, and in point of fact, you find the passage on the specific page and you read it to me. The words are exactly as I have spoken them. You are puzzled when I display great joy and say, 'Oh, I didn't know that. That's the first time I've heard that!' because previously I've quoted the passage to you by heart. And yet I'm telling you the truth. I'm not telling lies. I truly didn't know it, because I'd never read it before. The moment I told you the paragraph, at that very moment the grace of God, the Holy Spirit, revealed it to me. But I heard it for the first time when you read it to me, because I'd never read it, and it makes an impression on me and I'm overjoyed that you have confirmed what the grace of God has revealed to me. Let me give you another example.

One day the abbot of the Athonite Monastery of Megisti Lavra was speaking at the Archaeological Society at seven o'clock in the evening. I 'went' in prayer and I saw him. I listened to his talk for about half an hour. The hall was packed with people who were listening very intently. And what did I see? I saw that perspiration was showing on the abbot's outer cassock. It was pouring from him as he was speaking. And when I phoned you to ask you how the talk went, you said:

'It was very good. Everyone was very moved by it all. But he was streaming with perspiration!'

It's a mystery! 'Everywhere present and filling all things…'

On another occasion a group of four or five of us went on an excursion to north Evia. The car was passing through beautiful countryside. Plants, trees and flowers to the left, and on the right the sea stretching out to the horizon. All was perfect, clear and bright. No one was speaking. Suddenly I asked my companions:

'What do you see outside? What you are seeing at this moment, I, blind though I am, see too, through your eyes.'

I started to sing:

Your eyes are my eyes,
Your eyelashes mine,
Your two hands are keys
That open my heart.

This song, of course, is a popular song, but we take it metaphorically. Do you understand? There are other eyes, the eyes of the soul. With the eyes of the body you can see within a certain range, but with the eyes of the soul you can see the dark side of the moon. You see with the eyes of the body. I see the same things through grace even better, more clearly. With the eyes of the body you see things externally. With the eyes of the soul you see more deeply. You see externally, I see also how things are internally. I see and read the soul of the other person.

All those who loved and adhered to their elder took from him the charisma which he possessed

God gave me this grace as a result of my obedience to my elders. All those who loved and adhered to their elder took from him the charisma which he possessed. Saint Prochoros took from Saint John the Theologian. Saint Proclos took from Saint John Chrysostom. Saint Symeon the New Theologian from his elder. And in the Old Testament we see that the Prophet Elijah gave his gift of prophecy to his disciple, the Prophet Elisha.

Then Elijah took his mantle, and rolled it up, and struck the water, and the water was parted to the one side and to the other, and they both crossed over on dry ground. And as they were crossing, Elijah said to Elisha, Ask what I shall do for you, before I am taken up away from you. And Elisha said, Let there be a double share of your spirit on me. And Elijah said, You have asked a hard thing; if you see me as I am being taken up away from you, it shall be so for you; but if you do not see me, it shall not be so. And as they were still walking along, they walked and talked; and behold, a chariot of fire and horses of fire and they separated the two of them. And Elijah was taken up in a whirlwind as it were into heaven.

And Elisha saw and cried, Father, Father, the chariot of Israel and its horseman! And he saw him no more. Then he took hold of his own clothes and rent them in two pieces. And he took up the mantle of Elijah that had fallen from above on Elisha, and Elisha went back and stood on the bank of the Jordan and took the mantle of Elijah that had fallen on him from above, and struck the water and it was not parted; and he said, Where is the God of Elijah, affo? And he struck the water, and the water was parted to the one side and to the other; and Elisha crossed over. And the sons of
4 Kings *the prophets who were at Jericho saw him over against them, and they*
[2 Kings] *said, The spirit of Elijah has rested on Elisha. And they came to meet him,*
2:8–15 *and bowed to the ground before him.*

The Prophet Elijah struck the waters of the Jordan with his mantle and they were parted to the one side and to the other. And so the two of them passed across to the other side on the dry path that had been formed. And then did you see what Elisha asked from the Prophet Elijah? He asked for twice the grace and he received it with his elder's blessing. Once Elijah had been taken up to heaven, Elisha raised up the mantle which his elder had thrown down on him, and struck the waters of the river with it. The waters, however, didn't separate and weren't pushed from side to side, because he hadn't taken the blessing of the Prophet Elijah. Then Elisha said, *Where is the God of Elijah, affo?* Where is the God of Elijah, my elder, now? And what does the Old Testament say thereafter at verse fourteen? *And he struck the waters, and the waters were parted to the one side and to the other; and Elisha crossed over*. This time the waters were parted because Elisha realized his error and asked for the blessing of the Prophet Elijah.

Nothing works without the blessing of your elder. Nothing is achieved without grace. These are things that you will understand truly when grace comes. When the Holy Spirit comes it will teach you all things and bring everything to your remembrance. This is as John the beloved disciple says: *But the Comforter, the Holy Spirit, whom the Father will send in my name, he will teach you all things, and bring to your re-*
John 14:26 *membrance all that I have said to you.*

God gave me the charisma to help me become good

I have told you many times that I never expected the charisma, nor did I want it, nor did I seek it. My elders told me nothing. This was their way. They didn't teach me with words, only by their attitude. I learned everything from the lives of the saints and the books of the Fathers. The

Fathers didn't force things, they didn't ask for signs, they didn't ask for special gifts. And I never sought special gifts, only the love of Christ. Nothing else. God gave me the charisma to help me become good.

When I see something by the grace of God, I am very joyous deep down — with joy in the Lord. When the grace of God visits me, when I look at and read someone's soul through divine grace, at that moment the divine grace fills me with an enthusiasm. The divine grace is expressed by an enthusiasm which brings a kind of friendliness, familiarity, brotherliness, union. After this union there comes a great joy, such joy that my heart is as if about to break. I am afraid, however, to express myself. I see, but I don't speak, even if the grace assures me that the things I see are true. But when the grace informs me to speak, then I speak. I say some things which God enlightens me to say from my love for everyone. I do it so that people may sense the embrace which Christ extends to us all. My aim is for Christians to be helped and to be saved, caught up in a communion of love with Christ.

Forgive me for speaking to you like this. I never ask for God to reveal something to me, because I don't like asking Him. I believe this is contrary to His will, that it is not polite and that — even worse — I am coercing Him. But I say the prayer 'Lord, Jesus Christ, have mercy on me' in a supplicatory tone and then I abandon myself to Christ. Whatever He wills. Whatever He Himself reveals.

God conceals so many mysteries which He hasn't revealed to us. God reveals some of these to the person who loves Him, if he lives in the desert. He sees them, but he doesn't speak about them all, only what God permits him to say. Whereas a person who lives in the world in the midst of things and amid all the means of communication may not understand and know nothing.

Now that I see all things, I feel very, very humble. How can I explain to you..? God protects me. He sends His grace to me. And I say, 'To me, so humble and so unworthy! What does God want from me?' And yet God loves even sinners like me and wants them to become good. The grace of God does such things.

This charisma is a gift from God. It comes of divine grace, but it up to the person to preserve it. A person loses his spiritual gifts if he is not careful. Care is required in these spiritual matters. Don't tell others about the secret spiritual experiences you have. It's not right. In that way we lose the divine grace. Look at our Lady. She kept silence. She didn't tell Joseph about the secret of the Annunciation. The Angel told him. Joseph was sleeping and he heard the voice of the Angel. It came mystically, soundlessly, with confidentiality. 'Let none of the uninitiated touch.'[*] Be careful! God conceals Himself greatly, so much so that we think He doesn't exist. He appears to those who have been made worthy of the gift of humility.

I ascribe everything to God for His glory. I believe about myself that I am an old rusty pipe which, however, conducts crystal-clear living water, because it wells up from the Holy Spirit. When you are very thirsty, you don't think about whether the pipe along which the water flows is plastic, metal or rusty. You're interested in the water. And in spite of the fact that I'm ready to breathe my last, people come to my humble self. They have nothing to take from me. I have nothing. Only Christ has everything.

When a person is filled by the grace of God, he becomes different — his soul leaps! He hears His voice and his soul rejoices. Grace impels me to suffer the same thing. My voice changes, my face changes, everything changes. I have learned to boast, not about my own achievements, but about the grace of God which insistently and overtly wishes to pull me towards it, with all that it has been revealing to me in the course of my life, from the time when I went to the Holy Mountain as a young boy. But I always have the same feeling that I have never succeeded in living with longing for Christ. How laggard I am! How far off! For all that God has given within me, my soul condemns me greatly. I have within me a fear. I reflect on those words of Holy Scripture which say: '*Lord, Lord, did we not prophesy in your name, and cast out demons in your name, and do many*
Matt. *mighty works in your name?' And then I will declare to them, 'I never knew*
7:22–3 *you; depart from me, you evildoers.'* I think of this, but I don't despair. I
leave myself to the love of God and His mercy and I repeat those golden words from the prayers of preparation for Holy Communion:

I know, Saviour, that none other
has, as I have, sinned against You,
nor done the deeds that I have done.
But this again I surely know:
neither magnitude of errors,
nor multitude of transgressions,
can surpass my God's great patience
and His love for man unbounded.[†]

[*] Cf. Canon of the feast of the Annunciation, 25th March (*Irmos* of the 9th Ode).
[†] Prayer 7, by Symeon the New Theologian.

When we say these golden words, which were written by the Fathers, with faith and devotion, it is as if we were experiencing them ourselves.

Out of my love for you I tell you some of the things God reveals to me

I tell you many things that are deep, inner and personal. Perhaps some people might misconstrue me for not keeping secret those experiences which God reveals to me and for telling so much. They might say that I am self-seeking for telling about my experiences. I do it out of my love for you, my children. I do it for your benefit, so that you may set out on this path. What does Solomon the Wise say? He expresses this somehow or other… He says: *Neither will I walk with consuming envy, for such a man shall have no communion with wisdom.* (Wisd. 6:23 [DC]) And, yes, he says: *I shall not hide mysteries from you.* (Wisd. 6:22 [DC]) Wise Solomon does not want to hide the wisdom of God. God moves him to reveal the mysteries of wisdom.

What I am doing in telling you what God gave me is apostolic too. Saint Paul says this in his letter to the Romans: *For I long to see you, that I may pass on to you some spiritual gift in order for you to be supported, that is, that we may be mutually encouraged by each other's faith, both yours and mine.* (Rom. 1:11–12) To *'pass on'* means, Have you received something? Then pass it on out of love. You don't believe that you have something of your own. It belongs to God and you pass it on. This is true humility. Whereas a fanatic, an Old Calendarist,* will say: 'Look at that! He's talking about himself. That's egotism!' Saint Paul does this '*in order for you to be supported*'. It's like a tree that bends over when the wind blows strongly; that's what happens to people too. For that reason you need to put in a stake as a support, so that the tree doesn't bend and grow aslant. If someone is bent, he develops askew and so becomes insensitive and isn't worthy of God.

Of course, silence is best for the mysteries which God reveals within us. But, you see, what happened to Saint Paul can also happen to us. Saint Paul says: 'I have been a fool! You forced me to tell you this out of my love.' (Cf. 2 Cor. 12:11) Saint Isaac the Syrian gets upset in the same way when he is forced to tell the mysteries and the deep experiences of his heart, compelled by love alone. Listen to what he says: 'I have become a fool, I cannot bear to

* Following the introduction of the New (Gregorian) Calendar in Greece in 1924, a breakaway Old Calendarist Church was established which became synonymous with conservative zeal.

keep the mystery in silence, but I become reckless for the benefit of my brothers…'* He did what I have done all those years ago!

And I, wretched fool, out of my love for you, tell you some of the things that God reveals to me. But I, however, have a very deep sense in my heart that someone else is saying these things. I believe this very much, because I see something and immediately thereafter I feel my weaknesses very intensely, because it is not out of saintliness, nor out of anything else, but out of God's love for me, for He wants me to become good. But only to very few people do I tell the things that God reveals to me, because the person must be spiritual in order to understand them. A scholar may see or hear something and recount it or write about it and in conclusion say: 'Look, Plato says the same thing.' But this is not what is happening here, because we may use the same words, but with a different meaning.

When I don't want to say anything about the things I see, you shouldn't force me, because I have learned to be obedient. I am very malleable and simple and when I don't want to give something and then under pressure I do give, I regret it afterwards. This is my weakness, which comes from my habit of utter obedience to my elders on the Holy Mountain.

And when sometimes I see that someone is heading for disaster in his life, I can do nothing about it. I point it out to him a little, but he doesn't understand. I can't intervene strongly and compromise his freedom. It's not an easy matter.

There, amid the pine trees, we witnessed the greatness of God

Many times, with the grace of God, I have entered into another state. My voice has changed, my face has entered a cloud of divine light. This has happened to me on the Holy Mountain and also elsewhere. It happened to me in the village of Agoriani on Mount Parnassos in the chapel of the Holy Trinity, and two girls who were with me, Vasiliki and Panayiota, saw me. The church inspired me; it was a little country chapel. Let me tell you what happened there.†

As we were walking through the forest on Mount Parnassos we encountered a little chapel. It was dedicated to the Holy Trinity. We

* Cf. *The Ascetical Homilies of St Isaac the Syrian*, Holy Transfiguration Monastery 1984, p. 297.

† This event occurred in 1972. [The two girls mentioned here are the two women who collected all the material from which the present book was compiled.]

entered the church and I went forward to the Holy Doors. The two girls stayed at the church entrance. From the very first moment, I was filled with enthusiasm there. I saw the life of the church. I saw many things from the past in there: priests celebrating on feast days years before, the prayers of saintly people, the out-flowing of the suffering of so many sorely afflicted souls, at one Liturgy there was a very saintly bishop... With enthusiasm I started to sing by heart canons and other hymns and most especially the hymns magnifying the Holy Trinity. I felt an ineffable joy, my voice became as I had never heard it before, as if from a multitude of a hundred people, sweet, strong, harmonious, heavenly, *like the sound of many waters and like the sound of mighty thun-*
derpeals. I raised my arms, my face shone, my expression became Rev. 19:6
changed. I had entered into a spiritual state. And in an instant the sky became a cathedral vault and the pine trees with their branches brazen candle stands...

The girls were standing three yards behind me. They tried to record that voice on a cassette recorder, but I didn't allow them. I saw what they were doing and stopped them. I have learned from when I was young on the Holy Mountain to preserve secrecy... But days later, after we had returned to Athens, I had a wistful longing for those hymns of praise. I wanted to hear that voice again. I regretted we hadn't recorded them. I said to the girls:

'If only we had that singing now... It was so beautiful! How we would rejoice to hear it! That voice was not human, it wasn't my voice, it was the voice of the grace of God. I would love to hear it and to go back to that day. There, amid the pine trees, we witnessed the greatness of God. Didn't we? How wonderful! We lit a fire there and set the forest ablaze!'

I experienced on Patmos the event of the Divine Revelation

We once went on a pilgrimage with George and Katy P. to Saint John the Theologian on Patmos.* It was early in the morning. I felt the grace of Saint John was choking me. There were people in the cave of the Revelation. I was afraid that I might betray my feelings. If I allowed myself to express my feelings, people would pass me off as a madman. I controlled myself. I went out of the church. It is not good for other people to see the experiences of our mystical communion with God. So I whispered

* This event occurred in 1964.

to the others and we left. In the evening of the same day the church was quiet. There were only the three of us. There was no one else in the church. Before we entered I prepared them, saying:

'Whatever you see, don't move and don't speak.'

We entered devoutly, without noise and in silence, simply and humbly. We stood before the Divine Revelation. We all three knelt down. I was in the middle. We fell on our faces. We repeated the Jesus Prayer for about fifteen minutes. I felt empty. No emotion. Nothing. Desolation. The adversary, the devil, had understood and wanted to impede me. 'These things cannot come about by plan,' I thought to myself. I repeated the prayer, I wanted the prayer — or rather, I neither said the prayer, nor did I want it, because when you say the prayer and desire it, the adversary sometimes realizes it. It is a very delicate matter. You cannot ignore the adversary on your own. Even to ignore him you need to do so with divine grace. It's something inexplicable.

Pay close attention. I didn't apply any pressure; I didn't push matters. We mustn't approach these spiritual things with force. I went outside. I looked at the flowers as if I wanted to show indifference to the fact that my soul would not open up. I looked out to the sea a little. I re-entered the church, placed some charcoal in the censer and lit it. I placed incense on the charcoal and censed a little and then my heart opened. The divine grace arrived. A brightness came to my face, I became possessed of God, I raised my arms and started to weep. Tears flowed continually from my eyes. At one point I fell down. My companions told me that I remained prostrate for twenty minutes…

This miracle that happened to me on Patmos is a great mystery. It has great significance. I saw the event of the Revelation. I saw Saint John the Theologian and his disciple Prochoros. I experienced the event of the Divine Revelation, exactly as it happened. I heard the voice of Christ from the cleft in the rock…

Don't tell this to anyone. Lord, Jesus Christ… May God have mercy on me. Why did I tell you? Tell me… I told you, so that you would learn to give yourselves over, gently and without force, into the hands of God. Then He will come to your souls and fill them with grace. If the adversary places obstacles in your way, disregard him. Do you understand? That's what I did. I occupied myself with something else when I realized that something was intervening. This is a matter with great profundity.

I tell you these things, but it's not good for me that I tell you. I have the feeling that I ought not to say them… These are mysteries; I cannot explain them. The only thing I say is for everything to be done simply, humbly and gently. When you desire and expect to be united to God, when you coerce God, He doesn't come. Rather, He comes 'on a day when you do not expect and at an hour you do not know.' The manner is most holy, not something you can learn as a technique. It needs to enter your soul mystically, so that you take it into your heart through the grace of God.

Cf. Matt. 24:50

APPENDIX

Saint John the Hut-dweller

In the Lives of the Saints edited by Saint Nikodemos the Athonite, the short notice about John the Hut-dweller reads as follows:

> The 15th of January.
> Commemoration of our holy father John the Hut-dweller.
>
> *Denying the world, the boy left his earthly hut,*
> *and in heavenly meadows, a new hut he pitched.*

This saint was born in Constantinople in the year 460 during the reign of Emperor Leo the Great; his father was a senator named Eutropios and his mother was called Theodora. At an early age, indeed, while he was still at elementary school, he secretly left his parents and teachers and, joining himself to a monk, went to the monastery of the Unsleeping Order and assumed the monastic habit. There he exercised himself in an exceedingly austere way of life. The devil, however, troubled the youth with love for his parents, and so the saint resolved to face and defeat the enemy. How and in what way? First the saint revealed everything about himself to the abbot of the monastery and asked for his permission to return to his parents. And so, having received a blessing from each of the monks in the community, he came to his father's house as a pauper dressed in rags and unrecognisable. As a beggar, he received from his father a tiny patch of land near the entrance to his home, and there he built a tiny hut and dwelt there preserving his identity unknown. The blessed man was pained when from his beggar's shack he saw his parents passing before him with all their worldly vanity and, even worse, he was obliged to endure insults and maltreatment from the servants.

After spending three years there with great self-denial and deprivation, he foresaw his coming death. Thereupon he called his mother and made himself known to her through a gilded Gospel book which his parents had had made for him while he was still a schoolboy. As soon as he had made himself known, the blessed man fell asleep and departed to the Lord.

The Skete of Kavsokalyvia

The Skete of Kavsokalyvia lies on the wooded slopes of the south-eastern extremity of the Holy Mountain peninsula where the foothills of Mount Athos drop sharply into the sea. This area of the Holy Mountain is associated with some of the best known figures in the history of Athonite monasticism. Peter the Athonite, the earliest known hermit on the Holy Mountain, lived here in the 9th century.

The name 'Kavsokalyvia', 'Burnhuts', derives from another famous hermit who lived here in the 14th century: Saint Maximos the Hut-Burner (1270–1365). Saint Maximos, who devoted his life to cultivating the prayer of the heart divorced from all worldly cares and all worldly possessions, would construct for himself a makeshift shelter from leaves and branches and live in it for a time, then he would burn his hut and move to another location.

Saint Maximos lived at the time of the so-called 'Hesychast' controversy, in which the Eastern Church sought to defend her experience of the gifts of divine grace in the lives of the saints in the face of criticism from the increasingly influential philosophical theology of Latin scholasticism. Saint Gregory of Sinai (1255–1347), one of the protagonists in the 'Hesychast' controversy, found in the person of Saint Maximos a living vessel of those gifts of divine grace, a man in whom the fruits of the Church's tradition of prayer and asceticism were made manifest. The *Life of Saint Maximos the Hut-burner** contains an account of the meeting between Gregory and Maximos on Mount Athos in which Saint Maximos's gifts of discernment and clear sight are very evident; Gregory succeeds in persuading Maximos to set aside his mask of pretended folly and reveal the secrets of his experience of the prayer of the heart. An extract from this dialogue between Saint Gregory and Saint Maximos is included in the collection of texts on vigilant prayer known as *The Philokalia*.†

The ascetic ethos of Saint Maximos left an indelible seal on the area. This heritage was preserved and cultivated by his disciple and

* Written by a contemporary of Saint Maximos, Theophanis, Bishop of Peritheorion. Another Life of Saint Maximos was composed by his disciple Saint Niphon.

† *Φιλοκαλία τῶν Ἱερῶν Νηπτικῶν*, vol. 5, pp. 104–7, Astir, Athens, 1976. An English translation of the first four volumes of *The Philokalia* (translated and edited by G.E.H. Palmer, Philip Sherrard and Kallistos Ware) has been published. The final fifth volume of the English translation is still awaited.

biographer Saint Niphon (1315–1411). The cave chapel of Saint Niphon, which lies thirty minutes walk to the south-west of the present-day skete, opposite the islet of Saint Christophoros, is frequently mentioned by Saint Porphyrios. Saint Neilos the Myrrh-streaming (1601–51), whose chapel is also mentioned by Saint Porphyrios, is a further characteristic figure of Athonite monasticism who lived in this area.

Saint Akakios the Younger (d. 1730) is honoured as the founder of the present-day skete of Kavsokalyvia. The characteristic organization of a skete is a central church, the *Kyriakon* or *Katholikon*, which is surrounded at easy walking distance by scattered separate hermitages, each inhabited by one or more hermits. The *Kyriakon* at Kavsokalyvia, which was completed in 1745, is dedicated to the Holy Trinity. In deference to Saint Maximos the skete became known as the Skete of Kavsokalyvia. The hermitages grew up to the east and west of the ravine which cuts through the mountainside. Previously Saint Akakios had lived as a hermit for some twenty years at a higher altitude at a location known as 'Metamorphosis', the 'Transfiguration', a site on which Saint Maximos had earlier established a small hermitage. On account of the extreme cold, however, Akakios was obliged to move further down the mountainside. The cave in which Saint Akakios himself later lived lies in a precipitous situation some fifty metres from the sea.

During the 18th century monks from the skete of Kavsokalyvia played an important part in the revival of Greek letters and spiritual renewal on the Holy Mountain. The skete came to be known especially for its woodcarvers and icon-painters and also for its hymnographers. The distinguished Ecumenical Patriarch, Joachim III (1878–84 and 1901–12), also lived for a time as a hermit in Kavsokalyvia, attracted by its beauty, peace and serenity.

At the beginning of the twentieth century the skete comprised some forty hermitages with a total of 120 monks. During the years in which Saint Porphyrios lived in Kavsokalyvia the skete was enjoying a period of great spiritual blossoming.

A monk is inalienably bound to 'the monastery of his repentance'. Here in Kavsokalyvia Saint Porphyrios found discerning spiritual fathers and ardent ascetics, here he was initiated into the monastic life, here he underwent his most powerful formative experiences, and here he received his gift of grace. Moreover, he had fallen in love with the great natural beauty of the skete and he never ceased to consider it as his spiritual home.

Map of Evia and Attiki

Map of Mount Athos

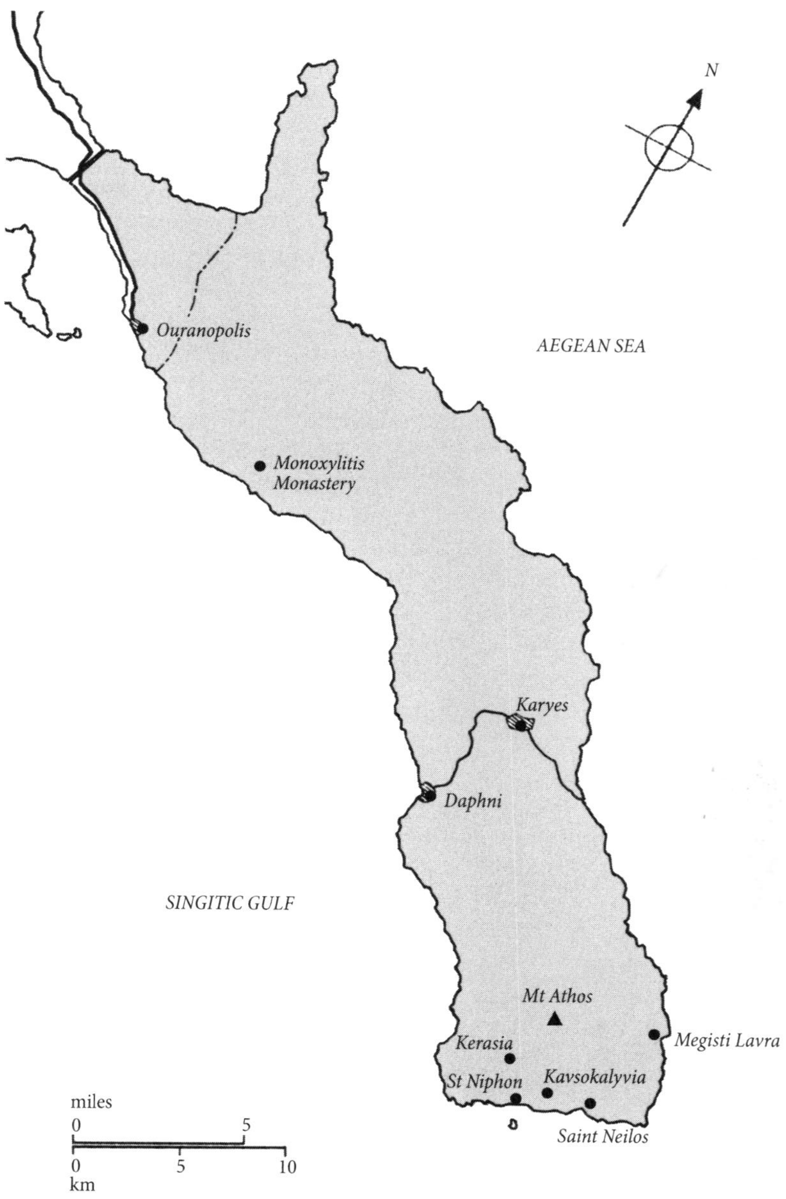